Group Counseling and Psychotherapy with Adolescents

Group Counseling and Psychotherapy with Adolescents

Second Edition

Beryce W. MacLennan and
Kathryn R. Dies

Columbia University Press
New York

Columbia University Press
New York   Oxford

Copyright © 1992 Columbia University Press
1st editon (MacLennan with Naomi Felsenfeld) copyright © 1968 Columbia
University Press

Library of Congress Cataloging-in-Publication Data

MacLennan, Beryce W.
    Group counseling and psychotherapy with adolescents / Beryce W.
MacLennan and Kathryn R. Dies.—2nd ed.
        p.   cm.
    Includes bibliographical references and index.
    ISBN 0-231-07834-X
    1. Group psychotherapy for teenagers.   2. Group counseling for
teenagers.   I. Dies, Kathryn R.   II. Title.
    [DNLM: 1. Counseling—in adolescence.   2. Group Processes.
3. Psychotherapy, Group—in adolescence.   WS 463 M164g]
RJ505.G7M33   1992
616.89'152'0835—dc20
DNLM/DLC
for Library of Congress   92–13563
                                                                            CIP

♾

Casebound editions of Columbia University Press books
are Smyth-sewn and printed on permanent and durable
acid-free paper.

Designed by Teresa Bonner
Printed in the United States of America
c 10 9 8 7 6 5 4 3 2 1

Contents

Contents

Contents

Group Counseling and Psychotherapy
with Adolescents

Introduction

This book was first conceived to address a number of concerns. Too many youth were identified as having difficulties only when they were in serious trouble. We wanted to encourage educators and care givers in normal settings to be alert to the needs and problems of youth before serious troubles arise and to use their understanding of group characteristics and methods to help youth live healthy, satisfying lives and avoid crises and serious failures. Second, too many troubled youth were reluctant to admit to problems and, when referred for treatment, dropped out or for months resisted facing their problems. We wanted to describe ways to bypass this resistance and build alliances with youth, as well as enlist their interest in changing their behavior. Third, we found that when youth have many problems, comprehensive programs are needed that include counseling and psychotherapy. Youth with multiple problems need the context of their lives to change, and they must see opportunities for satisfaction and success in order for them to change as well. These goals remain the same in this second edition, but in many cases it has become more difficult to achieve them.

This book was first written in the late 1960s, and since then conditions for youth of all classes have become more disturbing and dangerous. The patterns of marriage have changed. There are many more single-parent families, families with both parents working, and parents who have divorced and remarried. With the feminist movement and increasing marriage breakups and re-alignments, the role of the family has become more confused. With increased population and the development of the Third World, the struggle for the "good life" has become ever more competitive.

Unprotected and promiscuous sex has become more danger-ous with the increased occurrence of AIDS and other sexually transmitted diseases. Dangerous drugs such as cocaine and am-phetamines have become more prevalent—particularly among poor youth—and youth in general are adopting unhealthy habits, smoking, drinking, and having sex at an earlier age. Adolescent pregnancy is more frequent. More teenagers have abortions, and more babies are being born disabled by drugs or disease. Homi-cide has increased in the inner cities as has suicide among all classes of youth. Domestic violence has become more visible. With the deterioration and destruction of low-cost housing, homelessness, even for families, has become a serious problem.

In the late sixties the battle for civil rights was in full swing, and riots were exploding in the cities. The women's movement was in its infancy, and in spite of the Vietnam War, the middle class still felt affluent, with intellectual youth exploring the possi-bility of an improved quality of life beyond providing for material luxuries. In the nineties, although equal rights have ostensibly been granted, much discrimination against women and minority groups still exists, and many refugee groups from Central Amer-ica and Asia, with very different life-styles and values, are now competing with the more established minorities, further compli-cating the scene. In some states almost half the children, the majority of the poor, are of minority status, and in the twenty-first century the United States will be less dominated by the Euro-Caucasian culture.

New theories regarding women's psychological development are evolving, and women have made many gains in the workplace. These gains are associated with increased stress, however, related to the redefinition of male-female roles at work and at home, and to the lags in the development of an adequate child care system for single parents and for families in which both parents work.

There is more interest today in promoting healthy patterns of behavior in an attempt to prevent dangerous health habits among youth. Some school systems offer programs in family life, parenting, sex education, and programs that enrich the student's life. Teachers and school counselors help students increase their self-esteem, manage stress, and improve their ability to cope. It is unclear who benefits from each program, but it seems apparent, particularly when there are multiple needs, that more effective than education alone are programs that combine education with the development of coping skills and opportunities for alternative life satisfactions.

The various institutions concerned with the training or retraining of youth all have components that deal with the development of satisfactory human relations. Improved functioning can be achieved not only through changes in the individual but also through the reorganization of the structure and functioning of institutions, and through a change in the values and norms of society. There are several approaches to achieving individual and social change: (1) working with individuals alone or in groups to help them acquire the needed skills and knowledge to change; (2) creating new group pressures that impinge on individuals and move them to change; and (3) creating and changing community structures, institutions, or neighborhoods that can provide opportunities for youth to live satisfying lives. This book focuses on methods of working with adolescents in small groups. Life-style education and counseling help them solve problems of normal development. Psychotherapy and rehabilitation assist them to react differently to situations that cause them trouble and unhappiness. It is often difficult to distinguish between counseling and psychotherapy and sometimes it is preferable to treat both as essential elements of other activities, such as recreation, education, or employment.

Groups have many different dimensions and, to lead groups effectively, one must be able to analyze them at multiple levels and understand the implications of different leadership styles and different member groups. Chapter 1 describes some group characteristics that are relevant to the use of groups as agents of change.

Group counseling and group psychotherapy involve change for individual members of the group, as well as the creation of a group climate that will in turn affect the individual. Thus, to be able to control groups of adolescents, it is necessary to understand the developmental level of each teenager in the group. In a heterogeneous society such as the United States, teenagers belong to many different communities, cultures, and subcultures, and we must understand these cultural factors thoroughly if we are to work effectively with adolescents. Chapter 2 describes the various stages of adolescence and discusses the cultural factors that influence youth.

Chapters 3 through 5 describe the approaches and goals used in adolescent group counseling and psychotherapy; some of the processes that we can identify as the groups move from initiation to termination; and some major themes that concern the adolescents in the groups. Chapter 6 discusses the particular characteristics of groups that are used in institutional settings and in private practice.

Group leaders must strive to understand their own reactions to the group as a whole and to the individual group members. In training people to undertake group counseling or group psychotherapy, it is necessary to make concepts meaningful; relate theory to practice; and increase the trainees' capacity to perceive and comprehend group and individual behavior and to react appropriately and with correct timing. In chapter 7 we describe the essential elements needed in training group counselors and therapists.

Finally, we want to emphasize that intervention should be undertaken only when group leaders have a clear concept of the program they intend to follow, firm control over the program, and the ability to evaluate the program's results. At the start, it is essential to establish a baseline. What is the population like? What does the intervention plan to change? Who will undertake the intervention and under what conditions? What part will the leaders play? What kind of interactions do they anticipate? What results do they hope for? How will they determine whether they have been successful? Then, if only in a rudimentary way, the leaders should check whether the program is proceeding according to plan and whether the interactions are as expected. Outcomes should then be examined and the program refined in terms of the results. Unfortunately, we find that very few reports go beyond a description of the group and its members to include even a simple evaluation of outcome, and almost none meet the criteria that would enable leaders to judge whether their methods achieved their desired results. We hope that this book will encourage group leaders to evaluate their groups more effectively and to refine their methods.

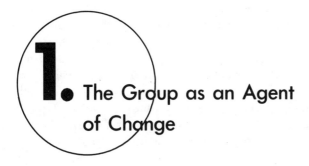

1. The Group as an Agent of Change

This book examines groups as vehicles for helping individuals change their self-concepts, their self-management, their interactions with others, and their way of life. Group conditions are established to

1. provide constructive experiences that will help individuals feel differently about themselves and others;
2. give support or provide motivation to individuals in their efforts to behave differently;
3. provide opportunities for group members to examine problems that they experience in their lives and allow them to share different ways of coping with these problems;
4. allow individuals to analyze their impact on others as this is experienced in the group itself.

To develop appropriate groups, we need to understand how groups are structured and how they function under various conditions. Groups can be analyzed at many levels and for different dimensions. We need to understand their characteristics and how such factors as size, leadership, purpose, and membership composition affect the group process. This chapter focuses on the contributions that basic small group theory and research can provide in developing effective adolescent groups for counseling and psychotherapy. Our emphasis is on small face-to-face groups, with a maximum of twelve to fifteen members. Intensive therapy groups usually contain five to eight members. We are also concerned with how the group relates to its setting and how that setting—a program, institution, or community—affects the functioning of the group.

Most of the important theories related to small groups were developed by the end of the sixties. Some elaboration and consolidation has occurred in the last twenty years, however, in addition to some new theoretical developments regarding group boundaries, family systems, and conflict resolution. Shaw in 1981 updated much of the social and psychological theory and research related to small groups.[1] Durkin related system theory to group psychotherapy, and several eminent family therapists, such as Minuchin and Bowen, have studied family systems and strategies of intervention.[2]

The Development of a Group

A group is a dynamic entity. It is not fully developed at the beginning but must in time create its identity, decide on its direction, determine its ways of operating, and become a small social system in its own right. It is composed of a number of individuals who come together for a common purpose. Group members must communicate and interact for the group to function, and therefore the size of the group is important. Members must be able to identify with one another, become acquainted, and define the purposes of the group implicitly or explicitly. They must develop a way of interacting and establish rules and limits, formally or informally. In order for the group to endure, it must be able to retain its members by satisfying their needs. This is called *group cohesion*.[3]

At the same time the group must be dynamic. Themes, alliances, levels of tension change as the group progresses. In systems theory, Von Bertalanffy has described a living system in which the group develops a dynamic equilibrium that permits the maintenance of a stable identity while progressively transforming the group.[4] As the group develops, members become interdependent. They become aware of one another, learn to trust one another, have meaning and concern for one another. If a member is missing or leaves the group, or if someone new joins, the group is no longer the same. The group becomes a part of each member's life. It becomes one of their reference groups and each has a sense of belonging to the group.[5] When a group ends, this means a change in the lives of all its members. Members may initially come to the group under pressure, but if the group is to become a viable entity, members must come to feel this sense of belonging and accept their part in the group and responsibility for it.[6] Thus, consent is ultimately crucial. Members come for some common purpose but also have separate needs, hidden agendas. There will be struggles within the group to reconcile these separate needs and pressure for members to conform to the demands of the group as a whole.

Members of the group also try to establish their position in the group in relation to other group members. They adopt certain roles. They select or assign leaders. A kind of hierarchy develops that is a focus of conflict and that rarely remains the same. Consequently, tension and dynamic interaction always exist within the group, and the climate of the group depends on these struggles. Contrary movements are always present, causing the group to fluctuate continually between change and temporary equilibrium.

Group members must take the initiative for groups to get started or continue, and struggles in the group may center on who will have the most influence and power. Groups vary in how they operate, in the kind of leadership that emerges, and the degree to which members participate. The amount of emotion, tension, and conflict, the kind of climate that is customary when the group meets, and the degree to which group members demand conformity or tolerate defiance, disequilibrium, and ambiguity also vary from group to group. Groups may start with designated leaders and a set purpose, or members may come together spontaneously with leadership and purpose developing gradually. Groups do not function in a vacuum but within a physical setting and in a larger organizational structure, either within a program, within an institution, or in an open community. The quality of the setting and the relationship of the group to the larger organization affect the group's functioning and impose limitations on it.

The differences between a group and a crowd are numerous.[7] Group members know one another and have a sense of identity, but a crowd is anonymous, its members strangers to one another with no sense of interdependence. They can come and go without appreciably affecting the whole. The ground rules of a crowd are established impersonally, by circumstances. Because no sense of personal responsibility to the whole exists, a crowd can easily turn into a mob. In a mob, and sometimes in a crowd, members surrender personal direction, judgment, and responsibility for decision making. Personal boundaries dissolve and members cease to think decisively for themselves. They follow chance leadership, are caught up easily in strong emotional currents, and often act in ways alien to their normal behavior. Emotional contagion, described by Redl,[8] where members respond to others by adopting the emotional expression of the group, is more likely to occur in crowds than in small groups, although poorly balanced small groups are also susceptible. This is an aspect of the concept of deindividualization in which individuals surrender their autonomy and their emotional control.

The Beginning of a Group

Groups may form spontaneously simply by people being together in similar situations, such as vacationers at a resort or children playing on a street. Or someone may take the initiative in calling others together, in which case there may be pregroup explanations and contract negotiations.

A new group is ambiguous and members strive to reduce this ambiguity. They want to learn what the group is about, what its purposes are, how it will operate, who will lead it, what the other members are like, how they will relate to one another, and what will be demanded of them. They try to develop structure and boundaries.

In the beginning, members deal with superficialities. They inquire about names and affiliations. They scrutinize one another and make initial judgments. They try to assess whether belonging to the group will be a pleasant or a painful experience. Because they are strangers, they feel vulnerable. They do not know what the others are like, how powerful they are, how much they can hurt them; consequently, they are reluctant to expose themselves and to trust one another. Involvement and intimacy take time to develop.

Names

People have primitive feelings about their names. One's name is a basic component of identity formation. When individuals are known by their names, they can be traced and held responsible for their actions. As such, power is given over to others. Names and titles provide information about a group member's position in the world. Names also have particular associations. They evoke memories from past experiences and often make attributions of others with particular names. They are expected to act in certain ways and fulfill certain roles.

Physical Assessment

When members first meet, they often seem to have little individuality. Although some stand out, others are hard to identify. People are judged initially by their physical appearance and outward characteristics; how they dress, their expressions, muscular tension, movements and gestures, grooming, tone of voice, and what they say. Again, judgments are made on the basis of past experience. Just as with names, members expect people who resemble others in their past lives to behave in similar ways, and members react to them as if they were similar. These expectations are the basis of transference, that is, relating to a person in the present in terms of past relationships with significant people in one's life, so that one attributes qualities and reacts in ways that may not be appropriate to present reality.

Cliques

As members become acquainted, cliques and alliances form. In a dynamic group, these will not remain static but will change, forming and reforming in accordance with the needs of the members at any particular time. Formal structure with the development of positions and ranks tends to interfere with this fluid and dynamic interaction.

Individual Defenses Against Anxiety

Individuals react to the insecurity and anxiety of becoming part of a group in different ways. Certain individuals remain very quiet. They do not want to risk exposing themselves until they are sure of their group. They may sit and say nothing, but they are very aware of what is going on. Others who are silent may be so anxious that they are not even aware of what is going on. They may go blank, may be overcome by fear, or may retreat into a world of their own and indulge in fantasy. Others who are silent may be expecting to be called on. They manage their uncertainties by being told what to do. Others, when anxious, begin to expect that they will be pushed around and gather their resistance to give as little as possible. Still others who are silent feel powerful, learning more about the rest than the other members know about them.

Many members attempt to deal actively with an anxious situation. Some members ask many questions. They try to get the leader to define the situation. They become good and eager pupils, or they place themselves in a superior position as the assistant to the leader and attempt to draw others out. Some members begin actively to assert themselves, to define the group in their terms, to struggle to gain mastery and overthrow the leader, or, if there is no leader, to assume this position.

Other members handle their discomfort through expressions of dissatisfaction and complaint. Often members will attempt to obtain allies by searching out those with whom they have something in common. Members may strive to establish their position by comparing themselves with others and taking the initiative in obtaining information from others for this purpose. Some members may engage in boasting, clowning, or talking about their problems. Others will talk incessantly and repetitively to cover their anxiety. Some members protect themselves by seeking out someone as the butt of the group and leading an attack on that member.

Group Defenses

The group as a whole deals with anxiety by attempting to reduce ambiguity. The members attempt to define their purposes and goals, understand what each wants, decide how they will operate, and find out how they stand in relation to one another. They look for someone to take responsibility for these interactions. If there are designated leaders, they expect them to take on these responsibilities; if they do not, members are likely to become resentful. They are evincing the "dependency demand," a mechanism identified by Bion as a group defense that is commonly seen at the beginning of a group's development.[9]

Bion was influenced on the one hand by Gestalt psychology—which views individuals within the context of their total social and emotional situation—and on the other by Kleinian psychoanalytic theory—which emphasizes the early months of an infant's life. He distinguished between the group's tasks, the overt content of the group, which he named the "work group" and underlying dynamic interactions, which he identified as "basic assumptions." He identified three principal group defenses at this second level, essentially ways in which the group resists change. He identified these defenses as the "dependency demand," "flight and fight," and "pairing," and each involves a a variety of group operations.

In the dependency demand state, group members may demonstrate helpless dependent behavior, complaining, asking for help, passive dependency. This dependency can manifest itself in the group by members talking about their longing to have the leader to themselves, asking for individual interviews, talking about how they hated sharing when they were young. It is important to recognize that such demands may have no basis in reality. An individual who claims he cannot talk about certain kinds of information in the group may not really be concerned with this at all. He may be motivated primarily by his desire to be taken care of or to be given in to by the leader.

Fighting can be clearly seen as a way to avoid getting down to business, although the real purpose is sometimes obscured by the sound and fury. A group may be unable to face any conflict and, consequently, whenever it reaches such a point may break up. A struggle focusing on who shall give or who shall do the work can successfully interfere with any change being accomplished. As a manifestation of flight, members may chatter about inconsequential subjects whenever they near an important or emotional issue, or they may come late or avoid coming to a session at all.

The third basic assumption, pairing, is often harder to identify. This occurs when the group sits back and allows two members to cooperate in diverting the group from its work. A clear example was seen in a group where a leader was asking the members whether they were satisfied with the group. Before anyone could talk, a supervisor, made anxious by this invitation to criticize, plunged into a long eulogy about the group, the leader, and how no one could possibly be dissatisfied, making it very difficult indeed for the leader to get to the root of any dissatisfaction. The supervisor successfully paired with the leader and cut him off from the group. Sometimes two members will talk with great mutual admiration about a subject of no particular interest to the rest of the group. The other members sit back and allow this to go on, thus evading the real tasks of the group.

Particularly in the early stages of the group, members are very concerned about whether it will be a "good" group, that is, a successful one, with status in the outside world. They become concerned that other members also think that the group is a "good" group. If there are several ongoing groups, they want their group to be the best.

Groups as Living Systems

H. Durkin and J. Durkin have examined the relevance of General Systems Theory for understanding group structure and process and a wide range of boundary operations.[10] H. Durkin has adopted Von Bertalanffy's concept of living systems that can restructure themselves and increase their autonomy.[11] She applies this concept both to the group and to the members' intrapsychic structure. A major factor within this system is the permeability of boundaries through which information and emotion can pass. Boundaries can be opened and closed to regulate the flow of these exchanges. J. Durkin has studied different types of interpretation and group experience, such as intellectual interpretations on the one hand and gestalt emotional experiences on the other, as they relate to change in the climate of the group and the control of the emotional reactivity of group members and the intensity of the group interaction, respectively. For example, intellectual interpretations and focusing on concrete problems both close off emotional expression. Boundaries can apply to many dimensions. Physical boundaries are one example. In this regard, members can be in or outside the group; they can bring images of their families into the group or exclude them. Different interactive subcliques within the group can form their own systems.

The group itself is a system within a larger system, such as an agency or a community. As the group forms and becomes more cohesive, the boundaries of the group become more visible.

Group Belonging

Members become affiliated and identify with the group as it becomes more cohesive. They belong and talk about "we," "us," "ours." There is a process of partial deindividualization in which the members identify with the group. They make the group a part of themselves and surrender some of their autonomy to the group in return for the satisfaction they gain from it. Thus, any slur on the group also reflects on them. If a member rejects the group and leaves, the others become anxious. Will everyone leave? Will the group fall apart and cease to exist? If the group is no good, are they also no good? They feel they personally have failed to satisfy the needs of the departing member. Group members experience anger at the leaders for failing to do their part in keeping the person who is leaving. If leaders want to add a new member the others may resist, because it will change the group and its pecking order and require them to rework issues of trust. Any group that is centered around a leader or leaders has some qualities of a family, and members compete for the leaders, for their attention and their love. There are always mixed feelings about other members because their presence means sharing the leader. Sibling rivalry is always a factor. Members have both the desire to work together and gain one another's support and to kill one another off. Thus when a member leaves, each member feels guilty that in some way he or she participated in driving away the departing member.

Group Stages

Groups tend to go through different stages depending on their purposes and goals. Bales and Cohen and other social scientists have studied the process of problem-solving groups in terms of identifying the problems, problem breakdown and analysis, and problem reconstruction.[12] In therapy groups, adolescents have been described as going through certain phases in their efforts to lead a more independent and self-reliant life: initial politeness and good behavior, griping, testing, and acting out, dependency and demandingness, mature problem-solving, and ultimately separation and self-reintegration.[13]

Dies describes in more detail one model of adolescent group development.[14] In the earliest stage of the group's life, there exists the task of "Initial Relatedness" during which the superficial bonding of group members occurs. The events of this stage have a social orientation and offer the safety of allowing for distance while exploring commonalities.[15] The group then progresses to "Testing the Limits." Even though group norms may have been clearly outlined in pregroup interviews with each member and in the initial session, questions of "Just how will this group be run?" or "Can this leader really be consistent?" are explored. Adolescents learn much from the confrontation, negotiation, and resolution of the "authority issues" in this stage and then proceed to a stage of "Working on Self." In this phase, group members share their feelings at a deeper level of commitment and, with help, may look into the common core issues of members. Surface issues of school failure, relationship break-ups, or parental conflicts are refocused on the central issue of "What does this say about me as a person?" As groups move to the terminal phase of "Moving on," members must deal with the important tasks of consolidating the learning that has occurred in the group and addressing the sense of loss that accompanies leaving. Learning how to adapt to loss is a critical aspect of healthy functioning and thus an integral part of bringing closure to the group.[16]

Dynamic Interaction as Essential to Change

For the group to become an effective agent of change, dynamic tension must be maintained. When a group is in equilibrium, no change is taking place. Change can only take place when there is conflict and the meeting of opposing views or when boundaries break and a flood of suppressed emotion enters the field of consciousness. When a group or an individual is in the process of change, no one knows the outcome. Inevitably, though, the individual and the group will be different. Individuals will have to change their concepts of themselves and give up certain beliefs or ways of behaving in favor of others. Consequently, for individuals to change, they must admire others who represent the "new." They must see advantages for themselves and the need to be a part of something new and exciting. Thus change always involves insecurity, anxiety, and discomfort, although it may also bring much satisfaction. Some degree of conflict is essential for change.

Because of these anxieties about change, groups become effective when they provide enough support so that members can trust one another, expose themselves, and test reality in the group. A climate must be created in which members can respect one another and in which confrontation can be undertaken constructively. There are always mixed feelings when change is desired, and change is achieved by working through this ambivalence in the group. Groups operate in terms of the values that are rewarded by the group. Thus, groups concerned with individual change should emphasize the importance of facing reality, the importance of respecting oneself and others, the willingness to become involved with one another and to become intimate and frank, and the ability to reveal the things that are of importance. If there are leaders, they should be willing to demonstrate these values in their actions and to ensure safety for members.

Intimacy is always a two-way proposition. It implies closeness, knowledge, and acceptance between partners. It necessitates willingness to trust each other and to reveal oneself as one really is. It implies caring for each other and is a means of combatting the essential loneliness of every human being. To be able to be intimate with another means giving up protective defenses that hide the internal reality not only from others but from oneself.

The Group as an Agent of Change

An intimate relationship implies that all who are part of the relationship reveal themselves. In most psychotherapy, therapists know the individual or the group members intimately; but the members do not know the leader. Existential therapists have challenged this position, believing that the intimacy of the "encounter" is the most potent force in treatment, that the capacity to be "real" in relationships is vital, and, consequently, that therapists cannot remain aloof.[17] Certainly, adolescents generally demand that therapists become real to them before they are willing to trust them. Thus, leaders of adolescent groups frequently find themselves more challenged to be self-disclosing than are leaders of adult groups.

The following conditions are necessary for the establishment of intimacy: face-to-face interaction; willingness to risk self-exposure; desire for closeness; a mutual demand for reciprocity; mutual attraction, trust, and some degree of predictability; and willingness genuinely to listen and respond to the needs of others. Because of these conditions, the larger the group, the more difficult it is to establish a climate of intimacy.

Trust implies expectation. When two people trust each other, they make demands on the other to respond in a particular way. One has confidence in the predictability of the other, an anticipation that the other will respond in terms of what is needed, an expectation that the other will not inflict hurt, and a belief in the other's consistency. Trust is justified to the extent that the individual is capable of perceiving the reality of the situation. Trust can exist without mutual trust. There are degrees of trust related to the degree to which individuals feel justified in lowering their defenses. Trust involves risk-taking. It is probable that human beings are born expecting that their demands on others will be met. The degree to which this confidence in others continues is a matter of life experience and capacity to adapt to reality. Disillusionment is the result of trusting unrealistically, of having expectations and making demands on others that cannot be met, or of one's environment being so unstable that one cannot predict outcomes.

Individuals vary in the degree to which they can trust others depending on their life experiences. Erikson believes that babies develop their capacity to trust during the first year of life and that the quality of life during this year is all important.[18] However, disillusionment, traumatic experiences, and betrayal at any age may destroy the capacity to trust and engender extreme suspiciousness. Learning to risk and trust in the protected environment of the group can improve members capacities to trust realistically.

Termination of the Group

As the group moves toward the end of its life, termination maneuvers are undertaken. Individuals must withdraw from the group and relinquish their group identities. They must now live independently or make new affiliations. There are anxieties and feelings of loss. It is as though a part of one has died. A world ends. To soften the blow and delay the process, members review the past and project themselves into the future, both in words and actions. They may relive incidents in the group. They will rework what they have learned and integrate it into their own personalities. Each will react to the ending in their own typical fashion: rushing into the future with joy, denying the loss, or grieving openly. The duration of termination operations depends on how long the group has been together. In a day-long workshop, the group will terminate in the last hour. If the group has been together a year, it may take two or three session to terminate. The intensity of termination will depend both on the duration and the quality of the experience.

Group Properties

As has been stated, groups can be studied at a number of different levels and from different points of view. Groups are conducted in various settings. They are of different sizes. They are organized

20

differently. All of these factors have implications for the way the group functions and what it can achieve.

To a great extent, what can be undertaken in any group is limited by what the community will tolerate. If a society does not permit open discussion of sex, no group run by a formal institution can adequately deal with this subject. The group's standing in the open community will influence the attitudes that members have toward their groups. The same is true of the relationship between the institution and the group. The rules of the institution set the outer boundaries of the group. Its function and entry regulations will determine the population that can be accepted into the group. In general, a group that has high status in the community and in the institution will find it easier to obtain members.

If a series of groups is to be undertaken, then the success of the first group is important.[19] If there is conflict and confusion of roles between the group leader and the staff of the institution, then the members of the group will be thrown into conflict. If there is conflict between the values held by the group and those of the members' other primary reference groups, group members, in adopting the group's values, will distance and alienate themselves from other intimate associations and may be presented with a choice between these other attachments and the group. This is a very important consideration when the family is an active force and in the treatment of delinquent youth and substance abusers. In the latter cases, youth may have to choose between their old friendship system and group treatment, which requires that they make new friends and adopt a different lifestyle.

In recent years, considerable attention has been paid to group boundaries. Boundaries that encapsulate systems can be viewed as many different concentric circles: within and around the individual, around cliques, vertical and horizontal interactions, around the group itself, and between the group and the institution or community. The boundaries drawn around the group may focus entirely on what goes on in the group. They may permit the drawing into the group of families and of experiences from other settings or different time periods. The group may focus very concretely or may include the reliving of dreams and fantasies.

The Physical Environment

The immediate environment of the group affects its climate and the quality of interaction in the group. The amount of space can limit the size of the group and affect the relationships between members. If there is too much space, members may experience feelings of insignificance, emptiness, isolation, and anxiety. If there is too little, they may feel cramped and confined or too close together for their present state of intimacy. The proportions of the room and its color and cleanliness add to or detract from the free atmosphere of the group. A long, narrow room makes horizontal interaction between members very difficult. Dark, dingy colors and poor lighting depress the mood of the group. Whether the group has privacy and can always have the room for itself affects what can go on in the sessions and indicates the institution's respect for the group.

The arrangement of the room and the spatial relationships of members to one another influence the functioning of the group. Because it is easier to talk when members look at one another, interactions are more spontaneous and member participation more general when groups are face to face. Rows of chairs may be satisfactory if communication is planned only between the leader and the group members; if all are to join in freely, a circle makes interchange easier. Another advantage of a circle is that it has no predetermined leadership position, whereas an oblong arrangement stimulates the development of hierarchy. Research has shown that participation is usually greater between members seated directly opposite one another than between those who are on the same side or segment of the oblong or circle. Positions also acquire emotional significance. A member who habitually takes a seat opposite the leader is often competing for the leader's position. A member who sits next to the leader may be hiding or seeking support. The presence of a table may serve as protection or a barrier, and an empty space may create anxiety or stimulate closeness.

Size of the Group

Spatial arrangements and group size are closely related. Hall has demonstrated that people of different cultures vary in the distances they maintain from one another in different transactions.[20] How close people need to be to one another to exchange intimacies or conduct business varies among cultures. As the number of members of the group grows, there is greater distance among one another, which seems to be one reason why large groups have more difficulty in becoming intimate. A second reason is that the more people in the group, the harder it is to get to know the others well and to trust them. Size also affects the amount of attention members can get from the group as a whole, from individual group members, or from the leader. This means that individuals in larger groups must have visibly more issues in common for the group to seem relevant to them.

Certain numbers have special properties. Simmel and many other later authors have pointed out the tendency of groups of three to break down into two against one.[21] A group of four, on the other hand, can work together or develop two competing or collaborating couples who may either fight each other or maintain a nondynamic status quo. In very small groups it is sometimes harder to maintain sufficient interest, excitement, and interaction, although a sudden temporary drop from larger to smaller numbers may facilitate intimate communication. If there is an odd number someone is likely to have the power to influence the decision between competing factions, to become a "swing" person.

Member Participation

Participation of members in the group, as we have noted, is influenced by the seating arrangements and the size of the group. It is also influenced by the way the leader conducts the group and by the composition of the membership. Vertical participation follows the style of a lecture, with a question-and-answer period; horizontal participation involves members interacting freely with one another. The more active the leader and the more responsibility the leader takes for structuring group interaction, the more the group tends to interact vertically. The more the members feel genuinely responsible for the group, the more likely they are to relate freely to one another. Sometimes a group will allow a member to monopolize the attention of the group for long periods, or permit two people to "pair" and transact their business together while the rest of the group sits back and watches. In such cases, group members are usually resisting carrying out the group tasks, although there may be vicarious learning.

The composition of the group is also important, that is, the extent to which it is made up of high or low communicators. Borgatta and Bales have found experimentally that persons who are naturally low participators are more responsive in groups of low or medium participators and that they find it difficult to be active in groups of fast reactors and highly aggressive participators.[22] Slavson and his followers have emphasized the importance of group balance in maximizing both member interaction and the group's capacity as a whole to be responsible to its members.[23]

Communication

Communication has been defined by Schachter as "influence," that is, a stimulus is sent out and affects a receptor.[24] This, of course, is then elaborated on: stimuli are sent to several receptors that react and then respond to the stimuli. Communication can then be said to be the stimulation of a chain, or network, of such interactions.

Ease of communication in small groups is affected by many factors:

1. Spatial considerations, as discussed above (the distance between "sender" and "receiver" and their relative positions in the group);
2. Interference of competing noise or interruptions;
3. The quality and comprehensiveness of communication;
4. Communication sets—differences in language and manner and differences in tone, expression, and accent. For example, in culturally and intellectually mixed groups, those who speak in intellectual terms will have to express themselves more simply and concretely and may have to learn street slang; those who communicate in street slang may have to modify their language so that others can understand them. Both can help each other;
5. Restrictions placed on communication in terms of direction (communication that must go through certain channels) or in terms of subject matter or form;
6. Roles and positions that interfere with free communication (certain statements may carry penalties, while adherence to certain other forms of speech or psychological attitudes may be rewarded);
7. Permission in the group to vent cognitive, emotional, or physical expressions;
8. The degree of structure and the type of leadership style and theoretical approach can either promote or retard intellectual discussion or emotional expression.

Communication can be verbal or nonverbal. Nonverbal communication is conveyed by gestures, involuntary movements, changes in tension and breathing, and facial expressions.[25] Verbal communication depends on people's style of speaking, speed and intonation, grammar, vocabulary, slang, and dialect. Both types of communication are tied to people's self-perceptions.

Although we are generally unaware of the preponderance of nonverbal communication, Birdwhistell estimates that speech accounts for no more than 10 percent of all communication.[26] Communication problems occur because of inconsistencies in verbal messages and conflicting verbal and nonverbal communications. This is best known as the "double bind," the psychological dilemma that arises when contradictory instructions are conveyed in the same message. Nonverbal communication can be better understood with the aid of audio-visual feedback.

Every culture has ritualistic communication sets used to ease communication and allay anxiety. Berne and other transactional analysts have also identified and described what they call "games," typical transactions between individuals in which a cue sets off a typical series of predictable interactions that are frequently detrimental to the goals of the individuals.[27] Groups are useful settings in which to observe, identify, and modify such games.

The efficiency of communication is affected by the nature of the task, the positions of the communicators, the availability of information and feedback, the consistency of the messages and cues, and the receptiveness of the communicators. This last quality is itself affected by several factors: the emotional level of the leaders and receivers and the climate within which the communication takes place, the status and previous value sets of the parties, the degrees of information held, the relevance of the message for the receiver, the degree to which the communicators accept their roles, and the amount of exposure to the messages and the setting in which the transaction takes place.

Leadership

A group's structure may be formal or informal. Leaders and officers may be appointed or elected into official roles, or leadership may develop spontaneously and fluctuate over time. The leadership in informal groups is likely to be less stable than in highly structured ones. Despite the formality of the group, however, leaders must have support to occupy a position of leadership, whether the leader is active or not. This support can be provided by institutions or superiors, by well-placed lieutenants, or by the general consent of the group or population. To be effective, leaders must have power, either in the form of force or coercion or by being in tune with the demands and needs of the members. The leader's effectiveness relies on the relative strengths and weaknesses of the leader and the group. Unless group leaders have, or can generate, powerful support, they cannot afford to deviate too far from the norms of the group or they will be rejected. However, a member can sense underlying discontent in a group, become the spokesperson for that discontent, and, inspiring other members, can become a new leader and change the norms of the group. Leaders may be attractive either because they can serve the membership or because they represent what the members would like to do or be themselves. Thus, although leaders can deviate from the norms, they should embody the needs of those they serve.

There are no typical leaders. Those who are leaders in one group may not be accepted as leaders in another. Moreover, leadership functions vary among groups.[28]

Some of the functions of leadership are to bring the membership together; to help the group identify its goals; to teach the group how to function; to help the group keep to the task; to be a model for the group; to present a value system to the group; and to facilitate the termination of the group.

Leadership activities may include: stimulating interaction; making suggestions; providing for the needs of the group; seeing that ground rules are set; influencing the goals of the group; keeping order; assigning tasks; planning for or with the group; deciding on membership; initiating action; and evaluating the group.

The more active the leaders and the more they take over responsibility for the group, the more dependent or defiant group members are likely to become. In groups where members are immature and increased maturity is a goal, the leader must help set limits and a structure that allows members largely to take responsibility for themselves within those limits.

The more inactive the leaders and the less structure they establish, the more a group is likely to function at a dynamic, emotional level unrelated to its stated objectives. Leaders significantly influence the tone of the group and the way it functions. They can affect the intrapsychic boundaries that open and close the flow of emotional expression. Leaders vary in the amount of authority given them by external and internal sources and the degree to which they delegate their authority in the group. If leaders delegate authority to the group for decision making and then withdraw this authority, they are likely to create a climate of discontent in which members will conspire against them. Lieberman, Yalom, and Miles found that the most effective leaders in counseling groups were those who generated emotional warmth and provided feedback but were neither overly charismatic and emotional nor too passive.[29]

When leaders promote a relatively unstructured group, the anxiety of members increases and they are likely to regress and relate to the leaders and to one another in terms of earlier significant relationships, i.e., transference. The group is perceived as the primary group, or "family," and group members are likely to transfer their ways of relating to family members onto others in the group. Family systems theorists have noted that individuals play specific roles within their families, such as "the sick one," the "spokesperson," or "the victim," and individuals may carry these roles with them into the group. Individual members and the group as a whole will also arouse feelings in the leader. The leader's response may be a typical or normal reaction or may be idiosyncratic to the leader. In some instances, however, leaders under pressure may also relate to group members in terms of their own early family experiences. This is called *counter-transference* and leaders must be alert to these reactions. Leaders must also be attuned to their own feelings and be able to use them as tools to understand and respond to members and the group. If leaders have trouble reacting appropriately they should seek consultation. If a group has more than one leader, the situation is more complicated because members react both to the two leaders individually and to the leaders as a couple. Further, the leaders react to each other as well as to the members and the group

Decision Making in Groups

Realistic decision making is based on the reality of alternatives and adequate consideration of probabilities, information about alternatives and hypotheses about consequences, and the prospect of implementing decisions. The following are important aspects of decision making in groups:

1. The process of effective decision making requires laying out the information, considering the alternatives and the implications, examining the desires and feelings of participants in the decision, and working out a course of action compatible with the goals of the members. In most real-life situations, decisions are made on predictions of outcome based on estimated probabilities.

2. Decisions in groups are made not only based on information but on the alignment of forces. Both the decisions reached and their implementation is affected by the balance of power in the group.

3. Decisions are made through the balance between two forces shifting to one side; decisions may be reversed when the balance of power changes within the group. When there is insufficient information, insufficient power to move the group in a particular direction, an equal balance of opinion between members, or uncertainty of members, no decision will be made or, if made, will not be implemented.

4. Decisions will be influenced by previous experiences.

5. Decisions will be affected by the prospect of rewards or sanctions.

6. Lewin demonstrated that the more people involved and participating in the discussion, the more likely they are to carry out the decision.[30]

7. Festinger demonstrated that the more difficult it is to make a decision, the more an individual is likely to stay with that

decision.[31] However, people have a tendency when making very painful decisions to regret those decisions as soon as they are made, such as decisions involving divorce, hospitalization, or abortion. It is possible that whenever a decision is made in a pressure situation and that decision successfully relieves the pressure, the individual is then unencumbered and forgets what was painful and what he or she was in fact trying to avoid. It is then that regret sets in and a desire to reverse the decision.

8. When groups polarize into subgroups that take extreme positions, it is difficult to reach a decision. Negotiations must focus on identifying major areas where agreement can be reached, narrowing the areas of disagreement, and drawing as many members as possible into a middle ground. A second strategy is to consolidate the group against an outside "enemy" or around a major group task seen as essential to all, as Lewin demonstrated in the "Robbers' Cave."[32]

9. The motivation of members affects the group's ability to make a decision. A decision can be more easily made when individuals either care very little or care very much about making that decision.

10. Decision making is related to value systems. If the permissible alternatives fall within the individual's or the groups' interests and beliefs, a decision will more easily be reached.

11. Structure and hierarchy can facilitate decision making and task completion, particularly in short-term groups.

12. If group members have already developed relationships with one another, it will be easier for them to reach a decision.

13. The boundaries and dimensions of decision making in groups include the following considerations:

i. Who can participate in making a decision either in an advisory capacity or in the decision-making process?
   a. The leader may make the decision
   b. Several influential members may make all decisions
   c. All members may participate
ii. What is the structure of the decision making?

   a. Formal voting or informal agreement
   b. Majority decisions, concensus, or decision by default
iii. The more the leader makes decisions, the more he or she fosters dependency in group members; if a change is made from leader to group decision making, hostility will be the first reaction and an attack on the leader may follow.
iv. If leaders delegate decision-making power to the group, it is important that the group understands the limitations of the delegation and that the group's decision hold true within these boundaries. In committees, the chairperson is an important figure in decision making, for the chair can decide who has the floor, can stimulate certain suggestions from members, can arrange when voting will occur, and has the casting vote.

Individuals and Their Roles

A social role is a prescribed pattern of behavior related to a particular position in a social group. Role is concerned with function and position within the structure of a group. People function in a group in terms of their perceived roles.

In formal organizations, roles may be clearly defined. In informal groups or fluid situations, a conflict in roles may arise between the needs of the situation, the expectations of others, and the views of group members about their own roles. However, even in well-established organizations where positions, jobs, power, and responsibilities are clearly allocated and defined, there may be marginal areas of conflict. Studies have shown, for example, that in hospitals there are frequent disparities between how nurses and doctors view their respective roles.[33]

In new and changing organizations there is often considerable role confusion, with consequent dislocation of functioning, conflict among individuals, and poor communication. When there is significant social or institutional change, people may find that the roles they were accustomed to playing are no longer relevant. Moreover, individuals may play a number of roles in different social groups and, sometimes, an individual's role may change over time in a particular group.[34] Changing roles may be the result of various factors: a change in the individual's own perception of the roles he or she should play, the pressure of other members, the changing composition of the group, or the demands of the situation. The roles individuals accept will relate to their self-image or concept of their own identity, their personal goals, and the opportunities and range of positions open to them. Individual self-concepts include how one views oneself; how one walks, dresses, speaks; and whether one perceives oneself as stupid, clever, attractive, ugly, a failure or a success, or as special, mainstream, or delinquent. Changes in positions, performances, or opportunity structures affect people's views of themselves and may exert pressure on them to change their sense of identity with resultant anxiety and conflict. This conflict is likely whether the change is viewed positively or negatively.

The formation of self-concept and role perceptions are influenced by people's innate capacities, the culture in which they find themselves, their primary group mores, the changing environment they encounter, and the significant persons with whom they identify. Individuals develop role conflict when they move into social groups with different demands, as when a small-town girl who still accepts the strict moral standards under which she has been raised moves into a big-town social group where the standards for full acceptance into the group are much more permissive.

Role flexibility. The capacity to play a number of different social roles with ease.

Role reversal. When individuals exchange roles or when an individual plays two opposing roles in different situations or at different times, as in some marriages when husbands and wives in time exchange roles of dominance.

Stereotyping. The attribution of certain actions or functions to certain positions or groups of people irrespective of the appropriateness or relevance of the attribution. Stereotyping is frequent in marriage where there are certain cultural expectations regarding the male and female roles. Partners bring role expectations from their own families and their own life experiences and these may not always be compatible. Early married life is a period during which the couple must accommodate their role expectations and work out more realistic roles that are more or less mutually satisfying, if the marriage is to endure. Individuals become stereotyped in groups so that their actions are viewed in terms of their customary roles rather than being critically evaluated. Minority groups are often stereotyped and are not accepted for their individual attributes. It is sometimes hard to change others' expectations of oneself. When individuals play the same kind of role in different groups, such as a leadership role, a passive role, the role of an instigator, coercer, provocateur, the leader's friend, an isolate, a scapegoat, or a clown, they are said to be consistent in their roles.

In small groups roles have specific functions, such as the following: [35] Clowning is defined as being funny by making oneself look clumsy, stupid, or silly. Clowning always involves drawing attention to oneself, usually in a self-derogatory way. It is an attempt to make others laugh. Purposes in clowning may be to disguise one's feelings of incompetence or lack of social ease, to gain acceptance for oneself in the group, to relieve tension, or to derogate others subtly in situations where one's lack of competence also reflects the inability of others to control the situation. Clowning may be tolerated because the group wishes to be diverted from its task.

The scapegoat. [36] Scapegoating is defined as the displacement of a group's anger onto an individual or group who may be inside or outside the main group. Conditions for scapegoating include a high level of tension (anger, anxiety, guilt, or frustration); a person or section of the group against whom the members could rightly feel angry but for some reason are not able to express their feelings; and a group or member who is seen as different, vulnerable, and open to attack. Such individuals usually arouse some irritation in their own right, by being provocative, extremely anxious, or condescending, or by displaying irritating mannerisms. The scapegoat may represent a quality that other group members dislike in themselves; or a leader, feeling threatened, may divert the group's anger onto the most vulnerable member. Scapegoated individuals are typically those who imply they know more than the rest or are more virtuous, who possess more and flaunt their fortune, who have very different interests and do not accept the values of the group, or who are the sickest or the weakest. The scapegoat may be victimized, ostracized, or run out of the group

Levels of Group Study

Groups can be evaluated in various terms: the content on which members focus, isolated themes, or the degree to which the group's overt tasks are achieved. The structure of the group can be analyzed, that is, its formal and informal hierarchies, cliques, member participation and positioning, member roles and alliances, and underlying individual or group defensive behaviors. Other areas to evaluate include the interaction between individual members and the group, the behavior of the group as a whole, the relationship between the group and the outside world, changes in various dimensions over time, and changes in how members function outside of the group. Whether we are studying a group to observe and understand its operations or to examine its efficiency in achieving certain goals, it is essential that we conceptualize our purposes and select the variables or dimensions that we plan to study. Whatever variables are studied, all of the data or samples can be used.

Lewin originated the concept of "field" as an area in which interaction takes place[37] and described the prevailing atmosphere of the group as the "climate." He was concerned with examining the tension within various fields and with the relationship of any particular "field" to the total life space of the individuals, life space being all the fields within which an individual plays a part. He conceived that although a field was an area of immediate interaction, many other fields from the lives of individual members were related to that immediate action in a ghostly fashion. In other words, individuals bring their significant relationships with them into any new interaction. General Systems Theory, which focuses on the opening and closing of boundaries, conceptualizes these phenomena somewhat differently. Lewin and his school have been concerned, too, with the positive and negative attractions, or "valences," that constantly occur in groups, the power struggles resulting from these tensions, and the dimensions of control that emerge. Modern theorists have been studying the issue of conflict resolution within and between groups, and techniques of mediation in problem solving.

Before expanding on the ways in which groups are studied it is important to note the concept of the primary reference group, first described by Homans.[38] Primary reference groups are the most significant, face-to-face cultural groups that influence individuals as they form their attachments, standards, values, and customary ways of behaving. The most notable primary reference groups are the family and the peer group. Of course any new group may also become a reference group for the individual, and the pressure of that group may influence its members to change their standards, values, and behaviors.

Groups can be studied by direct observation or by obtaining information from group participants. If direct observation is the method chosen, observers can be (1) participants, (2) inactive bystanders within the group, or (3) onlookers outside of the group behind a one-way mirror. In terms of organizing the study, observers can be (1) group members, (2) part of an intervention team, or (3) independent evaluators.

Three potential problems may affect observer reliability: perceptual misjudgments; emotional involvement and bias; and mechanical problems of recording and remembering. Trained observers offer a degree of reliability, but their training may limit the scope of their observations. During group sessions records can be gathered in the following ways: making films or audio or video tape recordings; writing shorthand or descriptive accounts of all or part of the sessions; preparing summaries of selected interactions; recording interactions in particular categories; checking particular events or interactions as they occur on a structured schedule; or tracking member participation. In recent years, video tapes have also been used within sessions to provide feedback for members.

Records collected after group meetings, relating to the group process or to members' reactions to the group, can take the following forms: a processed recording of the group in which a participant writes down everything remembered in the order in which it occurred; a summary of group events that essentially emphasizes particular values or dimensions; checklists related to group events; sociometric choices, that is, questioning that seeks to identify roles, cliques, and members feelings about each other; Q sorts of member roles; content analysis of primary data; ratings of group or member behavior; interviews or questionnaires related to individuals' feelings about the group or their impressions of what is going on; or physiological or psychological tests.

Certain difficulties are intrinsic in studying groups:

1. Most of the important data about what is going on at a dynamic level are inferential. Usually even the participants are unclear about what is actually occurring during a session.
2. Much of the communication is nonverbal and therefore difficult to observe, retain, and validate, although video tape recordings have greatly improved this capacity. These can be rerun a number of times after the session, and different sessions can be compared.
3. It is often difficult to know where one sequence of interaction ends and another begins. This may be a matter of judgment.
4. Many interventions are multidirectional; they may be ostensibly directed at one person, but may have relevance for another member, for the leader, or for the group as a whole.

The Group as an Agent of Change

Many systems have been developed for the recording and study of groups. Some of the most well known are the following:

1. Sociometric diagrams, developed by Moreno as part of his role theory, show the positions of members within a group.[39] They are constructed by (a) tracking participants' interactions, (b) asking group members to choose other members with whom they would like to associate for different activities, or (c) rating members in terms of their roles and capacities. General Systems theorists also use diagrams of concentric circles to show boundaries between and within systems and to illustrate stages in information exchange and feedback.

2. Symlog, developed by Bales and Cohen, is a system for observing groups at multiple levels.[40] It is a refinement of a system of interaction analysis developed in the fifties by Bales in collaboration with Borgatta. In this system, behavior, attitude, and content are described in terms of the same three-dimensional space. Multiple levels of behavior and content are analyzed, and the views of each participant and observer are described separately. Further, the system consists of both categorized observations by trained observers and adjectival rating scales. Based originally on field theory and group dynamics, it is probably the most currently utilized system for studying groups.

3. The Hill and Hill Interaction Matrix is a matrix that was developed to evaluate the effectiveness of treatment groups in terms of a particular therapeutic orientation.[41] The assumption is made that self-understanding is important and therefore the focus of therapy should be on the person rather than the group. The system holds that treatment involves change, which implies uncertainty and risk-taking, that people must be able to accept help from others, and that a change in behavior is most likely to occur by studying the present rather than the past. Four dimensions are studied: content, interpersonal interaction, willingness to work on problems, and work style. Groups are evaluated for their effectiveness based on these dimensions and in terms of the group's theoretical orientation. For example, in dealing with a group member's immediate problem, a group in which members evaluate their own feelings and are intent on helping or seeking help is rated higher than

one in which members are discussing group phenomena in a general way, talking to the group rather than to each other, and not focusing on the problem at hand. Similarly, the former group is also rated higher than a group that is intent on tracking down the historical origins of a member's problem in an intellectualized way rather than helping to solve the problem. The authors claim that the matrix can be used to evaluate groups along these dimensions that may have different purposes and that, consequently, would place different values on the dimensions.

4. Moos and his colleagues have also developed a system for examining and evaluating the quality of group climates and milieu. They studied the environments of small groups along a series of dimensions, such as expressiveness and dependence.[42]

5. Leary's system attempts to deal with both action and response. His categorization is inferential and therefore requires psychologically sophisticated raters. Dimensions of his system include managerial-autocratic and docile-dependent.[43]

6. Schutz's FIRO is an approach to understanding the role of intrapersonal dynamics on the interpersonal arena of the group. Individual predispositions for inclusion, exclusion, and control interplay as members struggle to define their roles vis-à-vis other group members. Although the FIRO requires trained raters, the FIRO-B offers a self-report measure for eliciting the personality dimensions of members according to their perceptions.[44]

7. Whitaker and Lieberman hypothesize that a group at any one time is concerned with certain problems at an emotional and dynamic level. They attempt to identify these "focal conflicts" and to select transcripts of interaction that illustrate the group's operations.[45] At a different level, transactional analysts identify "games," discreet transactions that may be repeated at different times and with different content.[46]

8. A number of workers have attempted to conceptualize leader operations that are essential to the creation of certain kinds of group climates or to the carrying out of certain group operations. The most famous of these is Lippitt's study of authoritarian, democratic, and laissez-faire groups.[47]

Multiperspective Outcome Measures

The foregoing discussion has focused primarily on studying and evaluating group properties and the group process. However, in evaluating the effects of group counseling and psychotherapy on group members, baseline and outcome profiles of each member must be developed. Although in everyday practice many constraints are placed on conducting large-scale, complex investigations, techniques do exist that are reasonably adaptable to the evaluation of outcomes in individual therapy groups. The guidelines for this type of research underscore the importance of (1) the use of objective measures, (2) the incorporation of multiple perspectives, and (3) baseline, outcome, and follow-up measurements.

Objective measures are those instruments that seek to record observable behavior or attitudes. These measurements may be research tools or tests from psychological testing batteries. They are intended to gather information that can be reported in a form that will facilitate our understanding of the changes that occur during the course of the intervention (in this book our concern is with adolescent subjects). Preferably, these measurements should be standardized on adolescent populations to provide viable comparisons of outcomes.

We emphasize *objective* rather than *subjective* measurement because in the real world of conducting and researching adolescent counseling and therapy groups, the investigator is frequently the therapist leading the group, or someone closely associated with the treatment process. This potential for a loss of objectivity argues for a more rigorous method of evaluation.

Objective measures may include questionnaires filled out by group members themselves, by group leaders, or by both; or they may be behavioral checklists completed by observers or significant others in the adolescents' lives. Examples of currently available measurements are listed in Azima and Dies.[48] To date, there are few instruments exclusively for adolescents; group leaders may have to reword adult measurements to fit an adolescent

39

population and place their interpretations in the context of the developmental stages of the adolescent members of the group being evaluated.

As mentioned above it is advisable to seek multiple sources for assessment data on the adolescents engaged in counseling or psychotherapy groups. One source of data may be a comprehensive psychological evaluation conducted prior to beginning group treatment. This type of measurement not only provides baseline data for evaluating change, but also affords the group leaders an understanding of individual personality dynamics that can (1) be used to facilitate the functioning of group members in the group, or (2) apprise leaders of potential problems that could impact on the group's development.

Other sources of information about group members include parents, teachers, peers, siblings, and the group leaders themselves. If the adolescent is referred by an individual therapist, that person can provide yet another perspective on the new group member. Collecting data from multiple sources is a time-consuming process. Nonetheless, it affords the opportunity to make more definitive statements on the outcome of the adolescent's course of group psychotherapy or counseling and enriches our understanding of why group counseling is deemed the treatment of choice for many adolescents.

There are times when group counseling or psychotherapy is designed to address specific goals, such as to increase specific coping skills, to change an individual's self-concept, or to help individuals adopt different life-styles or give up certain unhealthy habits. In these situations, the evaluation must include an analysis of individual functioning both at the beginning and at the end of treatment, and should follow group members over a period of time. Research has shown that most relapses to a former life-style take place within the first year following treatment but that there is also a significant percentage of individuals who relapse during the second year. Sometimes, several courses of treatment are needed before an individual can maintain a healthy life-style. In evaluating such changes, one needs to obtain information not only from the individuals themselves but from other significant persons in their lives.

Dies and Mackenzie, in the early eighties, assessed the state of the art for research on group therapy.[49] Relatively few well-designed studies, however, have evaluated the effectiveness of group counseling or psychotherapy with adolescents. Azima and Dies, in 1985, undertook a comprehensive review of current research on group psychotherapy with adolescents and found that only 21 percent incorporated any formal outcome evaluation.[50] The remainder of the studies reviewed were anecdotal material (51%), theoretical writings (19%), and reviews (8%). This indicates that the field could benefit substantially from the collaboration of researchers and clinicians in evaluating the wide range of methods practiced today.

While researchers need to be concerned with rigorous design, all group leaders should evaluate the group process to determine whether the interventions are being carried out according to plan. They should also obtain baseline and periodic individual evaluations, throughout treatment and in follow-up, to ensure that changes observed in the group are transferred into real life and are maintained.

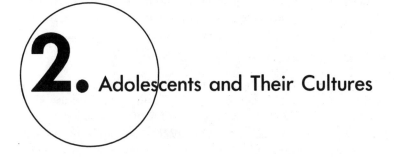

2. Adolescents and Their Cultures

Adolescence

Before therapists work with adolescents, it is important that they consider the nature of adolescence itself. Each stage of life has special tasks and intrinsic problems. In the Western world, at least, adolescence is a period of great change that marks the transition from childhood to adult life, and may be quite prolonged. During this time, boys and girls must establish their identities as men and women; decide the kinds of social roles they wish to play in the adult world, sexually and occupationally; and separate themselves from their primary families in order to become independent and envision the establishment of their own families. In today's world these tasks are made even more complicated by the uncertainty of the future. The frequency of marital breakdown and remarriage, the rapidity of technological change requiring retraining and career redirection in mid-life, the specter of global pollution, and political instability all create uncertainty for adolescents thinking about their future lives.

Early Adolescence

Sometime between the ages of ten and fourteen, all boys and girls begin to experience physical changes that increase their awareness of sexual differentiation. For the first time in their lives, they really begin to see themselves and are seen by their parents and other adults as potential young men and women. There is a great deal of self-consciousness about their bodies and appearances, and the youngsters begin to be preoccupied with their individual and sexual identity. They match themselves against and are curious about members of their own sex. There is much experimentation with different styles of living, dress, walk, and speech. They identify strongly with one another, compete vigorously, and want to be together a great deal. Implicitly, they seem to be asking: "What is it like to be a man or a woman?" In this period of early adolescence, there is relatively little interest in the opposite sex as people. Where sexual interest is present, it confirms either one's power to attract or one's inadequacy. Instinctual drives begin to build but are not well channeled, so they are expressed in fluid anxiety and mood swings. There is much self-doubt and self-preoccupation, and self-esteem is precarious. Adolescents are reluctant to admit to having problems. They often handle their anxiety by fluctuating between extreme reticence and idealistic verbosity, or between extreme physical activity or retreat into drugs or alcohol. Along with explorations of identity, there is also an exploration of values and an overvaluation of what is new and different.

At this time there are also intense contrasting desires: the need to be both dependent and independent, and the need for autonomy as well as for the security of being able to fall back on adults when life becomes difficult. If there is no one to depend on, some girls may fantasize that a baby will give them the love and support they do not find in their families. Boys may affirm their masculinity by getting a girl pregnant. Antiauthoritarianism and defiance are very easily aroused. Youth frequently choose behaviors that will be most hurtful to their families, such as using alcohol or drugs, being promiscuous and getting pregnant, running away, or failing in school.

As boys and girls begin to think of becoming adults, they must also begin to face the question of what kinds of lives they will lead when they grow up. For many this can be a time of panic and despair. Many children from lower-class backgrounds have no prospects of a bright future. They may feel that the gains from allying themselves with the drug trade or other criminal activities may be worth the risks of prison or death. Well-to-do children may feel unable to meet their parents' expectations and may drop out from the competitive struggle to achieve. Children from all walks of life can be afraid of the need to commit themselves to a career or to marriage, afraid of the thought of being a parent and the resultant long-term responsibilities.

Gilligan has emphasized the divergence in development between boys and girls.[1] Largely because of Western society's continued differential treatment of boys and girls, boys are encouraged to place greatest importance on independence, competition, success at any cost, legalistic negotiation, and precise calculation. Girls, on the other hand, are steered toward the development and preservation of relationships. Emphasis is placed on their responsibilities as caring persons, on their willingness to shift ground and avoid conflict rather than to win at any cost. Girls tend to be less theoretical and more pragmatic; boys tend to be more unstable and are more willing to take risks.

Regardless of the differences in the developmental paths of boys and girls, the prospect of becoming an adult and the altered perceptions of adolescents arouse in them much confusion and anxiety. Parents and children suddenly find each other attractive. In close-knit families, single-parent families, and families with stepparents and stepsiblings, this can engender panic that the adolescent expresses by fighting or running away. These new perceptions can also make for difficulty at school where boys suddenly become very sensitive about their maleness with female teachers and girls become provocative with their male teachers. Further, the intense identification adolescents have with members of their own sex is also a factor in the adolescent "crush."

When participating in group counseling, boys and girls are typically restless during this period of early adolescence. Conversation is often diffuse, confused, and diversionary. There is much giggling, touching, horseplay, and getting up and walking around. The attention span is brief, and the ability to stay with anxiety-provoking topics is limited. Group members struggle to stay with the topic for a while, then move away into gossip or physical activity.

Middle and Late Adolescence

Youth during early adolescence test out their potentialities sexually, socially, and occupationally, and, to a great extent, do so in terms of their feelings about themselves. Somewhere between fifteen and eighteen years of age, they begin to deal with the process of growing up at a level more related to the realities of their future lives. They begin to face in earnest the decisions they must make about the adult roles they will play in their work and personal lives. They begin to make tentative occupational choices and to deal realistically with their need to separate from their parents and become independent. They desire to know the opposite sex more intimately, and they begin to think about selecting a mate and establishing their own families. The intense interest in others of the same sex, typical of early adolescence, is subdued and turns into comradeship or a competitive relationship. In later adolescence, individuals tend to be more stable and gradually acquire an increased ability to relate to the opposite sex, to make decisions about how to manage sexual relations, and to conform to the mating customs of the group. Typically, those who choose a homosexual identity become aware of their choice during this time. Although the problems surrounding identity are still considerable, for most they are expressed less in general terms of what it is like to be a man or a woman and in more specific terms of what kind of a man or a woman one wants to be, what role one is going to play in life, and how one is going to relate to the opposite sex.

It is easier for adolescents in this later stage to admit that they have problems and are concerned about themselves. They are more generally willing to accept help and are able to sustain focused discussions for much longer periods. Ideally, as adolescents mature, there should be less tendency to fluctuate between dependency and independence, less emotionality, and a greater capacity to maintain oneself as an independent adult, taking more responsibility for planning one's life and for carrying out one's plans. In general, older adolescents are less impulsive and more able to express themselves in words rather than in physical behavior.

However, it is also in mid- and late adolescence when both genders get into more serious trouble. Very few teenagers between the ages of ten and fourteen attempt suicide, experiment with alcohol and drugs, become sexually active and have babies, drop out of school, or run away. By the time they reach fifteen or sixteen, however, the percentages of these events occurring increase to 11 or 12 percent nationally and much higher in high-risk populations. It is still true that more males than females find themselves in serious difficulty, but female delinquency and substance abuse is on the rise.[2]

Because adolescence is a time for youth to reexamine their standards and values, take stock of themselves, and think through what kind of adult lives they wish to lead, they frequently go through a period of rejecting most significant adults in their lives, rebelling against childishness and dependency. It is at this stage that the peer group becomes extremely important. It forms for the adolescents a pivotal reference group through which they can work out new standards, confirm their identities, gain support and security, and satisfy dependency needs without surrendering their newly found independence. Through the group they can gain status and a sense of belonging. Peer groups form a vital defense against feelings of loss of identity and alienation that can be harmful in adolescence and even lead to depression and suicide. For many youngsters who find it difficult to gain a place in society because of social or psychological difficulties or economic deprivation, the delinquent gang or drug subculture may provide a defiant reference group and become a main source of identification in their lives.[3]

The concept of reference groups is also important as a means of changing behavior. Counseling and therapy groups are essentially new reference groups that create their own standards, values, and ways of behaving. They can exert pressure on members to conform, and can challenge individual group members to explore the conflict between their old and new ways. The willingness of individuals to adopt a new reference group is always closely related to how they see themselves. It is also true that when individuals adopt a new reference group, changes will occur in their former self-images and in their relationships to their previous lives.

The important tasks adolescents face affect their feelings about themselves, their relationships with others, and their attitudes toward the world around them. These tasks include the adolescents need to (1)obtain a clear idea about the kind of person they want to be and the role they are going to play in life; (2)take responsibility for themselves, make plans, and carry out these plans; (3) sort out their feelings about what is expected from men and women and how they will get along with their own and the opposite sex; (4) think through and work out for themselves their own standards and values; (5) develop a self-image that they themselves can respect; (6) allow themselves to have feelings and to risk expressing those feelings when appropriate; (7) mobilize their energies into action; (8) increase their skills in coping with life's stresses and uncertainties; (9) learn to understand human interaction and to respond appropriately; (10) be willing to involve themselves with others and to give and receive help; and (11) understand the structure and functioning of the world around them and be able to assess and take advantage of opportunities realistically. More specifically, during adolescence teenagers must choose and begin to train for adult occupations; prepare themselves for intimacy, marriage, and parenthood; come to terms with themselves as men and women and learn how to develop sexual relationships; and separate themselves from their families and take on adult responsibilities. Early adolescence is concerned primarily with establishing a sexual identity and coming to terms with an independent life. Late adolescence is concerned with actually separating from the family, reaffirming one's standards and values, and making sexual and occupational choices. Gilligan believes that males are more concerned with separation and individuation, whereas females strive to maintain meaningful relationships.[4]

Cultural Factors

The forces that impinge on boys and girls during adolescence vary considerably depending on their cultural backgrounds. In recent years, the custom of studying adolescents in terms of their physical and psychological growth and development has been expanded to include the sociocultural analysis of the field in which their personalities have developed. To help young people grow to healthy maturity we need to understand their economic, social, and cultural backgrounds. Because it is impossible in our present discussion to analyze all the cultural implications of class, race, religion, neighborhood, family, and age groups, we will limit ourselves to certain general categories and the questions they raise pertinent to our discussion.

When working with groups, we need to know what life-styles, values, outlooks, and associations the adolescents bring to the group. Life-style is the pattern of behavior that results from an accumulated psychological and cultural heritage. It is observable and lends itself to study. Efforts directed at rehabilitation will involve changes in life-styles. Efforts directed at socialization should increase the range of adaptations within a life-style.

The problems of growing up in modern society are exacerbated because few meaningful roles exist for adolescents, and there are conflicting expectations for adolescents to be dependent or independent, children or adults. Adults tend to distrust the young, to consider them irresponsible, and to fear their competition. Many restrictions may be placed on adolescents. They may not be allowed to work, to earn money, or to leave home. Consequently, they cannot become independent. They cannot marry and assume family responsibilities before a certain age. They may not even be allowed to move freely in the community after dark, enter certain places of entertainment, or drive a car because their behavior is suspect. There are confused messages about sexual behavior and even about drinking and smoking. In some situations it may well be necessary for group counselors to work to change the environment and to reinforce the youth's natural inclination toward maturity. Group counselors and therapists need to develop an awareness of the effect their own group identifications and values have on teenagers who may come from similar or radically different backgrounds from their own.

Recent research has shown that many serious problems teenagers develop, such as school failure and dropout, depression and suicide, substance abuse and violence, running away, premature pregnancy, and sexually transmitted diseases, are highly correlated and associated with socioeconomic and cultural factors.[5] Another constellation of problems related to depression, anxiety, phobias, obsessions, and eating disorders may well be tied into another set of cultural variables, such as unrealistically high standards, perfectionism, or premature demand for performance, all of which engender insecurity and the fear of failure or success. Whatever cultural factors are at issue, however, all these problems appear to be highly correlated with family breakdown. It is important that we understand the economic, social, cultural, and environmental factors of adolescents when we come to assess their strengths and weaknesses.

The economic category is the easiest to delineate. "Poor" means insufficient earnings to feed, house, and clothe adequately and according to minimal standards. Up-to-date figures on individual and family needs are available through government statistical studies. If we know what the family income is and how many live on it, we can learn whether the youth come from destitute, poor, marginal, adequate, or comfortable economic situations relative to the city or area in which they live. We can also attempt to learn the kind of work being done for the money earned. We need to assess whether this work is above or beneath the educational or training level of the adults in the family. Is it "clean" or "dirty" work? Is it viewed with pride or disgust, or merely boredom? What do the youth know about their parents' work? From this information we can draw some hypotheses about the attitudes toward the value of education and training in this family and about their work habits. The family may be highly tolerant or disapproving of cheating. Parents who are intellectual or successful in business may be intolerant of teenagers who would like to work at a craft. Parents who have never been to college may have mixed feelings about their children getting higher degrees.

We need to know about the family's living conditions. Do they own their home, or what rent do they pay? Do they pay an unfair rent because of discrimination, or indeed do they have a home at all? A growing number of families are homeless today, with many repercussions on family adjustment. Living space is closely related to the numbers, ages, and sexes of those sharing the space. It is not uncommon for more than one "family" to share an apartment or rooms in an urban slum.

What is the community and the neighborhood like? Does it have a community feeling? Are there resources, such as parks, recreation centers, and transportation? To what extent is the population homo- or heterogeneous? Closely knit or open to strangers? Are there strong feelings in the community about religion, class, or racial and ethnic groups?

What does the word *family* mean to the teenager? What is the family constellation? A traditional nuclear family, one child and a single parent, five generations all living together, or a reconstituted family with a stepparent and stepsiblings?

Where does everyone sleep? Who shares a bed or a room? Is there any opportunity for privacy at home, a chance for one's own space? Many teenagers in trouble come from turbulent and overcrowded homes where there is little awareness of the youngsters' needs and struggles. There may be overt, promiscuous sex taking place in front of them. They may even be molested. Parents may be tolerant or disapproving of drug taking, or they may themselves be involved in drug trafficking or abuse. Parents may be alcoholic and there may be spousal violence. In many of these situations there is no protection for the adolescent. On the other hand, there are youngsters in counseling or psychotherapy groups who come from middle- and upper- class families who, to the outside observer, seem to have little to trouble them. These adolescents appear to be struggling, not with issues of survival, but with questions of value and identity in a successful family. These teenagers must find their place in the culture of the professional or managerial world. Although their environment differs markedly from that of the socioeconomically deprived, the core questions of "Who am I?" and "What is my worth and my role in life?" are experienced by youngsters from all classes of society.

How one conducts a discussion on the subject of sex with a group of teenagers depends very much on the background of the members. Boys and girls living in the slums often have had considerable sexual experience at an early age, whereas some middle-class youth are ignorant even of the facts of life. On the other hand, in middle-class families there is sometimes little physical privacy. Nakedness, bed hopping, and bath sharing may be common, which may be very stimulating to the youth. Open sexual practices may produce considerable anxiety.

Heredity and attitudes toward health care are important. Does the family neglect its health, or are members overconcerned? Is becoming ill an approved way of dealing with difficulties in one's life? Is the family attentive to the identification of disabilities, such as poor hearing or poor vision?

Eating practices can also be significant. Does the family sit down to eat together? If not, who does eat together? Is there no time or no space for regular meals together? A poor mother may not sit down because there are not enough chairs or table utensils. An immigrant family may follow the tradition of the mother and daughters serving the men. In some middle-class families everyone is busy going off to work, to class, or to a sports activity so that their timetables never coincide. In some highly successful upper-class families, busy parents may leave their adolescents in the care of housekeepers who serve them their meals. What is the attitude to alcohol in the home? Is there strong disapproval or excessive drinking? Or is alcohol an integral part of eating and used in moderation?

The language spoken in the home is an important element in the family's life-style. Is it adequate English, a foreign language, or a dialect? Are the patterns of verbal stimulus and response in the home active or passive? The implications here are many, particularly in relation to school and job performance. Language styles also have implications for the kind of counseling or psychotherapy one undertakes. Many middle-class youth are highly verbal and avoid reality with words or abstractions. In a different way low-income youth may do the same, using their unique language styles to con and box a therapist in, even though in general less educated youth work better in a setting that is concrete and closely related to real life.

The pressures to conform may differ in low-income and middle-class homes. The culture of delinquency may be hard to resist in poor homes. However, strong pressures to perform and a high degree of criticism in some highly educated families may also take their toll on adolescents, who become overly critical of themselves. As a result, adolescents may become prematurely conforming, rebellious, or even suicidal. Some girls may express their self-destructive perfectionism by starving themselves, or they may binge and disgorge as a sign of loneliness and despair.

What about responsibility? Too often youth from economically deprived homes appear to be irresponsible when, in fact, they are rebelling against premature, inappropriate, and over- whelming responsibilities for the care of younger siblings and the household while the mother is out struggling to make a living. Or they may feel it is critical to help support the family through illegal activities such as drug dealing. Middle-class youth may also be irresponsible but for other reasons. The family may not recognize the need to give adolescents opportunities to as- sume greater responsibilities, or the pressures to succeed may appear beyond the capacities of the teenager.

What opportunities are there for recreation in the home, and what are the family's attitudes toward books and reading, toward television and video? Who are the adolescents' heroes and hero- ines? Their favorite TV programs? This can tell much about their preferred life-styles and aspirations. What is the balance between their passive and active recreation, between the amount of time they spend alone, with friends, or with family?

What is the pattern of the family structure, and who does the fathering and the mothering? The number of single-parent fami- lies is growing and there are more than a million divorces a year. Moreover, many divorced and widowed parents remarry so that many homes contain more than one original family.[6] Very often both parents are working, and some families have not only chil- dren but dependent grandparents to look after. In some low- income, single-parent families where each generation has had children early in life, there may be four or even five generations in the home and individuals with some disability in each genera- tion.[7] In drug-ridden homes it may be difficult to find anyone who is responsible. With increased role flexibility between men and women, there may be great variation in who does what in the home. In a small number of families the man has taken over the traditional female roles of caring for the home and the chil- dren. In many single-parent families, there is no man around or there may be multiple dating partners. How do these different patterns affect the identifications of the boys and girls growing up in the home?

As the number of adults working outside the home increases, teenagers may be left alone at home after school or may go to after-school programs, visit with neighbors or friends, or remain on the street. Some children may have been caring for themselves after school until suppertime ever since the start of their school years. This raises the question of the quality and degree of supervision and protection offered the adolescents as they move from a more dependent position in the family toward a greater assumption of responsibility for their own care and behavior. In many middle-class families, parents are afraid to allow their children to experiment and make mistakes; they have difficulty trusting them. On the other hand, middle-class children often have opportunities for satisfying development through special interests at school and in their communities. However, some parents fill their teenagers' days with so many extracurricular activities that the youth live under great pressure.

Adolescents from socially deprived backgrounds face different kinds of problems. Since their early school years they have had to turn to their peers on the street for support. This exposes the youth to many risks and opportunities for premature experimentation. Their problem is to endure the environmental stresses to which they are subject while seeking meaningful roles with adequate opportunities for experiences that can help them achieve productive adult lives. Many have had bad experiences with adults and have little confidence in them. The more fortunate ones have a supportive adult at home or have been able to form a relationship with a supportive teacher or other appropriate role model in their community. We have found that feelings of inferiority and despair are often concealed beneath a front of rebelliousness.

Youth growing up in inner cities under economically deprived circumstances often have little opportunity to envision the choices available to them. The quality of schools may be poor and, except for the brightest among them, these youth may have experienced failure from early on in their lives. Cut off from the larger community, except for authorities who may well be conceived as hostile (police, school principals, and welfare officers), they may identify with the adults whom they view as successful, wealthy, powerful, and prestigious, even though these adults are living dangerous lives outside of the law. Moreover, the particular culture of the family and the neighborhood will influence how the youths adjust. For example, among immigrant youth, there will be a vast difference in the kind of support provided adolescent girls reared in strict and protective Japanese families where girls and boys are not allowed to mingle until they have graduated from high school, compared with the experiences of Southeast Asian adolescent refugees who have come to this country without their families and have had to make their own way. The experience of growing up will be different again in many Hispanic families where there is a close-knit, extended family network of support, but with limited encouragement to assimilate into the mainstream culture.

If, within the context of the group, we are trying to help adolescents change their ways, we must recognize that their efforts will be affected by their environment. Even though there may be some upset in family dynamics when middle-class youth change, it is likely that their socially acceptable adaptations will move them closer to the ideals and standards of their relatives, friends, and community. Their primary groups will reinforce progress as opportunities open up for them. For some middle- and low-income youth, however, particularly those who are drawn from a delinquent subculture, this is not the case. With such youth, the move toward greater acceptance in the larger society may mean abandoning ways of life that friends and family require in their familiar world, resulting in consequent estrangement for the youth. That changes in one element of an individual's life or of an institution or community may require alterations in many other factors must be considered in planning interventions. In unfavorable environments, special social, educational, and economic supports may be needed to reinforce prevention or treatment.

Schools have been criticized for failing to comprehend the educational needs of the economically deprived and, at the same time, for shortchanging them by expecting poor performance or presenting them with only a vocational experience. Although schools undoubtedly require many changes, they have become a community scapegoat as we view society's failure to rehabilitate the deprived. Large middle schools and high schools, with a huge student body and many hourly class changes, may confuse students and increase their sense of alienation, even in affluent neighborhoods. We must carefully question the adolescents we work with, be they affluent or poor. Questions related to parental and school pressures for academic achievement are relevant in affluent communities, whereas the school offerings and expectations in poorer neighborhoods should be explored. The relationship between youth and the school—the effects each has on the other and their expectations of each other—are important in any socioeconomic class. Many schools fail to identify youngsters with significant learning disabilities. Consequently, these youth often develop severe emotional disturbances because of frustration and loss of self-esteem caused by persistent failure. Recent attempts at establishing drug- free schools, if successful, may well set up a cultural conflict where drug dealing has become a major factor in the economy of the family and neighborhood. The danger of drug-infested areas may be a major stress factor for youth and family.

The feminist movement and the changing patterns in the American family have interacted to affect the roles of both males and females and their identifications and activities in adolescence. Although there is great variation in the extent to which equal opportunities for the sexes and changes in traditional sex roles have been accepted, there is a general philosophy that all careers should be open to women as well as men in accordance with their abilities, that girls and women should be able to take the initiative in developing relationships with the opposite sex, and that marital and parental roles should be worked out between couples in accordance with their inclinations. The truth is, however, that in many subcultures male dominance has not been surrendered and males feel threatened by bright and assertive females. Women are still mainly working in those careers traditionally open to women and are being paid less than men. Women have difficulty moving into areas of work where there are few other women, such as blue-collar trades, and they have difficulty reaching the top echelon in any field where there are few models of successful women.

Girls feel pressured to adopt habits that in the past were reserved for boys. An increasing number of girls are taking up smoking at a time when many boys are giving it up.[8] Girls are as likely as boys are to use illicit stimulant drugs but girls seem more reluctant to inject themselves with drugs.[9] Although both boys and girls seem preoccupied with body image, girls seem more concerned with slimness and boys with bodybuilding. Girls seem freer today to ask boys on dates, and paying one's own way is common. Where and how teenagers socialize varies greatly among subgroups, but the traditional dating patterns remain intact in many parts of America.

Most young women today expect to work. The once-popular ideal of getting married, rearing a family, and living happily ever after, never a realistic goal, seems to have been abandoned. Many women return to work soon after having a baby, even in two-parent families, and relatively few parents divide family responsibilities equally. Generally, the woman works and takes most of the responsibility for child and household care. However, there has been some increase in the time fathers spend with their children, and some divorced fathers fight for custody of their children. There are more than two million teenage pregnancies a year, although not all of these are brought to term.[10] Even so, the result has been a sizable accumulation of single-parent families, the majority of which are poor and headed by females, with the mother working or on relief. Again, there has been some increase in the interest of unwed fathers to assume a parental role toward the children they helped to produce.

In a society where sexuality is promoted daily in the media, teenage girls are largely unprotected. Moreover, even though schools have increased their educational programs in sex and family life, girls are still held primarily responsible for protecting themselves against pregnancy. Sexually transmitted diseases, such as syphilis, gonorrhea, and genital herpes, are rampant today, and infection with the AIDS virus is an ever-present danger.[11] Although sexual abstinence during adolescence is the only absolutely safe choice, many adolescent groups find this alternative unacceptable. Even though adolescents are aware of the next level of safety measures to follow, such as knowing one's sexual partner well, being monogamous, and consistently using condoms, many of them, particularly those who may be emotionally disturbed or involved in substance abuse, do not take these precautions.[12] Teenage sexuality is often impulsive, and teenagers frequently do not have contraception when they need it. Furthermore, teenagers with low self-esteem may have additional complications. Boys may bolster their masculinity by requiring their partners to have sex without protection. Girls may be unable to assert themselves to inquire about their partner's precautionary measures. After all, imagine a young girl brave enough to say, in the moment of passion, "I will not have sex with you if you do not use a condom." Girls may also want to have a child so they have someone to love and to love them when they feel alone and uncared for. The fact also remains that, in adolescence, boys become physically stronger than girls so that girls are in danger of physical and sexual abuse, rape, and incest.

Modern family patterns pose difficulties for both boys and girls. The lack of a consistent male figure in single-parent homes may deprive the boy of a masculine role model with whom to identify. It may leave the girl without any experience of a secure relationship with a man. If the single parent is the father, the situation is reversed. The girl will lack a feminine role model, and the boy may develop a negative or idealized image of women.

In stepfamilies, the adjustment to different parental surrogates and to additional siblings can be difficult and may take time to work out. Separation, conflict, divorce, and bereavement all create upset in the family which takes time to resolve.

To summarize, in the nineties some major challenges for our teenagers are related to the deterioration of the environment, both globally and in our inner cities; changes in sex role expectations in the development of intimate relationships, in the family, and at work; changing patterns of family life; work pressures and career changes; the problems of predicting employment patterns in the future; and the struggle to achieve healthy life-styles and avoid the use of addictive substances. Racial and ethnic discrimination is still a problem for our youth, particularly for the increasing numbers of minority youth, both native born and immigrant, who live in poverty. Consequently, in working with adolescent groups, we need to be knowledgeable not only about each individual but about the circumstances of their lives and the realistic pressures and opportunities to which they are subject.

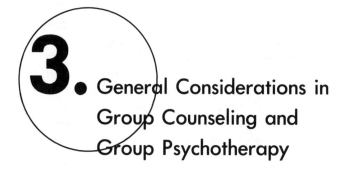

3. General Considerations in Group Counseling and Group Psychotherapy

Values of Group Experience

Group therapy is considered a particularly useful method for working with adolescents precisely because adolescents are generally reexamining their positions in relation to the adult world, because their feelings toward adults fluctuate, and because they are inclined to seek support, assistance, and confirmation of their judgment from their peers. The group situation has various advantages over individual treatment. Small groups provide a miniature real-life situation that can be utilized for the study and change of behavior. In groups, people expose their typical patterns of operation. New ways of dealing with situations can be learned in action. New skills in human relations can be developed, current problems resolved, and standards and values reexamined and altered. The group, skillfully conducted, can provide a mirror in which members can examine new visions of themselves, test these out in action with their peers, and find new models for identification. Moreover, when people are together in a group they lose the sense that they are unique and the only ones with problems. They feel less isolated. Their acceptance by the group and their ability to help others increase their self-esteem. Participation in a group can also assist adolescents in their struggle to achieve adult independence. Further, group participation is acceptable to some adolescents who fear or resist a close relationship with an individual therapist.

Groups are not necessarily positive, however. A group must become an efficient functioning unit to become a potent force and exert influence on the individual to conform to the group's expectations. Certain concepts are therefore important to our approach to group counseling and group psychotherapy, whatever the level and goal of treatment.

First, life is not static. It is never possible simply to solve a problem and live happily ever after. Life is always changing and one's role in life also changes over time, from infancy to childhood to adolescence to adulthood with its formal responsibilities, and finally to old age with its reduced physical capacities and the abdication of certain responsibilities. Everyone must continually face new situations. They must develop, adjust, and adapt, and find new solutions to new problems.

Group members need help in considering the kinds of skills they must develop to get what they want out of life and to avoid trying to achieve the impossible. To deal with life successfully, one must learn to face problems, to cope with a variety of situations, and to build satisfying relationships. The greater one's range and efficiency, the more satisfactory one's life is likely to be.

A necessary attribute in counseling and psychotherapy groups is the concept that people should help one another. This combats sibling rivalry and jealousy. It promotes the idea that there is enough for all—love, credit, gratification—and that satisfaction can come from helping one another obtain these. It encourages feelings of intimacy, trust, and interdependence. The capacity to be responsible for oneself and to accept responsibility toward others is emphasized. For example, in the excellent TV series, "The Power of Choice," [1] the leader's theme is, "You can make good choices or poor choices, but the choice is always yours."

To take part in counseling and psychotherapy means to accept the need to change. Although some adolescents accept this readily, many do not, and this raises the question of motivation. Certainly, it is difficult to see how change can occur unless there is contact and exposure to some agent of change. An individual is unlikely to change unless there is a change in the forces impinging on the individual, or unless there is a change in the intrapsychic balance. It can be that when individuals experience success their feelings about themselves alter; they become more secure and are more tolerant of themselves and others. However, forces may have to be created that present new dilemmas to the individual and militate new choices before any movement can take place.

Accepting Change and Admitting Problems

A special problem associated with therapy groups is the need for the patient to admit inadequacies or the existence of problems. It is essential to promote an atmosphere in which problems are accepted as normal. In such a climate, it is all right to make mistakes, provided one is willing to examine and learn from one's mistakes. It is also necessary to recognize that one cannot know everything or behave perfectly at all times. Failure is no longer a catastrophe, but an opportunity to learn and to try again. This implies an atmosphere of openness in the groups, promoted by the leaders' own attitudes. It implies further a tolerance and acceptance of oneself with all one's assets and liabilities, surrendering the need to be right, perfect, and omnipotent at all times. An increase in the adolescents' self-esteem is a critical element in this approach.

Counselors and therapists must recognize that resistance is an intrinsic part of the struggle to change. If there were no conflict, there would be no need for the group and no hope that change could take place. Resistance is the sign that members are involved. The problem then is to mobilize forces constructively so that the group members can move ahead and work through their problems.

Many group leaders like to start with a formal contract for individual members and for the group as a whole. This works well with members and groups where there is little resistance to coming at all. However, with some adolescents all that can be obtained initially is a simple agreement that they will try the group for a few sessions and then consider a long-term commitment. A group contract of some kind regarding behavior in the group is useful for all adolescent groups.

What Kinds of Groups for What Populations

Adolescents may seek help or information. They may be exposed to new situations that upset earlier adjustments. They may have long- standing problems that they cannot solve. They may require counseling in regard to normal activities, such as school, recreation, or job training. While counseling groups have always been fairly problem-specific, until the mid-seventies most psychotherapy groups with adolescents were generic and heterogeneous with the exception of groups that were run for delinquents,[2] for youth with learning problems,[3] or for pregnant teenagers.[4] By the early seventies some groups for adolescents focused on drug abuse[5] or physical disabilities.[6] During the latter part of the seventies and throughout the eighties there has been a considerable increase in problem-specific groups, possibly in the hope of reducing the duration of the group and making it more effective by restricting its scope.[7] Many current groups for teenagers focus on various types of addiction, such as alcohol, tobacco, or illicit drugs, as well as on eating disorders, adolescent abuse, depression, and school failure. Groups for pregnant adolescents are still quite common, and increasingly there are groups related to family life, sex education, and the prevention of sexually transmitted diseases, including AIDS. Groups are also focusing on specific psychological attributes, such as anger management, self-esteem, and assertiveness training.

There has been much discussion about what counseling, psychotherapy, casework, and therapeutic group work actually are and how they differ from one another. We believe there is considerable overlap and that boundaries are unclear. Two main divisions need to be considered. The first is the kind of counseling that is deemed necessary to help adolescents grow up and that applies to everyday life. This includes vocational counseling and frank discussions on such subjects as building friendships, acquiring values, or dealing with sexuality. Counseling that is related to normal activities, such as how to deal with a supervisor on one's first job or how to make decisions in a peer group, is also within this division. Youth who have serious mental health problems and disabilities may also be included in these groups, which are focused on the normal problems of everyday living. The second division includes counseling that mediates at times of difficult transitions or events in an adolescent's life and that deals with behavior, perceptions, or emotional reactions considered aberrant and disfunctional by society. This type of counseling is called treatment, psychotherapy, or rehabilitation. Varying degrees of leadership competence, education, and training are necessary for the different levels of group management, and this will be discussed in chapter 8. For purposes of simplification in our present discussion, however, we will talk about group leaders in general and refer to group counseling as an all-inclusive term.

Many counseling groups are a part of normal life and carry no stigma. However, whether treatment groups are held in youth counseling centers, child guidance or psychiatric clinics, mental health centers, doctors' offices, schools, or courts, they all imply that the teenagers need help. Teenagers have to recognize that something is wrong when they are getting into difficulty, unable to realize their potential, and have not successfully changed their situation on their own. From their perspective, in order to be helped, they must place themselves in a position dependent on the therapist and submit to the ground rules of the treatment. They must face the fact that they must change in order for the situation to change. This is particularly difficult for the teenager who already feels insecure and is striving to become autonomous and independent.

Teenagers attend treatment groups for one of three reasons: (1) They recognize they need help and are willing to seek it out; (2) treatment provides other advantages, such as belonging to a club where they will have companionship, interesting activities, and food; or (3) they are forced to attend by their parents, school, or the court. Only a very small proportion of adolescents are willing to admit openly that they need help. Many attend a group because there are other gratifications; the group may be fun, may provide desirable activities, or may be heterosexual and stimulating. Most attend because they are forced to. Institutional groups, of course, are frequently comprised of captive audiences. Although members may initially attend the group under duress, adolescents, in order to benefit and to change, must come to accept treatment and attend the group on their own behalf.

Thus, when we contemplate starting a group program, a number of factors must be considered:

1. How do we decide what kind of program should be established? How do we determine goals? What will be the group atmosphere? How will it function?
2. What is the population we are planning to serve, and what are its members' needs? How do we select and prepare members?
3. How large will the groups be, and how long will they last?
4. What is the function of the institution within which we are planning the program? What are its assets and limitations? How does the group program fit into the organization?
5. What resources do we have? Are they adequate? If not, can we obtain what we need in terms of personnel, space, and supplies?
6. What are the attitudes toward the program of all personnel within the institution, and what roles will they play? What administrative structure needs to be set up?
7. How will the groups be related to other programs in the institution and in the community?

General Considerations in Group Counseling

Although occasionally programs are established to train personnel or to carry on particular research, most group counseling and therapy programs are begun to meet the need of some service, either in the community or in a particular institution. Groups may be established because a youth counseling agency has a long waiting list or because many adolescents find it hard to respond to an individual therapist. Groups have been found to be particularly well suited to people who have a need to deny their problems and play interpersonal games. In schools there may be a need for groups that focus on vocational counseling, sex or drug education, problem solving and the clarification of values, or the management of learning and behavioral problems. Employment agencies may view group counseling as an aid in preparing youth for work. Groups may be established in hospitals to help adolescents deal with acute crises or to overcome the anxieties related to specific physical illnesses.

A group's goals must be related, of course, to the needs of its population, and the selection of members, methods used, and duration of the group will be determined by these goals. If the needs apply to the community in general, a decision must be made as to where the group will meet. All settings have advantages and disadvantages. Each institution carries its own image in the community. A school can be a pleasurable or neutral setting for many young people but for those who are in trouble or failing to learn, it may have disagreeable connotations and be a place they wish to avoid. For many such youth, having a counseling group meet in the school setting may well have to be mandatory or the youngsters will not attend, and this will affect the management of the group. Other settings may be preferable alternatives. A psychiatric clinic may be viewed as a place only for people who are crazy or queer, requiring patients always to recognize that they are in need of help. A group that meets in a recreation center is necessarily composed of members who come voluntarily and who expect to have fun and enjoy the group.

When setting up a group, the size and availability of the population must be considered. If a community psychiatric agency has only two girls in early adolescence who are applying for treatment, it may be difficult to start a group for them. Case finding will have to be undertaken in collaboration with other youth service agencies, such as the schools and juvenile services. Decisions must be made as to where and how the groups will be conducted: as classes or special programs within school time, as after-school clubs, or as counseling at the clinic. If groups are held in collaborating agencies, the administrators and staff of those agencies must understand and accept the group and its members. Scheduling problems must be considered, particularly if groups are held in a school. Most groups in outpatient clinics and private practice will be held after school hours. In specialty groups, such as drug abuse or child abuse programs, the focus will be predetermined and the groups will usually be part of a broader program of assistance.

Thus, groups may be established in various ways: membership may be drawn from agency waiting lists; members may be invited or assigned from existing agency populations, such as probation caseloads or school counseling cases; members may have to be specially recruited, such as when a clinic informs its sources of referral that it plans to start a particular kind of group and is ready to accept patients; or a recreation center may announce a group program to which all interested may apply.

Goals and Levels of Group Counseling and Psychotherapy

In all group therapy programs there are general goals for the program, goals for each group, and expectations with regard to individuals in the group.

It is not enough to say, "We think groups are a great idea. Let's start a group." All groups are not beneficial. Delinquent boys who band together in a group and reaffirm their delinquent standards are not being helped to establish a socially acceptable way of life. Similarly, a group that is suitable for anxious, shy, and constricted youngsters may well be unsuitable for sociopaths who already have difficulty managing their impulses.

Program goals, as we have stated, are related to the preconceived needs of the population. Within a group program, a number of different kinds of groups may be set up. Groups may vary in the degree to which goals for individual members are differentiated. The major concern in some groups is to establish a specific group climate that will be helpful to all members; in others, major focus is on the members' individual problems. In some groups, there are common difficulties; in others, members may be quite heterogeneous and the problems unique to each member. For example, in a group of youngsters who are learning to manage diabetes, a coma-free life will be a goal for all members. The group may be of short-term duration, concentrating on the requirements of a diabetic life, teaching members how to manage medication, diet, exercise, sleep, and stress, and helping them clarify their feelings and confusions about living such a life. However, a group made up of youngsters having difficulty managing the requirements of a diabetic life may move into other areas of their lives. Such groups may need to consider more general aspects of adolescent life. For example, the need to be dependent and to be taken care of conflicts with the desire to be independent and creates a power struggle between parent and child. In these instances, goals for each member will become individualized.

Treatment will need to be more intensive and will likely take much longer when the focus is on helping individual members change self-destructive patterns of behavior. If we identify such individuals in our short-term orientation to the management of diabetes, we may discuss with them more general considerations of how they manage their lives, and then assign them to a treatment group composed of adolescents who are manifesting similar basic conflicts in different life situations. When we discuss goals with individuals, it must be understood that the goals relate to what they want to focus on and what they might hope for themselves, rather than ultimate decisions about their lives. If later they decide they cannot give up a particular problem because it provides too much gratification despite the pain, or if they decide that they prefer to accept lesser goals than originally contemplated, that is their prerogative. The leader's task is to promote individual development, to assist group members in exploring situations, and to examine alternatives and their consequences. The goal of the members is to become sufficiently knowledgeable and realistic to make responsible and satisfying decisions. We may not always agree with the decisions of others, but we can never live their lives for them.

Levels of Counseling

There are four different levels of group counseling and group psychotherapy:

1. Groups set up primarily for prevention, including behavioral health and mental health education and for program information and member diagnosis;
2. Groups concerned with specific problems and their resolutions;
3. Groups related to general life adjustments demanding changes in a member's self-concept, self-management, and life-style;
4. Indirect counseling that arises out of other activities, such as playing, clubs, skills and craft groups, teaching and training settings, and work groups, and that emphasizes not only problem-solving but the actual life experiences provided in the program.

All these levels may be applied to, or adapted for, healthy youth, youth who are at risk for a breakdown, and youth who have serious long-term problems.

Scheidlinger has also conceptualized current therapy groups into four categories that are similar to ours but grouped somewhat differently.[8] He has not designed a separate category for groups with specific problems but has made a category for self-help, peer counseling, and mutual-help groups. We have placed these within our other categories. Scheidlinger concurs with us that when teenagers have many problems, group therapy must be allied with other interventions that address all the problems.

Groups for Prevention

Major efforts are underway today to help young teenagers adopt healthy life-styles, understand potentially dangerous habits, and cope with the challenges of growing up. Prevention groups held in school classes or counseling sessions in schools, youth services, and family agencies may include several types of group. Some of these are purely educational, providing information on healthy living, diet, exercise, and sleep, and on the dangers of smoking, drinking, drug abuse, and sexually transmitted diseases. Some groups are concerned with helping youth improve their coping skills.[9] These may be cognitive, such as problem-solving, learning how to say no, or reframing situations.[10] Groups may provide skills in the management of emotions, such as learning how to manage anger, how to relax to reduce anxiety, or how to be persistent and assert oneself. They may be concerned with the improvement of interpersonal relations, such as understanding family relationships, developing intimacy, choosing friends, and learning how and when to trust. Programs may provide growth experiences, increasing confidence and self-mastery through physical experiences, learning to work as a team, caring for young children, or developing peer-led mutual support groups. Many techniques, such as improvisational drama, games, and exercises, are used to help youngsters learn, and some prevention programs also provide opportunities for educational and career advancement. Prevention programs that are successful for high-risk populations generally combine several approaches, depending on the needs of the youth. Dryfoos provides an excellent summary of current programs for high-risk youth.[11] OSAP (Office of Substance Abuse Prevention) has also summarized the current status of mental health and substance abuse prevention.[12] States such as Wisconsin and Virginia have also provided details of programs and materials.[13] Many of these groups are highly structured. They have a curriculum, deal with problems sequentially, and their leaders are active and directive. The more experiential groups, however, tend to place more responsibility on the members, and leaders are required to be more sophisticated in their capacity to understand the underlying group dynamics. Some groups create a positive social structure that supports the youth in healthier living.

Program Information Groups

The goals of these groups are to transmit specific information about programs, to aid in referral, and to assist members to make the best use of programs. Some clinics, treatment centers, and hospitals conduct introductory programs that are usually in the form of lectures, with films and videos and opportunities for discussion. They may be held to transmit knowledge about certain courses of action, as in informational groups for pregnant mothers or unwed fathers in which members discuss the course of pregnancy or hospital procedures. They may introduce clients to the working of an agency. Groups may also be related, for example, to career development where a group comes together in a school or recreation center to consider the implications of selecting a particular career. Attempts may also be made in these introductory groups to present a new idea or to refocus the problem, such as helping parents see that an adolescent's problem may in fact be a family problem.

Orientation and information groups economize considerably in time. They may reduce isolation, guilt, or anxiety by recognizing a common situation, refocus the adolescent's and family's views of their problems, and clarify the members' feelings about what action they want to take. The leader in these groups is likely to take initiative and be quite active. There will probably be a fair amount of discussion between the leader and individual members and group participation may be limited. How active members are will vary, depending on the degree to which the leader encourages their involvement. Group size may vary from quite small to very large. The decision about size will depend on the number of people involved and the degree to which wide participation is desired; the more individual the participation, the smaller the group. Discussion is likely to be fairly concrete, using a question-and-answer format. The focus will be on reality but with some clarification of feelings about specific situations. Audio-visual aids may well be used and reading materials distributed,

Although there is some dynamic interaction as occurs in all groups, such as getting acquainted, establishing a purpose, deciding on a method of operation, and developing termination maneuvers, the teenagers in these groups are not likely to become overly involved and intimate with one another. If the aim is to lay the groundwork for a continuing group, however, the leader may deliberately stimulate the production of more intimate and bonding discussion.

Diagnostic Groups

Orientation and information groups where members are seeking solutions to individual or family problems may also combine a diagnostic component, which is helpful in understanding how individuals or families deal with one another. The size of the groups will then be held to no more than six to eight members. Such a group stimulates more discussion of personal material and encourages dynamic interaction. However, this more intense interaction creates other circumstances, for soon people begin to relate to one another more intimately, transferences develop, and the group becomes a cohesive whole. It is necessary to consider how much pretreatment diagnosis is essential and for what purposes, and how long a group may exist before being considered a short-term treatment. When working with resistive adolescents, it is preferable that they start therapy with the group therapist with whom they are likely to continue, even for the entry interview. Then when groups are started, we can expect that these adolescents will move into therapy groups. Teenagers do not tolerate transfers from one therapist to another very well. Precontracting is important so members do not feel that the rules are changing after they have made an initial commitment. Recontracting may be important at the end of the diagnostic period reflecting the change in focus.

Many clinics have started with a four-session series for diagnostic purposes only to decide that this was too long, for by the fourth session a group is well on the way to cohesion and members are developing relationships and beginning to settle down. Two sessions are probably adequate for diagnosis. Six sessions are already the equivalent of a short-term, problem-solving group.

Problem-Specific and Life Crisis Groups

Groups that focus on specific problems or crises, such as those that help youngsters make a transition from one school to another, prepare parents for the psychological adjustments of their first child, or debrief youth after a disaster, are normally short-term groups. The goal is to understand the ramifications of the problem and to explore alternatives for dealing with it, one's attitudes and feelings about the situation, and one's abilities to affect change, and then to determine a course of action. Group operations are thus limited to specific areas in members' lives, and discussion is likely to have relevance for all members through this commonality.

In such groups, leaders set the focus, then increasingly encourage members to discuss the problem themselves and to bring out their own feelings about it. They encourage both self-help and mutual assistance. The degree to which leaders will encourage group members to come up with their own information will vary, depending on the population and the setting. In terms of training members in self-reliance, however, the more the members are encouraged to act for themselves, the more effective the group will be.

Members, in examining their problems, can begin to feel intimate and can give one another support.There is also generally less acting out in these groups than in less focused ones because membership is usually voluntary and so members are more interested and concerned. Role playing can be useful in teaching youth how to deal with specific situations and to gain an understanding of how others may feel.

Because all members have a common focus and can learn vicariously from one another, these groups can be fairly large, up to eight–ten members. Selection does not have to be rigorous. Provided all members have a common problem, the group can sustain a wide range of other differences.

Problem-related and crisis groups take two forms. They may be short-term closed groups of predetermined length, or they may be ongoing open-ended groups, with members joining and leaving at various times, sometimes staying for relatively brief periods.

The group process in short-term closed groups is often accelerated, and the leader needs to be aware that termination procedures will usually begin in the last two or three sessions. In our view, it is possible to circumvent early and prolonged separation maneuvers without adversely affecting the final termination. In open-ended problem-specific groups, the relationship between individual members and between members and the group is likely to be less intense, and termination is individual rather than a group operation. In these groups, different facets of the problem are raised again and again as membership evolves and the needs of attending members vary. In view of these dynamics, most leaders treat each open-ended group session as an individual entity.

Groups for Life Adjustment and Changes in Life-Style

Life adjustment groups are concerned with the individual's way of life. They may be composed of youngsters in the process of transition from one stage in their lives to another or of teenagers wanting to make a more satisfactory adjustment, to learn more about themselves, or to resolve serious long-term problems. The goals are to help members understand themselves, how they relate to others, what they want out of life, and how their own behavior and feelings intrude. The group's goal may be merely to teach members how to work out their problems and begin a process of readjustment, or to help members work through deep-seated difficulties and achieve a radical change in their way of life and their perceptions of themselves.

Although these groups are generally treatment groups, they may be conducted for adolescents who wish to increase their self-knowledge or general competence, as in self-awareness groups or personal-development groups in school. Methods of leading these groups vary considerably, depending on the leader's philosophy and temperament. Leaders always set the time and place, and teach group members how to work together. Leaders may be active or passive, however, encouraging group members in varying degrees to be concerned with their relationship to the leader or to one another. Leaders may direct the group's attention to what is happening in the group or encourage members to bring in material from their lives outside the group or from their past. Leaders may emphasize the feelings generated by the group experience or encourage analysis of what is happening in the group. They may focus on content, on individual management of anxiety and resistance, on transference phenomena, on underlying themes, on member roles and group dynamics, or on restructuring the way individuals perceive and think about their problems and their assets.

Duration and intensity of treatment may vary considerably in these groups. There is no question that teenagers differ from one another in the ways they learn and the extent to which they can benefit from learning. Teenagers may not be able to respond or change at a particular time in their lives but later may react differently. Sometimes an individual is encapsulated in such a hard defensive shell that only intensive and prolonged exposure will break this down sufficiently to permit change to take place. At other times, during a crisis for example, individuals may be so receptive that small periods of discussion can set off inner reevaluations that will continue without further stimulation for some time. A single period of counseling or treatment is often not as beneficial as two periods with a break in between, at which time evaluation and consolidation of change can take place.

Selection and grouping are also matters requiring careful consideration in these groups. The more we require members to examine and possibly change their defense mechanisms against intense feelings and involvement with others and set in motion the development of transference, the more carefully we must select our group members. Central to this selection process is assessing whether individuals are strong enough to face these revelations or whether they will be forced to increase their defenses or regress to earlier and more primitive ways of dealing with intolerable situations, such as retreating from reality into psychosis. We need to be particularly careful in dealing with adolescents because their identity is still precariously established.

Choice of Individual, Group, or Family Therapy

There has recently been much experimentation with different group compositions, particularly with adolescent populations. Today we can emphasize the individual, the peer group, or the family. Much of our work with younger, middle-class adolescents includes a family emphasis because of the close involvement of most middle-class parents with their children and the primacy of the family as a middle-class acculturation agent. This may mean working with multiple family groups or with parents as a couple or in adult therapy groups, while the adolescents are involved in their own groups. With older adolescents and with lower-class teenagers in general, there is greater emphasis on the individual and the peer group because the teenager is already moving away from the family toward living independently.

When dealing with the family, we are more likely to be concerned with communication between family members. Limited abilities to interact effectively generates misunderstanding and mixed feelings leading to power struggles between family members. Goals of treatment are to help family members disentangle their individual identities and goals, increase their trust and autonomy, reduce family collusion, and focus on influencing the family as a group. With so many couples divorcing and remarrying, many groups today are concerned with the reconstitution of families and with reformed roles and alliances, as well as with grief over separation.

In the peer group, emphasis is frequently on the development of a new reference group within which the teenagers can provide one another with mutual assistance. Members help one another examine how they deal with situations and how they appear to others. They recognize the games they play to defend themselves. They establish a new set of standards and values and test out their sense of identity against the realities of the group.

There are important and intrinsic differences between working with teenagers alone, in small groups of unrelated peers, in a family, or in a group of several families. For example, the use of time in relation to content differs. The individual does not have to share the therapist's time or attention. The family is totally concerned with the problems of its members. When several unrelated individuals or families are placed together, they must share time and attention and endure periods when the discussion has no apparent relevance to their problems. In such groups members must learn how to truly be interested in others altruistically and how to empathize with others, as well as how to apply what they learn from others to themselves. In all groups members have opportunities to identify with other group members as well as with the leader, whereas in individual treatment there is only the opportunity to relate to or identify with the therapist or counselor. In family groups there are limited new identifications as one comes to see family members in a new light. Peer groups afford members many opportunities for identification, as do multiple family groups where members can identify with other fathers or mothers, with other sons and daughters, and so on.

Except in individual therapy, competitive feelings are likely to be aroused. Competition for the leader is often most intense in individual family groups. Opportunities for reality testing are more frequent and varied in multiple family groups and in peer groups than in individual or single family counseling. Transference is most complicated in multiple family groups, where there are parental transferences to the therapists, parent-child transferences between couples, and joint parent transferences to their children. Sibling transferences among all the group members become apparent, along with libidinous relationships between couples and rivalries between families. Thus, group members can form identifications not only as individuals but as couples, as children, and as families. In individual treatment, the individual's behavior in a group must be described; in family and group therapy, such behavior can be seen in action.

Communication is significantly enhanced in family groups as compared to unrelated groups. The established relationships often allow members of these groups to interact with one another more directly. Daily life is influenced more easily in task-related counseling groups as the work of the group is specifically relevant to routine life events. Members of peer groups who also meet outside the group can put much pressure to bear on one another and can influence their neighborhood or others in their institution. In groups composed of strangers, emphasis is entirely on helping members use the group to manage their own lives more satisfactorily and to enhance interpersonal skills. The more intervention is integrated with the lives of group members through the inclusion of family and friends, the greater the possibility for members to achieve change in the systems of which they are a part. This sets in motion a positive interactive cycle of change.

Concurrent and Conjoint Therapy

Choices must be made when teenagers and their families are involved in multiple therapies. Some therapists may choose to see all the group members in individual as well as group therapy, even when members may need different approaches in individual treatment.

Sometimes cotherapists will each select different members of the group to counsel individually. In outpatient and private practices, it may be useful for two therapists to run concurrent parent and adolescent groups, which would reduce transportation problems and make it easy to bring the two groups together from time to time. Sometimes youth are referred to a therapy group by several therapists; in such cases, communication between the group leaders and the individual therapists must be maintained and the parameters of confidentiality worked out. There are always advantages and disadvantages to any arrangement. Therapists should carefully think through what the transferential reactions and communication problems may be and ensure that any problems that arise can be openly discussed and resolved.

Approaches for Different Problems

Groups for teenagers suffering from serious mental illnesses range from short-term inpatient groups to long-term groups for schizophrenic, suicidal patients and those with incapacitating depressions. Eating disorders, anorexia, and bulimia are common among teenage girls today and some therapists specialize in this population. The eating disorder groups may be conducted in outpatient settings or, for seriously ill individuals, in hospitals.

It has been established that about 10 percent of those who become involved with dependency-inducing substances become addicted and need specialized intensive treatment programs, such as those provided in a therapeutic community where individuals participate in a variety of groups. These may include groups concerned with basic education about drugs and their effects, with coping skills and self-esteem, with supervision of milieu and work, and with cognitive restructuring. Often groups are designed specifically for girls who historically have been in the minority in these communities but are now increasing in number. Some groups are also concerned with identifying and managing individuals who crave drugs, and this extends into outpatient treatment as relapse prevention or mutual help groups.

Although therapists are increasingly conducting problem-specific groups, many still run long-term heterogeneous groups in outpatient settings for adolescents who are experiencing a wide variety of psychiatric problems. These groups are conducted within a range of theoretical orientations,[14] such as identity group therapy,[15] psychoanalytic work,[16] cognitive behavioral approaches,[17] and interpersonal orientations.[18] With the evolution of gender roles, more therapy groups presenting a feminist perspective are being conducted.[19]

Indirect Counseling

Because adolescents are often particularly resistive to admitting that they have problems and already feel so insecure that concentrating on their weaknesses can increase their resentment and malfunctioning, efforts have been made to build both socialization and rehabilitation into other activities. Groups, established for therapeutic recreational purposes, can provide youngsters with many opportunities to learn how to deal more effectively with one another and to increase their self-esteem. Members can talk over problems outside the group with sympathetic peers and group leaders. Counseling can be included as part of classroom management or job training. The major focus is on creating a positive group climate and on the strengths rather than the weaknesses of group members. Much is achieved from the relationships between group members and from experiences in the group itself. These groups afford ready opportunities for achievement, reality testing, and for confronting the effects of one's behavior on others. Problems can be dealt with in a constructive way in relation to actual situations. The quality of the interpersonal experience is as important as any verbalization and discussion of problems.

Such groups do not generally have highly selective criteria for admission, and they may even form naturally. They may be of short or long duration. They often meet for much longer sessions than do counseling or therapy groups because interpersonal growth and change is only one reason for the group's existence; formal learning and fun also take up much of the group's time.

Regression is kept to a minimum in these groups. Fantasy and unconscious thoughts are discouraged. Rather, the group is concerned with ego development and with reality, with such matters as how people see themselves, how others feel about them, what they can do, what they want to do, what they believe in, and how they manage different situations. The emphasis is on the here-and-now, with members interactions with one another and with the leader.

As we have discussed in regard to groups for substance abusers, group counseling is frequently embedded in broader programs. For example, groups for pregnant teenagers may be conducted as part of general prenatal care for the young mother; long-term maintenance groups for young chronically mentally ill patients or substance abusers may be part of a general program of rehabilitation that includes case management, work training, and recreation, as well as specific group therapy. Groups for school dropouts may be included as core group counseling in a program of work training, supervised work, remedial education, and health care.

"Youth empowerment groups" are becoming increasingly popular. These are group programs that provide opportunities for disaffiliated youth, with the assistance of knowledgeable adults, to take on responsibilities and achieve change in some aspect of their environment. Some youth have organized a recycling business. Others have formed a youth credit union or an arts center. Still others have banded together to rehabilitate and beautify their slum neighborhood. The youth learn that they can have an impact on their world, which gives them a stake in the future as well as enabling them to acquire many useful skills that may help them later in life.

Choice of Theoretical Approaches

Group therapy with children and adolescents in their early years was based on some form of psychoanalytic theory, whether this theory was used only for understanding the dynamic group process or for actual interpretation. Slavson developed group therapy oriented to activity, interview, and analysis,[20] and Moreno developed psychodrama.[21] Both of these schools are still active today.

Carl Rogers, with an emphasis on unconditional positive regard, empathy, and reflecting back what the individuals were saying, had a strong influence on counseling during the sixties and seventies.[22] Truax and Carkuff also emphasized warmth and empathy and working within a positive transference.[23]

Adlerian theorists emphasize the importance of each individual's unique life-style, which portrays a singular pattern of thinking, feeling, and acting in the context of particular behaviors.[24] The group creates an environment for self-discovery and interpersonal awareness. Family therapy has had an effect on social work approaches and particularly on multifamily group therapy.[25]

Transactional analysis,[26] with its emphasis on interpersonal games, the confrontational techniques of the Gestalt movement,[27] and behavioral contracting[28] have in various combinations been particularly popular in the treatment of sociopathic delinquents and addictive personalities where denial, avoidance, and gaming are major defenses. Rachman's identity theory is also confrontational.[29] Glasser's reality approaches have been used widely both in schools and in youth counseling services throughout the country.[30]

Developments in psychoanalytic theory, such as the elaboration of object relations and Kohutian self-psychology, have not in themselves been widely discussed in the literature on group psychotherapy with adolescents. The Kohutian emphasis, however, on the therapist's positive transference, on strengthening self-esteem, on mirroring, and on the understanding of "twinship," or mutual identifications, is useful with adolescents who have poor self-esteem and need support.[31] Current developmental theory[32] is more explicit now than in the early days of group psychotherapy, although developmental stages were always considered and modern understandings, both of cognitive development and of the capacity for object relations in different personality constellations and at different stages of maturity, have been incorporated into other theoretical approaches.

Most group therapy with adolescents emphasizes either the treatment of the individual in the group or the interactions and relationships between group members. Yalom's interpersonal group psychotherapy has had a major influence on the field, synthesizing, as it does so well, the theories of earlier therapists.[33] Few therapists use Bion's group-as-a-whole approaches as treatment.[34] Many practitioners take note, however, of the underlying group resistances and may from time to time make group interpretations. Similarly, field force theory and boundary theories are incorporated into other approaches and broaden the understanding of group and family structure. Skynner in England has probably developed the most highly integrated theoretical approach in working with individuals, families, and groups of strangers, melding together group analysis, family therapy, Systems Theory, and behavioral techniques.[35]

Preventive approaches draw heavily on theories of coping skill development[36] and behavior modification.[37] Stress management[38] and cognitive restructuring[39] have also permeated the adolescent group therapy literature in helping youngsters deal with disaster, abuse, and more specific fears. On the other hand, therapists generally have been reluctant to use hypnosis and trance inducement with adolescents because of the instability of the adolescent ego.

There have been many theoretical developments in the last twenty years, and adolescent therapists have approached these selectively, adopting approaches and techniques that seem most suited to different personality types, problems, and levels of treatment.[40]

The Leader's Attitude Toward the Group and Its Members

A paradox of all intervention is that while leaders can be considered competent only if they are helpful to those with whom they work, they must not be so invested in group members that a change in any one of the members in a certain direction becomes the measure of a leader's own competence and self-respect. Pupils, patients, and clients must be respected as individuals who have autonomy over their own lives and who have the right to choose how they will lead their lives. The task of the leader is to establish an appropriate group climate within which members can understand their situations, feelings, and needs as adequately as possible and can make and carry out choices and decisions with full understanding of the implications of their choices.

Undoubtedly, all group leaders, and particularly those who work with children and adolescents, represent certain standards and values and present themselves as models for identification. When they are leading a group, they attempt to teach the group these standards so that members may have a beneficial influence on one another. Teaching their young how to live within the range of acceptable behavior and to accept their standards and values is the task of all viable societies. Thus, society rewards those who conform, penalizes most of those who do not, and permits a few mavericks to live deviant lives in view of their special value to the society. To obtain compliance, the connection between conformity and rewards, as well as penalties, must be clarified. In modern metropolitan society, particularly, there has been a disconnection between rewards and conformity. For this reason, deviant and delinquent groups have developed that have set up their own standards of operation and their own rewards for behavior that are inimical to and in defiance of the larger society.

Even if the rewards for conformist behavior are apparent, however, such behavior will still be rejected by many if conformity threatens individuals' autonomy, if they do not have confidence that they can succeed, or if they must sacrifice too much security to obtain the reward. Adolescent groups must help members make these connections and should be linked to programs that provide teenagers with support and opportunities for success.

Leaders are critical to the group. Through their selection of members and their direction, they will establish the group climate and influence its operations. A leader teaches a group how to function by (1) definite statements about how to operate and limits on what is permitted and not permitted, such as at the beginning of the group; (2) activities such as asking questions or focusing on certain levels of exploration; (3) selective attention, that is, what the leaders focus on or ignore; (4) attitudes expressed verbally or nonverbally; and (5) statements about standards and values.

Group leaders play many roles. They are teachers, reflectors, informants and resource persons, explorers, models for identification, clarifiers, interpreters, transmitters of values, supporters, and persons who care about and respect the group members and are there for them when the members need them. In their work, leaders can choose to emphasize one or more of these roles. What they choose and what levels they work at will depend on the population and on goals of the group. Leaders must know their population, understand the significance of behavior, and be able to communicate in the language of their group members.

The Use of Authority in Treatment

It must be recognized that no fundamental personality change or alteration in value systems or ways of life can be achieved except by the individual concerned, so that authority can be used only to (1) expose individuals to the opportunity to change; (2) increase motivation for change; and (3) keep the learning environment safe. Ultimately, individuals must invest themselves in their treatment or no change will take place.

Outside Authority in Groups

A group may be set up so that the leader is an independent, outside person who must follow the rules of a particular setting, but who has no authority beyond the limits of events that occur in the group.In these situations, even attendance is under the control of someone outside the group. In general, all that goes on within the room is confidential within broad limits; members may act in ways within the room that are not permitted outside. The leader is not ordinarily obligated to report transgressions unless they appear dangerous to the individual and the community; rather, the leader is there to help members analyze the consequences of their actions and to take responsibility for themselves. The group leader generally plays the role of a benevolent, trusting, neutral, and accepting individual, while maintaining clear boundaries within which the group can function effectively.

Leaders with Authority in Other Areas

Leaders may also be guidance counselors or welfare officers who in that role can affect the lives of group members. When they are leading groups, however, they abdicate that power in the group and do not maintain formal authority there. This must be clear to members who will have to accept the leaders in their two different roles. There are limits to this distinction, however. Leaders have certain responsibilities that they do not abdicate, such as conducting an outside investigation if members inform them about activities that may be harmful to themselves or others.

Authority of Group Leaders That Affects Members' Lives

Leaders may have power over group members. Members' performance in the group may affect privileges they can obtain. The leader or the group may be able to apply sanctions. This is often the case in token economies and therapeutic communities.

In probation groups, the leader or the group may decide whether an individual should be returned to court for violation of probation. A guidance counselor may have to decide or have the group decide what should be done about a member who is playing hooky. Performance in the group may decide when an individual is permitted to leave the hospital.

The degree to which leaders delegate this decision-making power to the group affects their role and position in the group. Leaders who make the decisions alone do not encourage their members to take responsibility for themselves. They increase member dependency on them. If leaders delegate decision making to the group, however, they must be clear on the limits of power they are willing to give up and on the limits the institution places on them.

Confidentiality

The definition of confidentiality in group or individual therapy comprises two main areas. It implies that (1) therapists or group leaders will not reveal what has been learned in the sessions to anyone outside the group; and (2) members will not reveal to others what has gone on in the group.

Obviously, agreement about confidentiality must be part of the ground rules of any counseling or psychotherapy. Of course there are degrees of confidentiality that can be established between members and leaders. First, in traditional casework and psychotherapy, the most usual agreement has been that the leader would not discuss any materials learned in the group with anyone other than agency professionals without prior consent of the individual concerned or at least discussion with that person. This worked relatively smoothly with adult neurotic patients who came for help because they were uncomfortable and wished relief. It becomes a different problem, however, when one is working with adolescents and their parents, or with youth with behavior problems where the individual is accepting counseling more or less because of external pressure and many agencies are involved.

Referring or collaborating agencies often apply pressure for explicit information. In these situations, general progress may be reported and specific problems communicated after discussion with the individual member. Detailed group interactions, however, must be kept confidential if members are to feel free to trust others and reveal themselves.

Group leaders are sometimes caught in situations where parents and adolescents each confide information to their own leader, or even to the same leader, information that would be important to discuss with all parties but that the youth or parent is unwilling to release. It is wise for leaders to clarify initially that family members will be expected to work out problems together and that the leader may call the family together if such problems must be resolved.

Delinquents who are in and out of institutions, and other teenagers who are defiant of authority, can trap leaders (as in one group where the leader had promised to keep everything secret and was then told by a member that the member had stolen the keys of the institution). Such juveniles can raise anxiety in the group by telling of crimes committed or about to be committed, such as taking drugs or intending to commit suicide, while at the same time withholding permission for anyone to take action. When members tell such secrets, leaders must explore why the information is being given in such a way and at that particular time. It often reflects a youngster's mixed feelings about getting help or controlling impulses. Sometimes the relationship to the leader is at issue. Teenagers who tell such secrets may want to know that the group leader understands and cares about them, either by allowing them to be responsible for themselves or by overruling them. Members may unconsciously want to prove at any cost that no one can be relied on or trusted. Leaders must be able to respond appropriately to the dynamics of the situation. Unless ground rules are clearly set, individuals, families, and groups can become trapped by the use of confidentiality as a way to resist change and avoid solving problems.

Leaders can never promise absolute confidentiality and, from the outset, must make it clear that they are obligated to pass final judgment as to whether information is so dangerous that an individual's wishes must be overruled. For example, in establishing a contract with group members and their families before beginning the group, leaders can explain that suicidal or homicidal thoughts, with plans to act on them, will be reported to the appropriate authorities. Moreover, leaders may indicate their practice to report alcohol or drug abuse if it becomes self-destructive. Adolescents and their parents may also be informed of the leader's obligation to report any physical or sexual abuse that occurs within the family. Although these confidentiality practices may initially create a climate of greater caution, in the long run leaders gain respect for their clear boundaries. Such openness prevents breaches of confidentiality for which no foundation has been laid.

Closely allied to the issue of confidentiality in the group, and often confused with it, is the leader's right to confront group members with actions and information culled from the youngsters themselves or from others outside the group. When teenagers are resistant to dealing in the group with incidents critical to their problems, therapists must use their judgment as to whether or not to confront the adolescent. With motivated neurotics, the patients themselves consciously want to help and, consequently, are willing and sufficiently strong to bring up their problems for discussion. When dealing with individuals who characteristically deny and avoid facing problems and do not take such responsibility, the leader's task is to inspire members to take responsibility for themselves. At the same time, the leader must be free to confront members with information gleaned from other sources.

Finally, while it is important that group members feel free to discuss any part of their lives with one another and learn to trust and help one another, it is also important that a code be established prohibiting the teenagers from gossiping about one another outside the group. In groups where members have contact with one another in their daily lives, such as in school, institutions, or training centers, and where mutual help is considered central to the operations of the group, members are expected to bring up one another's problems in the group if they know about them. This runs counter to self-protective, antiauthoritarian systems, such as the child-adult or delinquent systems, in which lower echelons classically band together against the power structure and only "squealers" betray their peers. For group members to be able to help one another, they must feel there is a unity of purpose between group leaders and members that can eliminate the antagonism and the dichotomy. Even though such freedom is encouraged within the group, it may well be that care must be taken that members do not use such information as weapons against one another with authorities or peers outside the group.

Single or Cotherapists

There has been continuing controversy over the use of single therapists or cotherapists. The major advantage of a single therapist is that the transference relationships are less complicated. In cotherapy, group members develop transferences to each therapist and to the therapists as a couple, and the therapists have realistic and transferential relationships to each other. A single therapist need not be concerned with these dimensions or with the compatibility and style of another leader. There is less chance for members to play one leader against the other. Communication is also easier with a single therapist, particularly when families and other agencies are involved, because the single leader takes full responsibility. Time need not be spent on bringing the other leader up to date and on making sure that each one's role in the group has been worked out. One therapist is also less expensive than two, a consideration when money is a factor.

Cotherapists have been used for various reasons: to simulate a complete family with a mother and a father; to provide experiences with both male and female adults; to play different roles in the group, such as the more authoritarian therapist and the more permissive one; or to provide different dimensions, such as health information, education, and counseling. Two therapists are often used in groups of very disturbed youth, where one therapist can care for an upset child while the other attends to the group. Sometimes in private practice, two therapists will bring their

91

adolescent patients together to form a group. This can have advantages or can cause problems, depending on the members' needs, because such an arrangement resembles a reconstituted family with stepparents. Sometimes cotherapy is used as a vehicle for training, in which case one therapist is clearly the leader and the other an assistant. What is less defensible is when two therapists get together to lead a group because they may have underlying fantasies of attack from the group and want mutual support or because they may wish to have someone take over when the other needs to travel, attend conferences, or take a vacation. There may be problems if members sense that the therapists are adopting cotherapy for their own ends. When cotherapists are working together, however, they must learn to know and accept each other, be comfortable with their different styles, and take time to process together what goes on in the group. Cotherapy is like a marriage; leaders should enjoy working together and be able to serve as models for group members in terms of how they work out any problems between them. If there is unresolved conflict between leaders, this will inevitably be disturbing to group members and create problems for them. Under these circumstances, therapists should seek outside consultation in order to protect the group from any unpleasant side effects resulting from their differences. When a cotherapy team works well together, their effectiveness is enhanced when they can resolve differences in the group. Given that many adolescents do not have models for the productive working through of differences, coleaders can provide a valuable learning example through their behavior.

Selection and Grouping

One can find many discussions in the literature of how to select members for counseling and therapy groups. Questions are raised as to whether one should have unisexual or heterosexual groups, groups of patients with one symptom or many, or groups composed of members who behave in the same or in different ways.

Frequently, however, there is little discussion of several prior questions: why we select members for a group, whether we should select members, and, if selection is appropriate, who should make the selection, the group members or the leader.

It is important to remember that there are two orders of selection: first, the selection of members who are suitable for a particular kind of group program and, second, the composition of members in a group.

Why do we select at all? What are the purposes of selection and grouping? First, we assign individuals to a particular kind of group because we know it is designed to meet their needs. Sometimes we merely describe a service and let people select the service themselves. Even in this case, however, the group must always be appropriate and relevant to the needs and goals of the individual. Second, selection is made in an attempt to screen out people who will not benefit from the service. Third, it is designed to economize by putting people together with similar needs, thus rendering the group more efficient. Fourth, we select in order to create a particular kind of group where the members will work together optimally.

Are there individuals who should never be placed in groups? We can probably imagine a group that will benefit almost anyone, but matching members to the group most appropriate for them is important. Groups for withdrawn or very disturbed youth require more structure and perhaps more therapists than do groups for more stable teenagers. On the other hand, some youth really need the undivided attention of one therapist, some youth are very disruptive to the group, and the problems of some youth are so enmeshed with the family that family therapy appears the only solution.

We sort people into groups to provide particular interactions that we expect will be beneficial, to develop a particular climate, and to promote control of the group through the interactions of its members. We avoid putting members together who will have a detrimental effect on one another. For example, a group composed of teenagers who are all hostile and antiauthoritarian will make a group difficult to lead and may result in reinforcing antisocial attitudes. Too many depressed, passive youngsters may cause the leader to do all the work and reinforce dependent attitudes. The degree to which we have to consider group composition will depend largely on our group management. A highly structured group, in which the leader takes primary control, is much less dependent on its membership than one in which the leader provides little active direction. Consequently, the composition of a highly structured group is of lesser concern.

Our selection criteria is inevitably related to our goals, and how much we need to know about individual group members depends on these goals. If we are setting up a short-term counseling series, a series on how one goes about choosing a career and finding a job, for example, we may decide to open the group to all interested youth or only to junior or senior high school students. Or we may be particularly concerned with a certain class of student who is selecting a career and whom we want to assist in finding appropriate work, in which case we would become more selective. We become even more selective if we decide to invite only school dropouts or retardates who are unable to live in the community and who need help in finding and preparing for sheltered work.

In grouping, we must consider the degree to which differences can be tolerated in any group. If adolescents are working on general life adjustment and reviewing their values, they will find it harder to work together if they come from very different backgrounds. If they are focusing on solving a commonly held problem such as an eating disorder, however, their backgrounds and general life situations may be less important than their families' dynamic interactions and their feelings about themselves. More difference can be accepted and even welcomed. It is usually undesirable to include in a group one member who is very different from the others, whether in sex, class, race, or diagnosis, for that member could easily become a target of group hostility. If group members are angry at the therapist or have become overly anxious, they may discharge their emotion on the group member who is different from the others and make that person a scapegoat for the group.

In a group of teenagers struggling with how to manage their lives, we are concerned with developmental levels, age, school grade, life-style, and social class, for teenage values and ways of behaving vary greatly from one grade to another and among those who are older or younger. In a group of teenage mothers, however, who are trying to face their pregnancy and decide what to do about their babies, these factors would not be of primary concern. Rather, the problem of teenage pregnancy would be the central focus so that everyone would identify with the problem and the discussion would be relevant to all.

Whether a program includes both boys and girls or only one sex depends on the group's purposes and the age and developmental stage of the youngsters. Because adolescent boys and girls are intensely preoccupied with their sexual identity and the need to compare themselves with others of the same sex, most groups in early adolescence are composed of members of one sex only and are usually led by a member of the same sex. Boys at this age tend to be rebellious, seductive, or self-conscious with a female therapist and girls tend to be provocative with a male. Sometimes male and female cotherapists are useful to help adolescents understand how to develop sound relationships with men and women. If the group is focusing on a common problem such as diabetes, however, there seems no reason why both sexes should not be included. Older adolescents can often benefit from understanding the point of view of the opposite sex, although they sometimes prefer unisex groups if they are exploring intimate matters. Older teenagers often attend heterosexual groups more readily because they find the interplay between the sexes stimulating. In heterosexual grouping, developmental stage as well as chronological age should be considered. Girls of fifteen are often quite interested in boys, whereas many fifteen-year-old boys are still largely concerned with school, sports, and other boys. Many feelings are attached to a teenager's age and grade. If a group member has to admit that he is older than others but in a lower grade, he may well feel inferior to the others, an important factor to consider in grouping.

Individuals who may receive appropriate treatment in one group may not fit into another. A very poorly controlled schizophrenic may do well in a highly structured, relatively unstimulating group but may fall to pieces in an unstructured and permissive activity interview group. Thus, negative outcomes can be minimized by thoughtful attention to the selection process.

Whereas leaders in schools and residential settings do not have a choice, leaders in an outpatient setting may try to establish groups made up of strangers or may work with naturally formed groups of teenagers. The latter has the advantage of the youth knowing about one another's behavior in the real world, which can reduce denial. They also can help and support one another outside the group. They may have "secrets" or divide into cliques, however, which can make management of the group more difficult. Members of groups made up of strangers may feel freer to talk about their families and friends without concern for confidentiality. They are also likely to demonstrate relationships and behaviors in the group similar to those in their real lives and test out new ways of reacting to them.

Preparation and Group Contracts

Group leaders have become more concerned in recent years about ensuring that members referred or selected for groups are aware of the group's purposes, the reasons why they have been invited to attend, and how the group will function. The extent to which prior interviews are required will vary with the nature of the group.

In starting problem-centered groups, groups that are an integral part of other programs, and orientation or diagnostic groups, we may merely invite teenagers to attend or may ask agencies to refer members who have specific, defined characteristics. In these circumstances, a contract with members regarding how the group will function will be developed when they meet for the first session. If groups are being set up where the composition of the group itself is important, then more data must be obtained. It is usually preferable to interview each candidate personally or at least see them once in a small diagnostic group.[41]

The Pregroup Contract

Even if a group program is planned for teenagers as part of the normal socialization process, prospective members must know why the group is being established, what its purposes are, how it will be conducted, who the leader will be, what the group expects of the members, where it will take place, under whose auspices, at what times, how long it will last, and how it will be paid for. They should be encouraged to reflect on why they should be included and to formulate what they expect to obtain from the experience.

The In-Group Contract

When the group starts, general rules must be clarified regarding the conduct of the group, such as behavior in the group, taking turns in talking, listening to one another, no physical fighting, management of lateness and nonattendance, and confidentiality. Even if members are resistant to treatment, an agreement should be reached that they will at least attend the group for a specific number of sessions.

Whatever preparations for the group are undertaken, the group's purposes must seem relevant to the candidate. For example, if teenagers deny that they are having difficulties, it is unlikely they will accept a general invitation to attend a treatment group. We must decide whether resistances should be worked out through individual contact or whether the resistance might be bypassed if the teenager would join another kind of group, such as a recreational club or a career-preparation group that would include counseling. Sometimes youngsters have had such bad experiences with adults that no initial one-to-one contact is productive.

On the other hand, there are teenagers so fearful of being part of a group that they must first become comfortable with the group leader alone. Youngsters who are being forced to come for treatment and are denying their need for it should be seen alone by the group therapist. Their attitude needs to be assessed and a strategy for involvement developed. Some youngsters feel that they are always being forced into situations without regard to their own feelings, that they are just pawns in adult games. With these adolescents, therapists must show their concern and leave them free to choose. Other youth, however, feel that no one cares about them. In these cases, leaders must demonstrate how much they care for the youth by insisting that the teenager attend the group for at least a few sessions. Such strategy decisions are often based on nonverbal communication, the adolescent's walk, expression, style, and tension.

Interpreting the group to members should always be in terms of its particular focus, and to an individual in terms of that individual's needs. It is customary in our society to consider personal problems as private matters. Youngsters may well question why they might be required to talk with a group of strangers about the troubles they have making friends. It could be pointed out that perhaps in just such a group they could begin to learn why they have these difficulties, for as the group forms and members become acquainted they will be able to demonstrate their particular patterns of relating to others and members can share their reactions.

In preparing teenagers and their families for treatment groups, it is often necessary to refocus the problem. Parents bring their adolescents to clinics and complain about their children's difficulties or bad behavior. Adolescents are often angry at being made the focus of the family difficulty. They may even feel it is their parents' problem. They may be right, for trouble with the children often obscures basic difficulties between couples. At some point these problems must be restated, more in keeping with reality. It is often useful to discuss with the whole family at the start those problems that the whole family seems involved in.

When parents are part of the problem, one cannot help the teenager without also helping the parents, for the teenager's improvement changes the dynamic balance within the family and the parents are likely either to create further upset or withdraw the teenager from treatment.

Group Size

The size of the group will be determined by its purpose. If a group is assembled solely for the purpose of disseminating information, with little personal discussion and few member interactions expected, the group can be large. If everyone is expected to take part, twelve members would be an appropriate limit. When close relationships and intimate discussion are desired, it may be preferable to reduce the number to eight or ten members. If the group plans to discuss intimate material, an even smaller group of four to six members may be preferable.

A second factor to consider in deciding the size of the group is the nature of the members. Members who are reticent and shy or those who wander off into daydreams are more easily involved if groups are kept small. If members do not attend regularly or are poorly motivated, it is wise to add extra members. If members find it difficult to be interested in others, a small group is preferable. On the other hand, where there is a common problem and members can learn from one another's experiences, a larger group is quite productive. For example, in a group of single teenage mothers where all shared a common situation and faced similar decisions, not all the girls wanted to talk. Some felt they learned a great deal from listening to others who wanted actively to present their problems. Therefore, a large group of twelve to sixteen girls was manageable in which shifting subgroups of girls participated, depending on their individual needs. A discussion of the implications of giving up the baby was moving to all, even though only four of the twelve girls present took part, because the topic had significance for everyone. Conversely, when members are examining their own particular situations in detail and trying to understand how they feel and what they are doing, groups should be small, even though other members may have similar general problems. When one girl states in a group that someone has molested her, even though all girls may have fantasies and anxieties about rape, there are very special elements in this particular situation that must be explored. The girls must be able to trust one another and the leader. The group should be small enough so that those concerned can take an active part in the discussion. If a group is focused on the behavior manifested in the group, then everyone must have a chance to examine his or her own behavior.

Duration of the Group

Groups vary in the length of time they last. They may assemble for only one session, as in many diagnostic or information groups; they may be limited to a certain number of sessions; or they may last for several years. The shorter the duration of the group, the less radical the change likely to occur, although this may not be true during periods of crisis or if intense situations can be stimulated. Sometimes the resolution of a particular problem can have a great effect on the group's overall functioning. Problem-oriented groups with homogeneous populations are likely to be short in duration, from five to twenty sessions, whereas groups with heterogeneous members tend to last longer, for one or two years. Open-ended groups may go on for several years even though individual members only attend a few sessions.

Groups can also occupy the same number of hours but the hours might be condensed into a rather short period or spread over a longer span of time. Although differences in the two have been hypothesized, no one has indeed proven that a group held over an intensive period, such as a day, a weekend, or a week, has a different effect than one held once or twice a week for several months or years. Therapists who have worked with reconstituted families have reported a preference for longer sessions. Their claim is that the multiple roles in the family are so complicated that it takes time to clarify them and it is difficult to draw any conclusions in a standard hour-and-a-half session. Groups for very disturbed youth are often quite brief, perhaps only half an hour, because their attention span is short.

It is assumed that intimacy is more easily achieved when meetings are more frequent and that greater emotional intensity can thus be stimulated. Defenses are less likely to be reinstated when sessions follow one another rapidly. On the other hand, space between meetings often gives individuals time to think independently, to work out their own difficulties, and to realize their doubts or anxieties. It also stimulates less dependency and may encourage more self-responsibility. Furthermore, emotional intimacy may not be desirable for some youth. Although friendship is supportive, intimacy may be too threatening for them.

Open or Closed Groups

Short-term or crisis groups may be open-ended. These include groups for adolescents in acute in-patient treatment, adolescent drug detoxification programs, and groups for pregnant teenage mothers. In such groups the problems and issues remain the same over time; the group therefore continues but members come and go. Once the group is established, it is easily maintained because some experienced members always remain to teach the others. Although the issues may change from session to session, over several sessions the different aspects of the common problem will have been addressed so the group is always relevant to its members. The content of the sessions is important for members, as the groups are primarily concerned with gathering information and helping members clarify their feelings.

Short-term, problem-oriented groups may also be conducted as closed groups with a fixed number of sessions. All aspects of a problem are covered in these sessions so these groups, too, are concerned with both information and clarification of feelings, as well as with determining a course of action. Members tend to become more intimate and have more meaning for one another than in open-ended groups, however, and the group itself goes through the beginning process, the intermediate stage, and termination. Short-term, closed groups may also be experiential, designed to help members develop intimacy or resolve specific problems in their relationships. These group members will also become close and will go through the typical group process.

Long-term groups may also be closed or open-ended. Most long-term groups, however, have periods when they are closed to new members. In long-term groups members develop close and meaningful relationships and the introduction of new members results in a disruption of the current interrelationships and generally a regression to a period of testing and mistrust. In some groups members may be introduced at a set time, such as every second month. In others the group will be conducted for six months or a year and then the members' progress will be reviewed. Some will terminate, others continue, and new members will be introduced at that time. Other intermediate groups, which last perhaps a year, may introduce no new members during the year. At the end of the year, the progress of all members is reviewed and appropriate decisions made regarding termination or referral to other groups or settings. The advantage of these closed groups is that the dynamic group process is not interfered with. Members get to know one another well and can follow one another's progress over time. The members also experience the group's development from conception to termination. A disadvantage is, however, that some members may feel constrained to continue beyond the time they could possibly have terminated because they do not wish to disrupt the group . Further, whenever a new group is started, a new group climate must be created and members must once more learn how to function in the group.

The Setting

When considering where a group program will be lodged, we need to consider the institution's image within the community, its functions, its organization, its resources, and its physical attributes.

As we have noted, parents and teenagers may harbor certain associations, good or bad, with a particular institution. It may be a place where pleasurable or disagreeable happenings have already been experienced. The institution may be associated with particular populations distinguished by race, culture, or class, and others may feel reluctant to go there. An institution may be considered of high or low status. Dropouts may feel differently about attending a training program at a university than they would about attending the same program housed in a school. A counseling group entitled "How teenagers manage their parents" housed in a recreation center may attract many youngsters who would not agree to attend essentially the same group held in a community mental health clinic and presented as an opportunity for teenagers to work out problems they are having with their parents. Clinics are for "the crazy" and problems mean inadequacy. Teenagers are particularly sensitive to these implications. It must be noted, however, that success breeds success. If the first group held in a clinic goes well and members benefit, both authorities and teenagers are more likely to support future efforts. If teenagers who are known to be hooked on drugs are able to break free and start living more successful lives, other drug addicts, in their moments of despair, will be attracted to the program. Teenagers also have their favorite hangouts, just as they have their own language and style of dress and hair. Sometimes it may be useful to treat the group wherever they hang out.

When a program is housed within an institution, it must be fully accepted by that institution and complement its function. As McCorkle and his colleagues discovered long ago when they attempted to run a permissive group in an authoritarian and punitive institution, difficulties abound and the program can well be sabotaged.[42] Any group program should be integrated within its milieu, and the various parts of an institution should reinforce each other. Group goals should be congruent with the defined goals of the institution.

It is understood that the administrators of an agency must accept, want, and understand the group program. Further, anyone who deals with the teenagers must also understand and accept the program and consider how their roles relate to it. If a group is led in a school, the teachers, principal, assistant principal, counselors, school nurse, school psychologist, students, and parents must all reach some agreement about the group's purpose, how it should be conducted, how their roles interrelate, how they will communicate, and how they will handle crises. If power struggles develop among the staff, this will be reflected in the group. If staff who are referring or preparing youngsters for the group do not understand the program, they may not be convinced of its value and may be unable to prepare candidates effectively. If they are not accepting, they can sabotage the group, through conflicts in scheduling, problems with space, and so on.

Rules determining the group's operations must be worked out. Who sets the limits? If adolescents leave the room where the group is meeting and race through the building, is this acceptable? If not, who stops them and who is held responsible? These arrangements will vary with the purpose of the group and the method through which it is conducted. Who will handle nonattendance at groups? If there is trouble in other areas of the teenagers' lives, should this be reported to the group leader or left to the individual member to bring up?

Communication procedures must be established. What kind of information and records does the group leader need? What information does the institution need? How will contact be maintained between staff and other services?

Someone must be responsible for the administration of the group program, someone who has sufficient interest and power to see that the group's needs are taken care of. Membership must be maintained, space reserved, and supplies obtained, if necessary. Timing is important in setting up groups, and often a program can fail to get off the ground because of poor organization.

Decisions about the nature of the group will also be affected by the qualifications of the staff and the availability of supervisors.

These issues will be considered in more detail in later sections of this book.

An institution's physical attributes must be considered. Discussion groups require a room large enough to hold the requisite number of members and one that can be reserved regularly and without interruption. It is destructive to a group to have people walking in and out, for privacy is usually important. If the group must suddenly be moved because the room is requested for other purposes, the impression is that the group is not valued and the teenagers will feel they are being treated like second-class citizens, usually a sensitive point with them.

A group's atmosphere can be affected by the size, shape, and color of the room. A long, narrow room tends to have a sobering effect on the group and to limit participation because of the seating arrangements. Research has shown that participation is facilitated and more widely spread when members are seated in a circle and that the distance between members influences the type of communication. Hall has demonstrated that in every culture the distance between persons who are conversing intimately is much less than when they are transacting business.[43] Spatial distance, size of the group, and quality of discussion are all closely related.

The kinds of seats provided will also influence the group. Sitting around a table tends to be more businesslike and less relaxed than lounging in comfortable chairs. Providing a specific place for the leader, such as at the head of the table or in a different kind of chair, has implications for the conduct of the group. Such an arrangement lends itself to a more directive approach. In a permissive group, leaders may vary where they sit or even move slightly out of the circle.

If activities are planned, adequate space must be provided and supplies available. Too small a room builds up pressure. A very large space allows for evasion and adds to feelings of diffusion and anxiety. With younger adolescents who are likely to leave the room untidy if there are activities, there should be time to clean up at the end of the meetings and a place provided to store supplies. Further, the leader should not have to feel anxious about repercussions if the room gets messed up.

Although the majority of groups are conducted in agencies, hospitals, and institutions, some teenage groups are undertaken in private practice and there are some differences. For example, recruitment may be more difficult in private practice. Younger teenagers often have to be driven to the group and then there is the question of what to do with the parents who bring them. Should there be a concurrent parent group? Should they wait in the waiting room? Should they be required to leave and return? If the members car pool, does this create subgroup dynamics that will have to be dealt with in the group? The therapist is entirely responsible for the ground rules and management of the group in private practice and there can be no question of a split between institutional and group leader authority. The location of the therapist's office, whether in a medical building or private home, will also carry its own implications.

Use of Activities, Games, the Arts, and Videos

Activities, games, trips, role-playing, and meals have long been used in groups for young teenagers. There has been a marked increase, however, in the use of games, exercises, and video tapes for problem-specific and prevention groups. Examples are the Ungame,[44] the Love Game,[45] and the video "Learning to Manage Anger."[46] Many therapists have also used art in teenage groups,[47] Frances and Schiff music,[48] and Miller poetry.[49] Some therapists have used video feedback to help group members realize more vividly their impact on others, and Weber found that video playback in an in-patient group increased the adolescents' ability to respond more warmly.[50]

Program Coordination

A major problem in modern society is the coordination of different programs. Certain matters need to be addressed: the development of over-all community standards and expectations; the meshing of education and career planning; and the provision of cultural and recreational experiences that will enhance and buttress the adolescent's life and provide opportunities for initiative, emotional satisfaction, and outlets for the teenager's energy. Youth with many problems may need concurrent programs: health care, child day care, transportation, a place to live, help in developing a social life, as well as groups for remedial education, drug treatment, job skill training, and counseling.

In setting up a group program, the following factors must be considered:

1. The needs of the population must be identified and purposes, methods, and goals clearly defined.
2. There must be an adequate number of adolescents who require the same form of treatment. Members must be selected and grouped appropriately in terms of the kind of group and the level of operation.
3. The group's duration should be related to its purpose.
4. An adequately trained leader must be available or one who has some potential for and interest in leading groups and can obtain supervision or consultation.
5. The program must be interpreted to all concerned and individual resistances among the staff worked out.
6. It must be recognized that the group setting and the relationships between the group, the institution, and the community will set the limits and influence how the group will be run.
7. All persons concerned with the group and its members must be clear about their respective roles.
8. The limits of confidentiality should be clearly recognized by all.
9. Methods for the effective evaluation of the group and program control should be worked out and established before the group begins.
10. Integration of services with program planning for individuals is an important aspect of any intervention with adolescents, particularly with poorly motivated youth. Whenever possible, problems should be treated within the normal institution and

strengths and tasks should be the focus rather than difficulties and weaknesses. Integration of therapists and programs also includes regular feedback and close collaboration so that problems can be identified and worked on as soon as they arise.

11. When youth have many different needs, these may have to be taken care of concurrently if group treatment is to be effective.

4. Process and Maneuvers in Adolescent Groups

All groups follow a certain progression, whether the group lasts an hour or for several years. Members must become acquainted, establish a common purpose, decide how they will work together, conduct their business, and eventually disband. In groups that continue over a span of time, of course, much more has to occur. Relationships develop between members. Members join forces for leadership and position. Emotional demands are made on the group, the members, and the leader. Members learn to trust and care for each other. New standards and ways of behaving are created and upheld by the group. A continuous dynamic interaction takes place. Eventually the group must end and members separate to continue their lives independently.

The Beginning

Whether the group is an educational, counseling, psychotherapeutic, training, or recreational one, members initially expect their leader to structure the group and tell them how to operate. If leaders do not play an active role, the group becomes anxious and often resentful. Members will begin to pressure leaders to undertake these tasks. Adolescents, even though they wish to be independent, are no exception. They often dislike the suggestion that the group is to function as they see fit, although if leaders do impose a structure on the group adolescents are quite apt to oppose these suggestions. The more leaders define the group's structure and the more responsibility they take for its operation, the more they foster dependency and potential rebellion. With a moderate amount of guidance, adolescent group members can function in an independent, therapeutic manner. For example, in a recreational group for young boys strictly programmed by the leader, the members did not learn how to plan for themselves even though they met weekly for a year. With a new leader who gave the boys freedom to plan, they were able to take full responsibility after only a very short period of confusion. Most groups (even those consisting of psychologically handicapped members), if given a free hand, will learn to develop their own internal structure, come to decisions, and make plans in a very few sessions. Adults are all too prone to keep members dependent, to feel that youngsters are "not ready" for responsibility, and thus to prevent members from growing and developing.

From the start, group members struggle to become acquainted with each other, to establish a pecking order, to establish trust, cohesion, and commonality. Mutual introductions are usually a formality and names are not absorbed at the first go-around. Members gradually ask each other increasingly intimate questions. For a time, however, most groups hesitate on the edge of self-revelation. If formal roles are not established, members test out each other's strengths and weaknesses, as well as the leader's strength.

Testing Operations

In the beginning, all group members are concerned with mutual identification, their acceptance into the group, their relationship to other members and to the leader, the quality of the group, and the degree to which they can trust each other. They test out the leader and the group. They are concerned with the following issues:

1. What will the leader and the group members think of me? How do I rate? Will they like me?
2. What are the other members like? Can I trust them?
3. Is the leader competent, trustworthy, dependable? Who is really in charge?
4. What kind of group is this? Is it a good group? Can I get what I need in this group?
5. What do the other members want to do in this group, and do I want that too?

Members in counseling and therapy groups are also anxious about admitting problems and are sometimes afraid of being considered crazy or of being rejected if they do.

In the ongoing conduct of the group, leaders need to be clear about their own values and the limits of what they will tolerate in the group, for members need reassurance that they will not be permitted to disrupt the group completely and that they will not be hurt or hurt others. This is particularly true of early adolescents whose emotional stability may be precarious and who may act out impulsively. Emotional contagion is an important factor in this period. This does not mean that leaders should start out with a long list of prohibitions delineating the limits, but rather that they should be personally secure in what they will or will not allow. For example, in pregroup interviews leaders can state a few basic rules for participation in the group, such as attendance requirements, confidentiality, and no physical violence. From the beginning leaders model desired behaviors that will form a norm for the group, such as taking turns, exhibiting active listening skills, and providing constructive feedback.

Adolescents do not want to be able to overcome and defeat the leaders. They will try to do so, however, because they need to know whether they can trust and rely on the leaders in their struggle for self-sufficiency. Secretly they will hope that the leaders can maintain control for, if not, they will view the leaders as weak and of no use to them.

Testing in adolescent groups may include any number of operations. Members may gripe against authority; attack the leaders verbally, directly, or indirectly; or see whether leaders will permit behavior that members know is not allowed. Members use their manipulations as tools against authority to try to anger or intimidate the leaders or to elicit disapproval and rigidity. They appear to be engaging in power struggles, testing whether they can defeat the leaders or whether the leaders will betray them. In their anxiety and anger, members may scapegoat and attack others, seeing if they can drive a member out of the group. By testing whether the leader will play favorites or be pushed into defending and protecting the weakest, members are challenging leaders to display their own weaknesses.

Absence and Lateness

Absence and lateness can be manifestations of individual or group resistance but in either case are disturbing to the group. Members should be encouraged to examine these behaviors as an offense against themselves, something preventing them from getting the most out of their group sessions. Moreover, the pregroup contract should require that all such problems be taken up in the group. If a member is absent because he or she is particularly anxious or upset, however, the leader may first have to talk over the situation with the individual before it is discussed in the group. Later, in the group, the leader can provide support while the member shares his or her anxiety with the group.

During the beginning phase when the group is developing an identity, members are often concerned about whether they are going to form a worthwhile group. They are afraid to lose any members, afraid that if a single member leaves the whole group may fly apart. The slightest difference or disagreement between members makes everyone anxious. The following is an example of a group discussion after a member has threatened to leave:

C: Well, what's he trying to prove by saying he's not coming back?

G: Did he express why he wasn't coming back?

B: Well, why do we have to get off on him again? Why don't we talk about who is angry? We're angry right now.

F: I'm angry, and I'm angry at A because he's not coming back.

C: That's right. I am too.

F: Because for him not coming back and taking that attitude—

G: (interrupting) The whole group falls apart—

F: The whole group is lost—

G: When one person stops—

C: The minute we say anything at all.

F: That's what I was told when I wanted to drop out of the group. If one quits and another one can quit, and another can quit . . .

D: If this is to go on week after week and I know if A comes back everyone is going to sit here afraid to say anything.

P: I think it should be settled with A sitting here.

DR. T: Why are you afraid of saying things? What is this feeling that if he drops out the whole group disintegrates?

F: Well . . . if he drops out, if it happens to him and it hurts him, so next week we'll say, poor J sittin' over there and there was something, we were irritated about what he said, so we jumped on him and the first thing he goes home and says he is not coming back.

F: Then you have no group, so why the hell did I come here for— I just wasted all this time.

DR. T: No one has said that. In fact you know the group is not going to fall apart. A member comes to get help. It is the responsibility of others to help him face his difficulties, even if he finds this hard and sometimes painful.

During such a period of anxiety, the leaders should allow members to express their concerns before helping them gain a realistic view of their impact on the group process.

Facing Difficulties

As the group becomes more cohesive, members feel more secure with each other. Differences can more easily be faced and anger with each other can be expressed. If members threaten to leave when they feel ill-treated by the group, the entire group becomes anxious and guilty. Unless the leader intervenes, these feelings may inhibit the members' capacity to face their differences, to express feelings, and to disagree. When such a climate prevails, problems cannot be worked out.

Whatever kind of group is conducted with adolescents, a non-defensive posture should be fostered. Group members need to recognize that difficulties and differences are natural, that they should be concerned for each other and help each other stay with problems and work them out. In fostering this attitude, leaders must be able to examine and discuss their own behavior without insisting that they are always right. If adolescents complain that the leader did not help enough, did not tell them what to do or stop them from making a mistake, it may be an excellent idea to examine what went into the leader's decision and posture and whether he or she took the appropriate attitude. If members understand that the leader does not have to be perfect, then group members can also make mistakes, and everyone will find it easier to face their mistakes.

Members and leaders may disagree about what an appropriate reaction is. A leader may have one purpose in mind, and group members may want something else. Members may want to satisfy their dependency needs, whereas the leader may be concerned with having members recognize their own strengths in facing difficulties. Leaders must be able to accept the difference and clarify their own position. For example, a boy who had always been overprotected by his mother provoked another boy into a fight. He then called out to the leader, "Help me, help me." The leader paid no attention, and the fight finished quickly with the provoker receiving a punch on the nose. The boy turned to the leader in a rage and said, "Why didn't you help me? I called to you." The leader replied calmly, "I didn't think you needed any help. You are big enough to take care of yourself." Group work is not manipulation. Its goal is to move toward self-determination. In discussions, the leader will first acknowledge the importance of the members' concerns and then encourage discussion in a nondefensive manner. Because a primary goal during adolescence is to develop skills in productive confrontation and negotiation, the leader's willingness to engage the members provides an excellent opportunity for experimentation and change.

Competition

Competition goes on constantly in groups: competition with the leader and for the leader and for the attention, control, or approval of the group. Members of the group secretly compare themselves with the other group members. Subtly or openly, the youngsters try to establish a pecking order, although in a dynamic group in which members are growing this never becomes static. Some vie openly for leadership in the group. Others sit back and observe the situation. Still others move into accustomed roles of the sick, the weak, or the isolate. Some individuals compete by working diligently on their problems, by being good, or by currying favor with the leader. Others compete with attention-getting, disruptive, boastful behavior. Still others compete by being plaintive, stupid, or silent. Whatever method is used, group members unconsciously recreate for themselves the roles they are accustomed to playing and use the kind of defenses and resistances they normally use at home. These defenses are then open to analysis and change.

In some families the only way youngsters can get attention from parents is to cause trouble. Trouble is rewarded with attention even if the attention must be paid for with negative consequences. The same is true of displaying stupidity; some children get no rewards for success but, although approval may be unobtainable, they do get attention if they fail. These patterns are repeated in the group. In one group, for example, a girl who felt she was stupid would begin to create a physical disturbance or talk about some meaningless gossip whenever another group member reported any success in school. The competition for attention and the various ways the girls in the group tried to obtain it were discussed. The girls' feelings of worthlessness and their inability to feel loved and accepted for themselves were revealed, after which the need to be disruptive died away.

Member Roles

When considering prospective members for group counseling or psychotherapy, it is useful to know the roles they normally play in their families and among friends as they are likely to reenact these in the group. Group members can play many roles: the coleader; the questioner; the finder of quick solutions; the consoler; the conformist; the one who is weak, sick, or special; the silent one; the stupid one; the victim; the one who blames others or defies the leader on behalf of the group; the superior one. As the group progresses, members may also try out different roles and practice new ways of relating to others.

In any counseling or therapy group, members and leaders find it difficult to tolerate a member who consistently denies any difficulty and assumes a position of superiority. One must recognize that such members are usually insecure. They need to prove themselves, as well as to keep from exposing themselves. Such attitudes usually give the individual trouble outside of the group as well. These individuals need support in feeling more secure. Once they feel less anxious they will have less need to be perfect. Leaders must understand the problem in order not to get annoyed, for although it is good to have heated discussions and for members to confront each other, it is important not to encourage the group to attack each other in a destructive way. If members can share their feelings and reactions in the group, however, offenders can become better able to hear the feedback and to alter their behavior.

Teenagers who insist on finding immediate surface solutions

and who give endless advice may be popular at first, but after a time they begin to annoy the group because they cut off feelings and discussion. The leader can point out to such youngsters that the members are not yet ready for a solution but are interested first in examining what is involved and exploring some options. The leader might also inquire why these youngsters need an answer so fast and ask how they are feeling at the moment. Ambiguity and lack of clear directions may be difficult for these teenagers to tolerate.

The defenses members adopt in groups are usually significant of the way they perceive themselves and the way they have obtained satisfaction in the past. All defensive operations carry satisfactions as well as limitations. A boy who was having difficulty performing in school, although he was intelligent, continually acted stupidly in the group. His comments were always off the point. The group members grew irritated. Some attacked him and others were supportive, and so he became the focus of attention. The leader asked why he was always missing the point although he was bright enough to understand, and asked what advantage this behavior had for him. It was finally revealed that he had not been able to compete in his family with his father and elder brother, both very aggressive, but that he received attention and protection from his mother by appearing weak and stupid. In the family, as in the group, he had divided the members and created a conflict around himself, thus gaining attention even at the price of failure. Once he recognized this maneuver, he was able to stop acting stupidly and to mobilize himself to learn and succeed.

Individual Resistances

In counseling and therapy groups, individual members or the group as a whole avoid involvement in task-related discussions by means of a number of operations known as resistances. These resistances are most likely to develop during the second phase of the group but can reappear at any time when anxiety is high.

Individual members resist through silence; inconsequential chatter that avoids important issues; diverting discussion from painful subjects; obsessing, that is, repeating thoughts and ideas that could be important but that are not dealt with; intellectualizing, that is, divorcing content from feelings; refusing to take responsibility by denying behavior and feelings; fighting; being late or absent; monopolizing the group's attention; vacillating; or listing, that is, elaborating on categories and classes of people, things, or events that are irrelevant to the problem. Some members demand help and ask others to make decisions for them. Some focus on the problems of others and assume the role of helper without revealing their own feelings and problems. Still others boast, withhold information, or question without analyzing the problem or following through with a solution. Some agree and comply on the surface but without revealing any genuine feelings.

Collaborative Resistance

Members also join with others in collaborative resistances. Mutual support and admiration can link members in less than productive alliances. Joining in diversionary tactics that are physical or verbal, such as competing with others, fighting, or setting up cliques that splinter the group, all impede the work of the group. Members may also be secretive or discuss important material outside but not in the group. They may allow other members to monopolize the group's attention; engage in group silence; combine to intellectualize, argue, or gossip; or criticize absent members but avoid bringing up the same subject when they are there. The group as a whole may develop a habit of lateness or absenteeism. All these resistances are important to the leader, whether they are individual or group-centered. How the leader deals with such actions will determine the group's direction and movement. When the leader fails to help the group deal with such individual or group resistances, the group's usefulness is reduced.

Monopolization

In many of these operations, the group as a whole uses an individual's resistance in its own desire to avoid dealing with the tasks at hand and to avoid change. Monopolization is an interesting example. Frequently, group leaders are plagued by an individual member who constantly takes over the discussion and holds the floor so that no one else can express an opinion. There are a number of reasons why individuals may behave this way. They may have a strong need to obtain the group's attention at any cost. They may be preoccupied with themselves and their own problems and unable to take any interest in others. They may be unable to tolerate silence and become so anxious that they have to talk if no one else moves in fast to take the floor. They may use talking to prevent the group from bringing up disturbing subjects. They may be unable, because of their anxiety, to let go of a subject once they get started. They may need to reassure themselves of their status by proving they are knowledgeable or by holding the group's attention.

Other group members do not have to permit such monopolization. There can be many reasons why they go along with it, however. They may feel that the monopolizer genuinely needs attention and support and so they remain silent out of concern. They may also identify strongly with the other's need to talk and feel that to break in would be hurtful and a hostile act They may want to force the leader to intervene. Sometimes a monopolizer makes other members so angry that they are afraid to deal with the person for fear of attacking too severely. They may also welcome a relief from having to face their own problems. They may sense that monopolization annoys the group leader and so they support it as a means of attacking and defeating the leader. The monopolizer may be genuinely amusing and the members enjoy the flow of talk at least for a while. Sometimes the monopolizer is actually the spokesperson for the group, supported by all.

In dealing with the problem the leader must understand the individual's motives and those of the other group members. The leaders have several choices. They can allow the talk to continue with the expectation that the group members will eventually become so bored and restless that they will deal with the problem themselves. The leader can ask the group why they are allowing one member to do all the talking. They can raise a similar question with the individual. They can pose a general question, "What is going on here?" They can be more directive by suggesting that others should participate or by asking questions of others, thus demonstrating the need for wider participation. They can analyze the situation as they see it. In making their decision, they will consider not only the positions and motives of the individuals and the group but also the group's level of operations, its goals, and its developmental stage.

If the leader chooses to intervene directly, it is important to produce a shift in participation without appearing to criticize the monopolizer. For example, the leader might say, "John, may I stop you for a moment? You are saying a number of important things, but it is hard to think about so much at once. Let's see how others are feeling about what you've said." With this intervention, the monologue has been interrupted, John has been positively reinforced for taking the risk of talking in the group, and the leader can then verbally or nonverbally invite other members to join the discussion.

Avoidance

Members of a group sometimes want to talk about a problem that has great significance for them, but they are anxious about tackling it. They will use a variety of diversionary tactics, and the leader must help them face what it is they really want to talk about. The following example begins with M saying that her father was in the hospital for a leg injury. The leader asks questions about her father's condition but there is no response. The girls are busy exchanging nuts and gum. When there is relative quiet, D says she wants to talk, then she has nothing to say and mutters that she will keep it to herself. L asks what she is going to keep to herself? D responds, "What I've got on my mind." L persists in asking what is on her mind. The leader wonders whether D can talk about why she cannot talk. D says that she will be getting the hospital report that day. M tells the group about her report card, and there is some talk about school. The leader asks why no one responds to D's remark. L says she told her father she was going to be a "dog psychiatrist" to take care of him. There is general laughter. The leader again points out that they are not responding to D. The girls seem to be listening. Then D says, "Last Thursday I got the shock of my life. I'm going to have a baby."

Adolescents are adept at forcing adults into decision-making roles. Leaders must be on guard against taking over responsibility that belongs to the group. This is particularly true in the formative group sessions where the youngsters are exploring the limits of what is acceptable and unacceptable, and are testing the leader. Allowing the leader to adopt a typically authoritarian role can permit the individual or group to slide along relatively uninvolved. They will engage in obsessing, that is, repeating issues that could be important but are not dealt with, in an attempt to force the leaders to impose structure on the group and strict procedures. Members complain, vacillate, boast, and refuse to take any responsibility in order to force leaders into the role of parent or teacher. Leaders may acknowledge these maneuvers without offering specific directions to the members by saying, "It seems that a lot of energy is being spent on avoiding talking about X" or "What do you think would happen if you were to talk about X?"

Physical Activity as Tension Release

A high proportion of all communication between humans is nonverbal, and certainly we see many examples of this in adolescent groups. Teenagers indicate their feelings and attitudes readily by their posture and muscle tone, their clothes, their make-up, their hair, their facial expressions, their gestures. In the group, they easily become restless. They are often like a flock of snow geese, rising, walking around, sitting down again. They will feign sleep, or sometimes even fall asleep. They touch each other, wrestle, giggle, grimace. They may push their chairs back from the group, lean out the window, or even try to walk out of the group when issues become too anxiety-laden. All these movements are mechanisms that members use to release the tensions inherent in group therapy.

Significance of Silence

Silence is one of the most potent means by which groups and individual group members can express themselves. Moreover, silence also can be extremely difficult for adolescents to tolerate because of their general inability to handle anxiety. Two dimensions of silence concern group leaders: group silence and the silence of individual members. Group silences can have many meanings. They can be reflective, as when members mull over some experience or idea that has just been presented to the group. They can be anxiety-laden, as when everyone is embarrassed and resisting a discussion or when members reach a point in a particular discussion that they find upsetting to pursue. Silences sometimes have a particularly dynamic quality, as when members are apparently girding themselves to reveal something very significant, a silence that the leader must not break. Sometimes, after solid work has been accomplished, silences can be relaxed, satisfied, and intimate. Of course silences can also be extraordinarily hostile and withholding. At times members may be determined not to work on their problems or may be very angry with the leader. Sometimes silences may be filled with depression and despair, lethargy or boredom. These are truly resistive silences.

How do leaders understand these silences and know how to deal with them? They consciously or unconsciously observe all the nonverbal cues and are aware of both the context of the previous discussion and the voice tones and expressions. Something else is presumed to be an intangible composite of all these elements, the quality of tension in the room, the group climate. No one understands what is specific to this atmosphere. It may be that members' individual reactions create pressure, humidity, and electrical discharges that add to the room's atmosphere and to which individuals are unconsciously sensitive.

The individual group member can use silence in many ways. Individuals may be silent, yet actively participate. Members may be playing a role that is typical for them, or they may indeed have withdrawn from the group. Some people handle their anxiety by "going blank." They blot out and cease to become conscious of what is going on. Others become sleepy when anxious and do not participate although they are physically present. Their presence may disturb and annoy other members, however, because they are concealing their thoughts and feelings. Others are silent because they are listening. Sometimes they agonize over the desire to say something, but they fear attack, derision, or exposure. Sometimes they are too slow to react and the group moves on without their input. Others are eager to take part, but they become too emotional and do not dare to express themselves. Some members are content to allow others to express their feelings for them. They ride along learning but do not themselves contribute. As leaders come to understand the underlying dynamics of the various silences, they can select an intervention strategy. For example, the member who appears to want to participate but fears attack or rejection may be invited to role-play. This allows the member to experience involvement in a forum that affords some protection so that future participation may seem less threatening.

Silent members can play two interesting roles. Individuals may fantasize that by remaining silent they have more power than the others do, for they know a lot about the other members but the members know nothing about them. Such individuals forget the purpose of the group in their effort to win a power struggle for control. In a second interesting reaction, members remain silent because they want to be asked to speak. They wait for the leader to turn to them. Sometimes they fix the leader with a demanding stare. They want the adult to show interest in them and to treat them as special.

Of course all these reasons for silence are significant of roles individual members assume. For example, members who blot out the group or daydream are expressing their difficulty in relating to others and becoming part of the group. They choose the role of isolate. Members who silently demand an invitation to speak expect to be treated as a favored group member. Those who are afraid to speak either expect to be made into victims or are afraid they will become the group destroyer.

Chattering and Horseplay

Chattering is frequent in adolescent groups. Methods for dealing with it depend on the type of group and its stage of development. In groups that are largely experiential, leaders are most likely to wait for their opportunity to open up more meaningful discussion. In groups that are task-related, it can be important for the leader to raise questions about the relevance of the discussion. Sometimes group members will try to shift the responsibility to talk about relevant material onto the leader. Leaders should not allow themselves to be enticed into this power struggle for they can always be defeated, but should remind the group that it is their group and consequently their responsibility to decide whether they want it to be a useful group or not. Teenagers are particularly good at provoking adults into battles over control and responsibility. In the earliest stages of the group, leaders are more likely to tolerate the superficiality of chatter but later on will bring the phenomenon to the group's attention. Horseplay may serve a similar purpose. It can also be a clearly competitive and attention-getting device. When one boy in a group of thirteen- and fourteen-year-old boys showed the leader a tape recorder he had bought, another immediately picked a fight with a third group member and drew the leader's attention away from the first boy. Once the fight had been attended to, the leader described the sequence and asked the boys what they thought about it. In the beginning stages of groups members may not be conscious of the meaning of the interaction but after a time they learn to understand what dynamics are being brought into play.

Scapegoating

Scapegoating, one of the most conspicuous of group mechanisms, is prevalent in all sizes and conditions of groups. It involves the displacement of anger and attack from its real object onto another person, or the sacrifice of one member for the good of the group. A typical form of scapegoating is the transfer of anger directed at the leader onto another group member. Another form is the symbolic expulsion from the group of a member who represents feelings or behaviors about which the group feels guilty and so they sacrifice the one member in expiation of their sins.

Members selected as scapegoats usually differ in some way from the rest of the group. They may have a different diagnosis or be of a different race or sex from the majority of the group. A member who emphasizes his or her own difference, whether it be a sickness,weakness, or superiority, is more likely to become the group's scapegoat. Further, youth who are hostile and anxious may stimulate hostility and anxiety in the group and become its target. This is particularly likely if they are naturally provocative and seem to be asking the group to attack or beat them. Finally, a group member who openly expresses impulses that group members are trying to defend themselves against is likely to be the target of attack. In general, the higher the degree of insecurity, hostility, and aggression in the group, the more likely scapegoating will occur and the less tolerance of individual differences there will be among members. Attention to grouping can reduce the likelihood of scapegoating, that is, following the "Noah's Ark" principle of including at least two like individuals in each category, such as gender, race, or diagnosis, in a heterogeneous group. The potential for becoming a scapegoat, however, cannot always be foreseen.

Although some members attract the displeasure of the group in their own right, they may become the group's scapegoat because of what they represent for the group: the embodiment of the group's guilt or the target of its anger. For example, a group therapist had to attend several conferences and left the group with his cotherapist. Members were angry because they felt he was putting his own interests first and treating them as though they were of little concern. They were afraid, however, that if they vented their anger on him he would abandon them completely. Instead, they attacked the group's weakest member, almost forcing her to leave the group. When the leader interpreted the members' behavior, their anxiety level rose, but they also felt free to express their negative feelings about the leader's absence and to explore their concerns about rejection and abandonment.

Groups for Younger and Older Adolescents

There are a number of differences in working with groups of younger and older adolescents. Early adolescence is concerned primarily with the establishment of a sexual identity and with the adolescent's beginning to come to terms with the need for an independent life. Late adolescence is concerned with the actual separation from the family and with the process of finding a mate and making occupational choices.

In early adolescence the individual often experiences much anxiety and confusion, which is reduced as the personality becomes more stable. This is reflected in various differences between younger and older adolescents. Younger adolescents are less willing to recognize and accept the existence of problems. They often suffer from greater tension and self-consciousness. They have less tolerance for anxiety, a higher degree of physical expression, and a greater need to discharge tension physically. Older adolescents, on the other hand, show an increased ability to stay with anxiety-provoking subjects. They are less preoccupied with physical changes and have less of a need to compare themselves with others of the same sex. Older adolescents are more interested in the opposite sex, and their relationships are more stable. Younger adolescents swing more frequently between the desire for independence and the need to be taken care of.

In view of adolescent resistance, it has often been thought more sensible to avoid directly confronting adolescents with difficulties and rather incorporate counseling into other normal activities, such as recreation, training, or even work. If groups are in fact set up for rehabilitation or therapy, however, the following principles should be considered. Because many younger teenagers are unwilling to admit they have difficulties, it is not useful to press for rehabilitation at the beginning of the group. At the same time the purposes of the group should be clearly stated so the leader does not play into and support the resistances of members. The leader might begin the group by saying that the group has come together so the members can help each other with the things that typically bother teenagers, and then suggest that they might first like to get acquainted. Older adolescents, aside from offenders and substance abusers who usually vehemently deny any problems, are more willing, right from the start of the group, to recognize that they have problems they want to work on. Many adolescents because of their mood swings, however, are worried about being crazy and have reservations about being identified as having special problems.

Younger adolescents are particularly self-conscious when they first meet as a group. Any new experience is an ordeal for them. It is often difficult for them to get started. They squirm, giggle, and whisper to their neighbors. Silence is difficult for them to tolerate, and anxiety tends to mount fast. If there is too much discomfort, the teenagers will drop out of the group. Several approaches can be used to deal with this problem. First, the leader can take more responsibility for maintaining the flow of the group and thus help to relieve tension and maintain anxiety at a bearable level. Second, having crafts available at a table, such as drawing materials, clay, models, or jewelry-making equipment, enables the young teenagers to withdraw into an activity during periods of embarrassment. As the group gains confidence, members can usually give up these props.

There are also a number of group activities in which leaders can engage younger adolescents to lay the foundation for future therapeutic work. At the initial session, for example, members can be given paper bags in which they keep writings or drawings about themselves that are easily identifiable to others. The youngsters can also write things about themselves that other group members are unlikely to know. These jottings can be shared when the teenagers choose to do so in the future. Members can also write their observations of other members that can be used later as feedback or to demonstrate progress. This activity is patterned after Johari's Window, which encourages self-disclosure before feedback.

A more structured type of group has also been used effectively with younger adolescents and with adolescent delinquents. In such a group, the day-to-day adjustment tasks are worked out for each group member; the group then discusses whether these tasks have been accomplished and, if not, why. Materials, such as stories about typical teenage problems, have also been used to stimulate discussion. Such aids are not necessary in the later stages of any group, and older adolescents can learn to work appropriately without them from the beginning.

In all adolescent groups, members have difficulty staying with a discussion that focuses on members' concerns, but their ability to do so increases with maturity. In most groups composed of younger teenagers, a great deal of chatter about mutual friends and day-to-day experiences leads into short periods of meaningful discussion. For example, one group spent some time exchanging names of boys; then one of the girls told how a boy she did not like kept wanting to kiss her. How did one deal with this? The girls discussed tactics, and then for a few moments talked about their feelings and anxieties of being overcome. The discussion then quickly changed. Older girls are more able to discuss the problem of being accepted if one does not go along with a boy's demands. Such a discussion typically leads to their feelings of not being lovable or desirable.

Sometimes a group resists an individual's attempts to deal with a subject that makes the rest of the group too anxious, as can be seen in the following example:

A: The only person I could usually count on is dead. I just want to be with that person. Last night was the first time my mother ever heard me say this.

B: I asked my mother if I could get my hair straightened and curled, and my mother said no. Someone was there and I said, "See how your best friend will do you Miss—" and my mother says "Oh, did you hear that?" My mother says everyone corrects her.

A: Will you let me talk?

C: Whenever I want to get my hair done, my mother will fix my hair.

B: My mother can't fix no hair.

The therapist intervenes to ask why, when A wants to talk about something of significance to her, the other girls are changing the subject. In this example the members are avoiding the anxieties related to death and separations. Once the members acknowledge the underlying cause of their uneasiness, they will be more able to tolerate fearful issues such as death. Younger groups often cope with anxiety and self-consciousness through motor discharge, and such feelings are dealt with in all groups by changing the subject to a superficial discussion. The therapist must decide what the group can tolerate at a particular time. Some rules can be established in the initial group contract, however. Generally, it is not desirable to allow teenagers to leave the room if they are anxious because this can become a major resistance and a disturbance. Whether to continue with a discussion or let it go, however, may often be left up to the individual member. Overall decisions regarding the setting of limits may be left up to the institution or the therapist, depending on the type of group. In activity group therapy, for example, the institution is the restricting authority and the therapist the benign authority. If there are cotherapists, one may help the anxious youngster while the other continues with the group.

Motor activity relieves tension and reduces anxiety. It is also a diversionary and attention-getting device. When one boy in a group began to describe how he had gotten three As on his report card, two of the others who had not done so well started throwing pieces of paper at each other and succeeded in diverting the group's attention away from the first boy. The therapist then asked the group to look at what was going on and examine the different ways the boys competed for attention: by being good, by pleasing, by succeeding, or by being disruptive during the discussion. The boys who had created the disturbance were able to see that they were angry because the other boy was succeeding in school and they were not. The more successful boys talked about their feelings of having to produce in order to be liked.

In an institutional group of girls, one girl had betrayed the confidences shared by the group, and the others attacked her verbally. She rushed out of the room but was later able to return and face their anger. In another group, the girls had spent ten minutes working on one girl's difficulty with her mother, who, the girl felt, disparaged her. There was a short pause, then one of the other girls jumped up and shouted, "Who wants to dance?" The girls all followed her lead and danced and sang for several minutes. Then they returned to the table and the discussion continued. Older adolescents may shout and thump the table, but are usually able to stay seated for the duration of the meeting. In these examples, motor activity allowed for sufficient release of anxiety to enable the youngsters to talk about the feelings that made them uncomfortable.

Personal relationships and moods are volatile in early adolescence. One moment a group member may be friendly to the leader and the next moment rejecting. Young teenagers are constantly challenging and testing the leaders and have a great need for them to be perfect. At this stage in a teenager's life, as parents know all too well, it is very easy to say the wrong thing or to infuriate the teenager with an indelicate phrase, so that group operations are much less stable than in groups of older adolescents. With older adolescents, once a positive relationship is established, it usually remains a solid underlay to surface disagreements and negative feelings.

Early adolescence is the period of maximum interest in others of the same sex, which further complicates group relationships. Girls and boys compare themselves with others of the same sex, and intimacy and affection are often mislabeled as homosexual. In the American culture, despite growing acceptance of homosexual adjustments, this can still occasion much anxiety. Moreover, because of fluctuations between dependence and independence in young adolescents and their need for a role-model, strong attachments also develop toward adults of the same sex. Both of these trends may be viewed as a sign of homosexuality by the young teenagers and defended against with intense anxiety. This can become a tremendous problem in groups of early adolescents and must be dealt with openly and reassuringly. Sometimes the group will start with talk of "queers" followed by provocative and anxious giggling, a sure sign of sexual interest. At such times, it is often desirable for the leader to comment that the members seem to be thinking a lot about homosexuality and suggest that they might like to discuss the subject and understand more about it. If this problem is not dealt with, the youngsters' anxiety may turn into uncontrollable acting-out in the group and can disrupt it. Adolescent groups become angry and punishing if the leader does not understand what they are trying to talk about or if leaders evade the subject. The leader's own capacity to feel comfortable with such subjects is, of course, crucial. The raw emotions expressed by adolescents often stimulate earlier, unresolved conflicts in the therapist, and the intense and open anger or derision of resistive youth can be hard to take.

Intense negative reactions that can develop toward the leader as a defense against positive feelings are sometimes more difficult to handle. Often it is enough for the leader to interpret anxiety about closeness and then to discuss the attachment with the youngster as a desire to have an all-loving parent, a desire that can never be entirely fulfilled. It may be that the conflict becomes so intense that a neutral outside therapist may have to intervene. Cotherapists can be useful in this situation.

Groups composed of older adolescents begin increasingly to resemble adult groups. The leader still must be more active than in many adult groups in helping the adolescents deal with their anxiety, in presenting a model for identification, and in stating values clearly. Older adolescents face their problems more freely, however, and take more responsibility in setting their own limits. There is less need for crafts, and there is much less expression through physical movement.

In older adolescents the focus is on the individual's separation from the family and on consolidating one's identity, whereas with younger adolescents, particularly in middle-class families, parents are usually deeply involved with the adolescent's difficulties. The problem is often a family problem; however, the adolescent is often identified as the "patient" and deeply resents this position. Whenever possible, the entire family should be counseled together at the beginning so that the problem is clearly defined as a family problem that requires family responsibility. Parents should be involved in treatment. No promises should be made regarding secrecy on the grounds that communication is often a problem between parents and adolescents and that this is something the family needs to work on. Groups composed of several adolescents and their parents show much promise in being able to work out family difficulties. In this method the family system that pressures and conditions the behavior of individual family members is the target of change.

The Values of Nonverbal Experience

Change does not come about only through discussion, verbal recognition of problems, or insight but also through nonverbal interactions and experiences. The value of work and recreation therapy is based on self-mastery, skill development, and the satisfaction of tasks completed and difficulties overcome. Improvement in self-esteem also comes from being accepted and recognized by peers and adults and from working as part of a team. In wilderness excursions, group members feel the power of nature, of a force beyond themselves, and experience the comfort and closeness of supportive companions. They learn they can extend themselves to meet new challenges. Therapy through the arts is also based on activity, on the expression of emotion through movement or painting, the release of creativity not previously recognized, and the gaining of a new perspective on problems through dramatic or artistic portrayal.

Activity group therapy is also primarily a nonverbal treatment. Therapists react to the youth in terms of their individual needs. They may help one member but ignore others when they ask for assistance. Members confront and learn to accept each other and themselves. In the early phases of the group, members re-create their problems. In the fourth session of one group, a girl, always rejected by her mother and known for her attention-demanding behavior in school, began to make demands on the therapist. By the sixth session, her demands for assistance were almost continuous. The therapist said nothing but responded to the demands. Some of the others in the group became competitive and also made demands. By the eighth session, the turmoil had died down. The girl settled into the group and her behavior improved at school. The acceptance and meeting of her needs in one setting carried over into other parts of her life and she no longer required continuous reassurance.

In another group, a boy who had always been overprotected by his mother learned through surviving a fight that he could stand up for himself. And in another group, a girl who at first lied continuously about her accomplishments learned that she could be valued and accepted for herself by the other group members. She came from a poor family and did not have fancy clothes. In an early session, when the girls decided to dress up for a trip, she did not go with them. Toward the end of the year, a similar situation occurred. This time she was able to say that she had nothing to wear. The other girls immediately said that they wanted her to come with them so they would not dress up either. This was the turning point in this girl's therapy.

Termination

The termination of groups should be considered on two levels: first, understanding the basic feelings and typical maneuvers involved in dissolving the group, and, second, resolving how to manage termination for the individual members.

Whether a group has been meeting for only a short time or has been an intensive long-term therapy or social group, if meaningful experiences and bonding have occurred between members, members will react to separation. Sometimes the group tries to ignore the fact that they are about to terminate. Other times, members relive the experiences they have shared in the group.

To avoid separating, group members may plan to meet again for what they hope will resemble "old times." As the group nears its end, members may frantically try to deal with all issues that concern them, withdraw interest, loosen ties, or express depression and anger. Leaders must monitor their feelings carefully and guard against joining the members' strategies in avoiding the confrontation with separation and loss.

While the group as a whole goes through these typical maneuvers, individuals may exhibit a range of reactions. Some outwardly deny any feelings, others desire abrupt termination, while still others experience anxiety and grief. Some members suddenly bring up an important problem that they have avoided up until then.

Termination is easiest with short-term, time-limited groups. In such cases there is a set date for termination. If individual members have unsatisfied needs, other arrangements can be made for them.

Open-ended groups that members may enter and leave at any

time must deal with termination and reformulation whenever a member leaves. When the composition changes, the climate of the group also changes, and as old members separate and new ones are added, the group briefly regresses to earlier stages of development in order to regain a sense of equilibrium, trust, and cohesion. In such groups, procedures are established to deal with the separation of those who are ready to terminate and the integration of new members.

In groups, where members start together and work intensively over a long period, questions arise as to when the group and individual members should terminate. Some members feel ready to leave but are reluctant to do so because of the attachment they have with the group. This problem can be dealt with by setting up a group for a specific length of time, then reviewing at that time what has been accomplished and deciding who wants to leave and who wishes to continue. In school-age groups, the end of the semester or of the school year is a convenient time to review a group's progress and decide who will stay in treatment and who will leave. Summer break helps consolidate gains, and lessens new problems and guilt that may surface about staying or leaving. If a number of people leave, the others will essentially start a new group with additional members. Some may even decide to move into a different group altogether. When new and old members start a new group together, the major problem to consider is the difference in psychological sophistication between the old and new members. Another method for managing termination in long-term groups is simply to lose and add members as individuals are ready to leave, forcing the group each time to face problems of separation, reintegration, and trust. This can be useful for members who have problems related to acceptance and loss of intimate relationships.

If some members are terminating and others continuing, feelings will be stimulated on both sides. Members who are leaving may feel a combination of relief, guilt, and anxiety about their future. Those who are remaining may feel abandoned and angry that they have done less well in the group. Most feel sad at losing friends. Intimate groups can be especially important to those who have had difficulty in developing close relationships in their lives. For such group members, it may be useful to foster ties outside the group to help them terminate more easily.

Who decides when a person or a group will terminate? In short-term groups, the leader or the program has already decided when the group will end. In long-term or open-ended groups, the leader, the group, or the individual members may decide. In treatment groups, it is customary to discuss within the group the question of whether a member is ready to leave. In this way all members help the individual decide. Continuing discussion and questioning usually makes it clear as to whether the member is ready to leave or not. Adolescents, particularly, should be encouraged to take responsibility for deciding on their own termination and for helping others come to a decision, because of their tendency to rebel against authority and their need to become responsible.

For the individual, the dissolution of a treatment group, a learning or training group, or a special-interest group means not only the end of an experience, anxiety about separation, and the loss of meaningful relationships, but it is also a maturing process, a recognition that one has reached a new stage of development and is ready to "move on." Members, by signaling their readiness to leave the group, indicate that they have learned new skills, have become more self-reliant and independent, and can do without the group's special support. Growing up, maturing, and becoming more independent involve a great deal of conflict and stress. This is why one frequently experiences a resurgence of dependency in the last stages of a group, just as adolescents, when ready to leave the family, may experience a wave of fear that makes them yearn for the safety of the family even as they struggle for independence.

Leaders and therapists may also have difficulty giving up a group or letting a particular member go. Particularly in long-term, intensive therapy groups, leaders must face and work out their feelings about separation. Being too emotionally involved with a member will make the termination process more difficult than it normally would be and, throughout therapy, leaders must guard against and seek consultation for this problem should it occur. Leaders must avoid creating the kind of attachment some parents engender that causes a child to panic when he or she strives for independence and to make a life outside the family. If members are permitted to remain very dependent on the leader, the therapist, or other group members, separation may cause more anxiety than they can cope with and the constructive effects of the group experience may be greatly impaired. Relationships within groups are prototypes of relationships in the outside world, but they should not be permanent substitutions for them. At some point, members must make relationships and interdependencies that will support them and satisfy them in their lives.

While the length of time, degree of involvement, and readiness to terminate will determine how difficult separation will be, termination should be viewed as a time of celebration, advancement, and challenge. The close and meaningful relationships formed in the group are not destroyed but are foundations on which members can build. They are supports that help them in accepting change, and the experience of building relationships and terminating them satisfactorily can be carried over and used throughout their lives.

5. Major Themes and Problems in Adolescent Groups

Identity development and confirmation is a vital part of adolescence. All adolescents are concerned with questions of who they are, what they can do, what they can become, how they feel about themselves compared with others of the same sex, how they can intrigue the opposite sex, and how they can separate from their parents and become independent adults. There is a progression in these questions. Young teenagers dealing with major bodily and hormonal changes pay a great deal of attention to themselves and their friends of the same sex. They are in the early stages of perceiving themselves as potential young adults. They are likely to be preoccupied with looks, mannerisms, dress, hair styles, and habits that will make them seem more adult. They begin to strain against parental restriction and family closeness. They move into their peer groups but are still making only tentative moves toward a career choice. They are largely unable to consider being truly independent and, for many, their sexual activities are still at a tentative stage. As adolescents grow older, they become more concerned with the opposite sex, with breaking free from parents, with sexual intimacy, with signs of adulthood such as driving and owning cars, with earning money and selecting a career. For many, the major focus of interest is outside the home, with peers, school, jobs, recreation, and their relationship to authorities other than their parents Throughout this period they have mixed desires. They vacillate between needing independence and wanting to be dependent. They are confused about themselves. They want to be responsible, yet free of responsibility. They are often enraged and depressed by unfairness and confused about how they will achieve their goals. The more thoughtful adolescents spend time ruminating on the meaning of life.

Today the world seems to have become more dangerous for adolescents. Statistics show that alcohol and drug-related accidents, drug overdoses, and drug-induced killings and suicide account for most adolescent deaths. Vandalism and violence are not uncommon in schools and neighborhoods. Sex-related diseases and AIDS are ever-present dangers. The daily news is filled with stories of world-wide pollution, natural disasters, and internecine warfare.

Who am I? What Can I Be?

Youngsters between the ages of ten and fourteen are often intensely preoccupied with the question of who they are. Their moods are unpredictable. They may appear confused and anxious, shy, or wild and defiant. They may become intensely self-conscious, act impulsively, spend long hours studying themselves in the mirror, or adopt bizarre styles, changing their looks and mannerisms from day to day. Older adolescents are more focused on how they relate to others and what they will become.

Adolescents want to be treated as grown-ups. They resent restrictions on when they must be home, where they may go, what they may do, and whom they may know, and they may adopt unhealthy habits as rites of passage. Smoking, drinking, and experimenting with drugs may seem adult and exciting. For some, alcohol and drugs become habits that ease self-consciousness, heighten pleasure, or dull the pain of school or family problems, rejection by friends, or despair of ever being successful.

Enhancing Self-Esteem

Groups that include the element of enhancing self-esteem may be general or specific, preventive or designed to treat particular problems. Within the context of the group, the adolescent, through self-examination and feedback, develops a clearer answer to the question, "Who am I?"

Prevention groups may run for a very limited period and focus on the following areas: building social skills and problem-solving abilities; becoming aware of one's emotions and managing anger, anxiety, or the "blues"; clarifying one's goals and values: becoming more assertive; and learning how to solve conflicts and to expect and manage periods of change. Groups may be combined to form prevention programs, such as those designed by Sure and Spivak,[1] Botvin,[2] Schinke and Gilchrist,[3] and Kramer and Frazer,[4] or focused on one problem such as improving communication skills.[5] Although prevention groups were first held in high schools, in many locations they are now starting in the fifth or sixth grade, as teenagers begin experimenting earlier and earlier. Some programs focus specifically on teaching teenagers how to experience success, whether through clubs and friendship groups or through activities. Activity interview groups have been successful for young teenagers who are not particularly verbal but who have problems in managing their emotions, dealing with authority, feeling good about themselves, and who lack social skills.[6] Some therapists, such as Rachman and his followers, concentrate on identity formation as a major element in therapy.[7]

Body Preoccupations in Adolescence

Boys and girls throughout adolescence are concerned with their bodies, their physical development, and their looks. Adolescence

141

has always seemed particularly difficult for the aberrant developers, particularly girls who develop very early or very late, boys who are slow developers, and youngsters who are extremely fat and flabby. In recent years, however, girls appear to have become increasingly concerned with their weight and a significant number suffer from anorexia nervosa, an extreme preoccupation with thinness, and bulimia, a mixture of gorging, purging, binging, and starving. Both problems stem from low self-esteem.[8] Anorexic girls come from families where parents are hypercritical or disengaged, and the girls themselves struggle for perfection. Even when emaciated, they think of themselves as too fat. If they do not receive help, they may starve themselves to death. It has been found that groups can be very beneficial for these girls.[9] In a group, the girls can confront one another with reality and give one another support and appreciation. Many of these groups eat together and encourage one another to eat properly. Thornton and Deblassie describe one group of anorexic girls who are all fourteen years old.[10] Lieb and Thompson lead structured inpatient groups for girls in a broader age range.[11] These groups focused on the problems the girls were having with their self-esteem, their perfectionism, and their obsessions with thinness and helped them reorganize their thinking, increase their self-esteem, and support one another in a healthier life.

Bulimic girls tend to be older adolescents, often in college. They are subject to depression and may be insatiably dependent. They, too, are never satisfied with themselves and frequently binge when they are upset. Bulimics are often unaware of their feelings of anger and rejection. They set up goals that they feel are imposed on them by others, such as parents, teachers, or therapists, and then feel they must fail in these efforts in order to defeat authority. Groups can be helpful in enabling these young women to face reality and understand what they are doing to themselves. Groups also provide support and friendship so they can begin to feel better about themselves. Osterheld, McKenna, and Gould summarize the literature on group psychotherapy within this population.[12]

Another body image problem, more frequent in boys and young men, is the desire for the perfectly developed body. Body-building can become an obsession. It can be tied into competitive sports and has led some youth to take steroids and mood-enhancing drugs to improve their capacities.[13] Coaches and trainers must set the appropriate tone in sports programs so that young people are able to do their best without having to adopt extreme measures to feel adequate or to compete. Many people today feel that competition and winning are overemphasized and that sports should be offered to all who are interested. They feel participants should be able to play at their own level and that having a good game and achieving fitness should be more important than winning.

Managing Feelings: Loneliness, Depression, and Suicide

Some young people have never learned to make friends. They were hurt as small children and cannot risk closeness and intimacy. Others find that changes and transitions often lead to loneliness. Youth often do not know how to make connections in a new situation, such as moving into a new neighborhood, entering a new school at midterm, or beginning middle school or high school, and they feel very much alone. Youth may also become discouraged and depressed if their family breaks up, if a close relative dies, or if they are rejected by a friend. They may despair of ever succeeding in school or fulfilling their parents' ambitions for them.

Groups are used to help boys and girls anticipate and defend themselves against despair.[14] In one group of high school students one girl stated that she could not shake her depression. It took hold of her and would not let her go. She felt she could not go on. Eventually she had told a friend of her feelings, and the friend told a counselor. A boy who had been in an accident feared he might not walk again and wanted to die. He thought of the poisons in the medicine chest in the bathroom. The therapist asked what had stopped him. He replied, "My family. They were always around, telling me jokes, saying how they loved me, telling me that I would be well again."

In a farm crisis group, teenagers shared with one another their fears of losing their homes and friends. They felt badly that their parents had failed in farming or in business. Some family members had begun to drink heavily. Some parents argued incessantly or were impatient with the kids. The teenagers felt helpless.

Even when they have friends teenagers may feel their friends are not available to them. In one group that was discussing suicide, some high school students made the following remarks:

> "Most people are gone when you need them and some wouldn't know how to help."
>
> "When I am very depressed I put on a facade and no one knows I am not all right."
>
> "I listen to others all the time, but somehow when I need them my friends are not willing to listen to me."
>
> "Sometimes it's just too hard. You are upset and then your friend wants to lay it all out on you."
>
> "My parents were breaking up. They were fighting all the time and I was alone with them."
>
> "I felt bad too, as if my whole world was disappearing."
>
> "I took some pills and went to the hospital. It was really helpful. I learned how to deal with my life and let other people know how I was feeling."

In another group of middle-class girls in junior high school who had all attempted suicide, the following discussion took place:

> JOAN: My mother is never at home. She comes back from work, is mad because dinner's not on the table. Leaves me to babysit for the kids while off she goes again. I can't stand it. I don't want to live. Last week I took fifty aspirins, but they took me to the hospital and pumped out my stomach. I didn't want to come here. It's no use.
>
> MARY: I've felt the same way. Nothing I ever did was right. I was caught in a trap. There was no way out. Somehow now

> I feel better—I don't upset Mom so much and she's nicer to me.

When they are extremely depressed, teenagers often feel they cannot do anything, cannot reach out to anyone. Sometimes they put their friends on the spot by asking them to promise not to tell and then confiding in them that they are about to kill themselves. One girl who had been in the hospital stated that you should never promise absolutely not to tell because you may have to in order to save your friend's life. Pritchard, in a video discussion of suicide, pointed out that suicide is a "permanent solution to a temporary problem" and that if one can just hold on, troubles will pass.[15]

Groups dealing with depression and suicide focus on helping teenagers, parents, and teachers recognize the symptoms of depression: behavioral changes, lethargy, changes in eating and sleeping patterns, moodiness and irritability, and wild behavior.[16] Sometimes youth will begin giving away their possessions and seem concerned about saying good-bye. Everyone should know how to deal with a cry for help. Groups for treating depression and suicide have been based on several models: interactional; cognitive restructuring; or behavior modification, with or without the use of medications.

Management of Anger

Teenagers often feel angry—at themselves, their parents, their teachers, their friends, their enemies. They deal with their anger in different ways. Some are afraid of their anger and become sullen and depressed; others are verbally or physically abusive; still others develop somatic symptoms or retreat into a fantasy world. Some groups are specifically designed to help youth deal with anger, become more assertive, and think through their problems before they react.[17] In other more heterogeneous groups, feelings of anger and ways to deal with these feelings are raised as part of a general discussion. Sometimes anger is tied into feelings of helplessness:

"Sometimes when I get real mad, I get tired of doing the same thing over and over again. I try to change it, but I can't do anything about it."

"If I get mad and argue with my sister—she's older than me— just seems like she is always right."

"My mother hollers at me—she made me mad, so then I told her I was going to leave home if she kept on hollering at me, but she knew I wasn't. So most of the time, I just go somewhere and cool off."

"How do you cool off?"

"Go somewhere and sit, put on an ugly look; you think about it, but you don't say nothing."

In another illustration, a girl describes the difference between feeling and acting out her rage:

GIRL: If you do something and something happens, you shouldn't put the blame on someone else. Like I'm saying, if you want to go somewhere real bad and you can't; like she had to take care of her little sister, maybe had the urge to put her in the closet.

THERAPIST: You are saying as long as you take the responsibility—

GIRL: I don't think it is right for you to let your urge like locking somebody in the closet or pushing somebody over a bridge or something like that. Suppose somebody had the same urge to do you like that. You wouldn't want them to do you like that.

THERAPIST: So it is natural to feel mad enough to kill somebody, but it is not right to do it.

GIRL: Not in a case like this—because I have a real nasty attitude, real bad temper, too. I wouldn't really do it, but I feel like it.

On the street in inner cities, youth are faced with daily violence, with sex, drugs, and fighting. Fighting is used to settle disputes or to obtain revenge, and is part of their maturation. Sometimes physical fighting replaces intellectual argument and depression as a means of overcoming boredom.

JEAN: We were on a picnic. Weren't nothing to do so I just ate up people's food. Messed up people's food.

MARY: Suppose a fight broke out, you would have liked that, though.

146

JEAN: You know my teacher said anytime there is a fight I am going to be there. I just like to watch fights. I try to push a fight if I can.

THERAPIST: Why do you think Joan likes to see if she can start something?

MARY: I guess she don't have anything else to do. So she looks for some kind of excitement.

THERAPIST: So there is nothing you want to do, and you get bored and then make trouble?

MARY: Yeah, I get the same way.

THERAPIST: Doesn't this get you reputation for trouble?

MARY: Uh huh—everybody fights. Everyone on the whole street— that's what everybody does.

Leaders suggest other ways of ventilating anger, such as taking a long walk, practicing deep breathing and relaxation exercises, creating pleasant images in one's mind, playing hard-driving sports, or punching an "anger bag."

In one school district students have been trained in conflict mediation and, if there is an argument, they intervene and help the protagonists resolve the issue.[18] In other programs, teenagers are taught to relax, take time out, move away from the situation, and think through how to solve the problem. One boy became angry because his mother nagged him all the time. He felt he wanted to beat her up. Once he began to examine what was happening with her and how she was feeling, he recognized that she was overwhelmed with the task of bringing up four children on her own on a small income and that his continual opposition was just too much for her to bear. He got together with his siblings and they began to work out how they could be more helpful, which in turn allowed her to calm down and be more tolerant of them.

Sometimes teenagers are anxious in the group and try to make the therapist angry or fight with one another to ward off their feelings, as seen in the following exchange:

LEADER: I'm interested in what you said about you all making me mad by giggling. I think giggling can mean all sorts of things.

M-1: You mean you're not mad with us?

LEADER: I just wanted to say that I'm interested in why you giggle. I noticed that when you started to talk about death, you started to giggle, too. Sometimes when people get anxious they giggle. It can mean all sorts of things.

M-2: Do you know why I giggled when we were talking about death. To get it out of my head. I can't stand to hear about nobody dying.

M-3: Sometimes I giggle when I'm embarrassed. I don't know what to say so I start to laugh and sometimes I can't stop.

M-4: I'm that way, too."

Fear of Violence, Disaster, and Death

It seems that a day does not pass without reports on the television news of domestic killings, lethal accidents, wars, and natural disasters. Many youth today experience these events close to home, with violence in neighborhoods, abuse in the home, or friends and relatives being hurt or killed in accidents. Discussions of these events come up in most groups, and some are specifically designed for youth who have experienced losses, frightening disasters, or acute or chronic physical or sexual abuse.

In recent years, mental health consultants, school administrators, and police have come together to work out ways to help students and school faculty deal with neighborhood shootings, major accidents involving students or staff, or the suicide or death of members of the school community. Staff are trained to work with whole classes or with small groups of students to help them express their grief, separate from the those they have lost, and come to terms with the event.

A few authors have reported on groups for children and adolescents after disasters, either to prevent or treat severe reactions. In some situations the youth have all experienced the same event, such as a flood, an earthquake, or a school bus or ferry accident.[19] The groups have dealt with establishing a relationship of trust, sharing experiences, and helping one another understand what happened and understand their feelings and reactions to the stress and grief. Youth are often upset by the randomness of the event, their sense of helplessness, that they cannot control what happens to them. As a result they often distrust the future. Stories, jokes, artwork, or a reenactment of events all help teenagers overcome their fears, allow them to grieve, express their anger at fate, learn techniques for managing future events, and accept the uncertainty of life. Gradual exposure to feared situations through exercises that recount the events, such as watching films and videos and role-playing, gradually desensitize the youth and help them master their fears. Youth also learn relaxation techniques and how to image events and leave themselves with happier feelings.

We are also learning that posttraumatic stress symptoms can go unrecognized and that some youth who are acting out and getting into trouble are really suffering from Posttraumatic Stress Disorder (PTSD). Doyle and Bauer report identifying disturbed and acting-out youth and treating them for PTSD in a residential setting.[20]

Since the first National Child Abuse Reports were published in the late seventies[21] we have become much more conscious of the prevalence of physical, emotional, and sexual abuse of children and youth in America. Although both boys and girls have been sexually abused, most groups that work with this population are reportedly for girls. Most of these groups have been short-term, lasting from ten sessions up to a year. They have usually had two female therapists and have been semistructured, combining education, games, humanistic experiences, and support and clarification of issues and feelings. Some groups have been closed with a narrow age range and have included only five to eight members, with regular attendance expected.[22] Other groups have been open-ended, longer-term, have included a wider age range, girls between eight and eighteen, and have generally included a larger population, from sixteen to twenty members, with an expected attendance of about half that number at any one meeting.[23] Some therapists run art therapy groups for this population.[24] Others prefer unfocused activity interview groups to help the girls feel at ease with one another before confiding their experiences, because typically these girls experience difficulty with emotions. They are fearful, angry, distrustful, feel inferior, damaged, and guilty. They may show avoidance behavior or express their disturbance in antisocial behavior, sexual acting out, or running away. They may experience sleep disturbances, eating problems, or somatic reactions. Trust is a major issue for these girls. Some try to avoid members of the other sex. Others appear confused about whom they can trust.

Whichever form of group therapy is used, the goals are the same: to help the girls share the event, deal with their feelings, learn to feel better about themselves, cope with their ambivalence and guilt about exposing the perpetrator, and learn to understand why adults molest them and why a parent fails to protect them. They learn factual material about how to deal with the courts and what resources are available to them. They receive education on the male and female bodies. In situations where the girls are living apart from their families, this separation must be dealt with. If a stepfather has been the perpetrator and the mother chooses to remain with him, the girl usually feels hurt and bitter. Groups for younger adolescents and less articulate girls make more use of games and concrete activities, whereas discussion is emphasized more with articulate, older teenagers. All groups will probably use some role-playing in the service of skill development. Most of these groups have not been evaluated. There appears to be a consensus, however, that the prognosis is better if the girls are able to admit frankly that abuse has occurred and if a family member is supportive.

Parents and Siblings

Absent or present, loving or abusive, parents are always central in the lives of their children. Even when a child is adopted or has never known one parent, the fantasies exist. Although a youth has separated from the family, is primarily attached to a peer group, or has run away, the voice of the parent is still heard, sending a message: "You are no good," "You are bad," "You are special," "I can't stand you," "We will always love you." In one-parent families, there are always questions of why the parent left, was it the youth's fault. When a child is adopted, youth are always wondering: "What were they like?" "Why did they give me up?" "What blood is in my veins?" Certain questions are inextricably bound into parental relationships, such as "What am I like?"; "Can I be successful?"; "Am I lovable?" In one way or another, parents are major influences in forming a teenager's self-image and in teaching children how to cope with situations and deal with their emotions.

The teenager's mixed feelings about dependence and independence are focused first on the parents. Throughout adolescence, youth are testing their parents' limits and that of other authorities, swinging back and forth between the desire to stand on their own and the desire to be taken care of. Teenagers want to make decisions about their own lives and they resent their parents having goals for them. Sometimes youth are confused by parents' mixed feelings regarding whether the parents actually want the teenagers to grow up and be successful. In a multiple family group where the teenagers were not doing well in school, the parents discussed how much they wanted their teenagers to go to college and how disappointed they were that their grades might not be good enough. One parent asked another, "You didn't go to college? How do you feel about your son going? Are you afraid you will lose him?" That parent replied, "I believe I am. I never thought about it before but I might have mixed feelings about my son, the lawyer, when I am only a construction worker." The son broke in, "Yeah, you are always telling me to do my homework and yet when I'm going to settle down you yell at me that I haven't done my chores." One of the mothers in the group was always talking about her baby when referring to her son, while at the same time complaining that her son was irresponsible. Another parent picked up on this discrepancy, and the son said, "I know I don't really have to do things because she will always do them for me."

151

In a group of adolescent girls, one girl complained that her mother was always nagging her and would not let her do what her friends were doing, go out with boys and stay out after midnight. She turned to a girl who was living in a foster home and said, "I wish I didn't have a mother. I wish I were like you and lived in a foster home." The other girl replied, "I wish I were you. I wish I had a mother who cared enough about me to set some rules." This sounded so funny to the others that they laughed, and the first girl said, "Well, I expect I do give her a hard time." Following this episode she became more reasonable, and her mother was also able to relax so the struggle between them gradually abated.

In another group, members were examining how teenagers and their parents nag and upset each other.

M-1: Sometimes you might bring up an argument and then find that you are wrong, but you don't want to admit it because you brought it up. You don't want to feel ashamed or embarrassed. Sometimes you don't want to admit you are wrong.

M-2: I don't bring up anything with my mother because she runs it into the ground.

M-3: Sometimes when I argue and I can't have my way, my mom will tell me I can't go somewhere and I follow her wherever she goes, arguing with her. She will tell me to go on out and get out of her face.

THERAPIST: So sometimes you nag her just as she nags you.

Today parents and children in many families have to accommodate to remarriage and adjust to new roles as stepparents and stepsiblings. There is often unresolved grief for lost parents and resentment against the stepparents who have taken their place. Stepsiblings are often jealous of one another and if there are babies in the new family, teenagers may feel excluded. Therapists such as Serrano often work with the splinter families that may have resulted from the marital break-up,[25] but teenage groups can also be helpful in allowing the youth to share their problems in a sympathetic atmosphere and work out ways to deal with them. Role-playing will often help teenagers understand what is happening in the family.

Teenagers play many roles as siblings. Brothers and sisters may be close friends and supportive of each other. They may be models for identification. They may also be sources of aggravation, rivalry, and jealousy or, if older, may lead their younger siblings into bad habits and bad company. Some teenagers may have been abused physically or sexually by older siblings. Unless it is a family group, it is not usual to include siblings in the same group. When one does, a situation is created where two group members have a preestablished and continuing relationship and are seeing each other much more frequently than are the other members. This creates an imbalance in the group and usually makes it difficult to function therapeutically.

Friendships, Secrets, and Sex

Friendships become particularly important in adolescence, and difficulties in finding and keeping a close friend come up many times in teenage groups. Differences in the adolescents' rate of development can split apart same-sex friendships when one friend becomes interested in the opposite sex before the other is ready to do so. When this happens, the friend who is developing more slowly often feels excluded. Some adolescents lack social skills and have difficulty making friends. They are too shy or too depressed to reach out or respond to others, or they may seem too awkward, different, or provocative to fit in easily with others. Groups can be useful in helping teenagers understand how they appear to others and in giving them a chance to practice their social skills and become accepted and cared for. Sometimes these groups are made up of youngsters with different problems and skills, as in a well-balanced activity-interview group. Sometimes they are specialized, as when a group of shy teenagers practice becoming less self-conscious and more outgoing.[26]

In early adolescence particularly, friends use one another as close confidants and enjoy having secrets. This is a time when lonely and depressed youngsters join cults or indulge in secret rituals as a way of experiencing a sense of belonging and of importance. Peer groups are important arbiters of habits, and teenagers urge one another on to try out smoking, drinking, drugging, and sex. Girls and boys during adolescence tend to band together, first in same-sex groups and later in heterosexual groups. These peer groups have great influence over the members and affect their speech, style, dress, interests, values, and habits. Groups that are designed to influence teenage habits in a socially acceptable way must be equally powerful to have an effect. Groups that are designed to delay experimentation with negative behaviors include social skills training; resistance skills training, such as learning to say no when one is under pressure;[27] and programs that encourage teenagers to take part in more interesting and challenging activities. These may include adventure programs such as "Outward Bound" trips,[28] profitable hobbies, special interest groups for art, music, or drama, or a range of sports activities. For example, one group of rebellious boys who had become involved with drugs and were in trouble with the law were formed into a group that made kayaks after school.[29] Ultimately they developed their own business. They became more self-reliant, learned construction and business skills, had fun on the weekends, learned how to work as a team, and of course no longer had time for drugs. Groups for developmental and preventive purposes largely focus on interpersonal relations and activity skills. To be most effective, they are multifaceted to address the youth's various social, cognitive, behavioral, and emotional problems. Agencies such as The Door[30] and Teen Link[31] serve many different needs and offer a number of different groups and programs under one roof.

Confirmation of the individual's sexual identity, management of sexual impulses in terms of one's culture, the capacity to become intimate with others of the opposite sex, and the selection of a mate are major tasks and problems confronting adolescents. Consequently, all areas of the adolescent's life have sexual implications and therefore sex needs to be talked about in adolescent groups. There is also much reticence about bringing sex into the open, for in Western society there have been traditional taboos on such talk that are still not fully broken down today. Moreover, there is a great diversity of opinion regarding what is appropriate sexual behavior for teenagers. Boys, girls, and leaders alike are therefore often embarrassed and reluctant to start talking about sex. It is a great relief to a group to be able to deal with sexual matters, for as an intimate subject it brings a feeling of intimacy and closeness to the group. To undertake this successfully leaders must feel free to allow the group to talk about sex. They must recognize and pick up indirect cues, and then indicate their willingness to allow such talk. If they ignore the cues, they convey the idea that discussing sex openly is not permitted. The group's anxiety is not dealt with, much anger and resentment is built up, and group members are likely to act out disruptively during the group and sometimes sexually outside.

In some school systems, such as the Irvington Board of Education in Irvington, New Jersey,[32] and in some families and religious groups, sex education is started early and children gradually learn about sex in age-appropriate ways. Many youth still receive no information except from siblings or friends, however, and as they reach puberty they become curious about sex, what it is, how sexual acts are performed, and how babies are made. Sophistication varies enormously among groups and although some boys and girls are sexually active at puberty, others are still quite naive in high school. Discussion in prevention and therapy groups must be geared to the level of sophistication of the members. Sex education today often will include contraceptive information and certainly should provide teenagers with a knowledge of how AIDS and other sexually transmitted diseases are contracted and how this can be prevented.

Often, particularly with boys, the first expression of concern is about homosexuality or masturbation. Teenagers become aware of bodily sensations and are interested in comparing themselves with others of the same sex, yet are afraid of the implication of

155

this intimacy. There are allusions to being queer. Giggling, teasing, and a high level of excitability are usually indications of a sexual undercurrent. Leaders should bring these interests out into the open and discuss feelings as part of normal development. There is both an affectionate, intimate aspect to these feelings and, in early adolescence particularly, a comparative and competitive aspect. Boys getting together to masturbate are enjoying a new skill and sensation. Girls in becoming physically close are retaining their early dependency on mother and thinking about themselves as future women. If homosexual interests continue, the reasons for this identification should be examined. Sometimes in girls it is an attempt to retain their mothers. Sometimes it is a fear of men, sometimes an identification with men, or sometimes a need to be aggressively in control. Boys may have been close to their fathers and obtained great satisfaction from them. They may have felt it safest and most satisfying to be a woman or to be passive, or they may be afraid or rejecting of women.

Adolescents in institutions often indulge in masturbation or in homosexual activities because of the lack of other outlets for the expression of emotional tension in general and sexuality in particular. They may feel troubled and guilty about this. They may also, if their stay is lengthy, come to find sufficient satisfaction in these practices to be loath to make a change to heterosexuality. Once the egosyntonic nature of the preference for homosexuality has been established, the homosexual identification needs to be accepted as a particular way of life that some individuals in every culture have chosen.

Sex should be discussed as a natural drive and as part of human relations. Teenagers need to recognize that the other partner is human too, has fears, needs, weaknesses, and strengths. It should be emphasized that it is most important to know and care about each other, to respect each other, and to consider the partner's interests as well as one's own. Sex is one component in intimate relationships and carries responsibilities as well as pleasures. If possible, boys and girls should be helped to recognize

156

that they may not be ready for sex and for its possible unwanted consequences.

As group members discuss intimacy, they examine the nature of the relationships between boys and girls, how sex is used by either partner, and the consequences of sexual relationships psychologically and socially. They need to learn how they can develop fully rounded relationships in which affection, mutual help and interdependence, intellectual stimulation, mutual interests, and sexual satisfaction are ultimately blended. They can explore together the range of relationships between different people and how they can protect themselves in the process of growing up.

Concerns vary between early and later adolescence. How boys and girls begin to get together and know each other is of central interest in early adolescence. The following examples are typical of discussions in groups of young teenage girls:

"I don't want to talk about boys. Sometimes when I'm walking down the street, some boy will come up to me and ask me my name and address, and I'll sometimes give my name and such and such an address that I don't even know where it's at."

"One time, I gave a boy a phony name, a phony address and phone number, and then one day I saw him across the street near where I live. I took off and ran because everybody around there knows where I live and my phone number."

"A boy asked me to go out with him. I didn't know how to say no because I didn't like him. I was so embarrassed."

In another group the girls were discussing a first date:

"Wilma, how old is he? Fifteen?"

"No, he's just a year older than I am."

"You're not supposed to go with anyone younger, are you?"

"Well, anyway, he came down here. He couldn't find nobody to go to the prom with him. I said, 'All these girls in the ninth grade and you can't find anybody?' He said 'No, give me some suggestions.' So I told him the girl downstairs. He said he had asked her and she already had somebody to go with ... so he asked me and I told him no."

157

"You're a fool. Is he good looking?"

"Yes, he's good looking."

"I said no, and then I said 'I'll think it over.' Then I asked my mother and she said I could go, so I'm going."

Boys and girls in our society are frequently poorly prepared for the sexual stimulus of adolescence. They are given very confused guidelines by an adult world that refuses to face and work through the issues. Discussion has to be geared to the life experiences of the youth. Although dating practices, containment of the situation, and delaying the initiation of sexual activity may be the approach with adolescents from protected environments, it is useless to discuss these notions with teenagers who have experienced sexual intercourse for several years. As we have already mentioned, a few school systems have excellent programs[33] and some schools offer Life Skills education that includes family life and sex education as part of a more comprehensive approach.[34] Scheidlinger has developed two excellent films on sex education for groups of teenagers.[35] The Rosenbergs present an intensive sex education program,[36] and a film—*When Jenny When?*—shows how young boys egg one another on.[37]

It is unrealistic to withhold information about birth control from adolescent girls until they have had their second baby. It is important, however, to help adolescents understand the implications of full sexual involvement, the energy absorbed in the culmination of intimate relationships that may be diverted from other essential tasks, and the possible consequences of the completion of the sexual act. Boys and girls who are sexually active often have difficulty with contraceptives. Some do not like to be "prepared" because it seems too planned and unromantic. Even those who usually carry condoms may, in the heat of the moment, fail to use them. Regardless of the threat of AIDS today, many teenagers still feel that pregnancy or infection can't happen to them. They may feel that they are invulnerable, or that they do not care about disablement and death. Some have given no thought to the reality of giving birth to damaged children. It is difficult for many youth to think beyond the moment, particularly if they are also involved in drinking alcohol or taking drugs.

In the group, leaders need to raise these questions: Why is there no thought of the consequences? What are the mixed feelings involved? How can teenagers protect themselves against their own impulses? Although not denying the urgency of sexual desire in adolescence, many teenagers who indulge in indiscriminate sex do so either because they are angry and turn their anger back on themselves or because they are lonely and unloved. They feel they are nothing, have nothing, and can be nothing, and the only way they can get anyone to care is by having a sexual relationship. Some boys want to prove their masculinity and some girls are afraid that the boys will have no interest in them whatsoever if they do not have sex. Some teenagers long for closeness to fill a void in their lives because of their own lack of self-esteem. They feel of no consequence and have no satisfactory relationships. They feel they have no talents, no charm, no attractiveness, no future, nothing but their sexuality. Often sex is not even enjoyable, but rather frightening and strained. The girls say that the boys do not want anything else, yet the boys do not feel better for having indiscriminate sex. They feel it is necessary to prove their competence and potency over and over again and do not really respect themselves or the girls. Even if they do not feel competent in other ways, at least they can be strong, masculine, and adequate sexually. If they can get a girl to have intercourse with them without protection, then she must really care for them. Yet, hasty exploitative sex can never be fully satisfying. One advantage of heterosexual groups is that the boys and girls can exchange their points of view and perhaps gain a better understanding both of their mutual problems and of their genuine differences.

Older adolescents are deeply interested in how to select a life partner, what marriage means, the role of sex in marriage, how and when to establish a family, and how to be successful men and women, husbands and wives, fathers and mothers. They ask: "What is marriage like?"; "How can I have a more satisfying marriage than my parents did?"; "How do you choose a life partner?"; "How do you know when you are really in love?"

Troubled relationships at home make consideration of these matters difficult, as in the following example:

JEAN: My mother and father fight all the time. I don't think I want to get married.

MARY: father left home and now my mother has to support all of us children. How can I know if the man I choose will be responsible?

In another group, Tom stated, "My father has been married and divorced twice. My mother has had two other relationships and neither of them worked out."

The management of roles in marriage bother the youngsters.

LEADER: Your feeling is that women should stay home with the children and men should go out to work?

M-1: I don't agree. Because if only the man works, he don't want to give you no money.

M-2: I live with my uncle and aunt. He works in the laundry and he works in a night club at night. He gives me money every time he gets paid, twice a week. When my aunt stopped working, he wouldn't give her no money. She had some kind of heart trouble or something. Anyway, after she stopped working, he stopped giving her money.

M-3: Nobody in my house works. Nobody but me.

M-4: Don't your mother and father work?

M-3: My father is dead. My mother says she is sick and can't work.

M-5: My mother and father are not together and every Friday I go up after he gets off work. He knows to expect me, and he can't turn me away because if he does, I call my mother's lawyer and tell him. Every week he's supposed to give us an allowance, me and my three sisters.

In a middle-class professional group, the youngsters discussed the difficulty of both parents working. They had all experienced coming home from school to an empty house and had been required to look after younger siblings and do many of the chores. Sometimes both parents had to work late, came home exhausted, and then would argue as to which parent would take on what household and child care responsibilities.

Teenagers are often disillusioned by the difficulties grown men and women have in getting along together. Adolescents, whether from poor or rich families, feel scornful and angry when parents preach faithfulness and self-control, yet act promiscuously themselves. The well-to-do youngster may have to contend with only one parent and the problems of working out relationships with parents who are divorced and remarried. Other youth cope with their mother's boyfriends who leave or are thrust out when living gets rough. They ask desperately how they can meet and identify individuals who will make good mates and how to manage more successfully than their parents did. Their ideals remain those stated by American society, but their expectations are that they will end up like their parents.

Getting Along in School

By the time boys and girls reach puberty and early adolescence, their capacity to function in school has largely been determined. Many are clearly in the fast track and designed to be successful academically. For them, the pressures are how to maintain the pace and how to make the most suitable academic and career choices. Some adolescents will begin to fail in school because of situational problems or because of interpersonal difficulties. Others will find that their gifts are not so great when they get into high school or college and compete with others at their own level.[38] Many of those who will get into trouble in adolescence have already been failing since the first grade and are two to four years behind their normal age level. In school they are bored or depressed, irritable, explosive or restless, or seek to escape as often as they can. Others are overwhelmed by the confusions of early adolescence, unable to meet the demands of moving into middle school, or seduced by the temptations of appearing prematurely adult. A sizable proportion of adolescents, perhaps 40–60 percent of those in poverty areas, do not make it into high school without major comprehensive interventions.

Moving out of elementary school is difficult for many teenagers. They are confused by the larger number of teachers and students and have difficulty finding their way from class to class. The increasing difficulty of the work challenges some, particularly if they already have other problems. The seduction of drugs and alcohol may add to the confusion. Many youth have difficulty adjusting to the styles of different teachers. Pleasing teachers, annoying teachers, or feeling there is no way to get along with a particular teacher ("Man, she is just bad news.") are common themes in the group. Some school systems have developed transitional groups.

Boys and girls feel the pressure of homework, particularly when they have many other interests, have no quiet place to work, or have to hold a job to stay in school. Training for the track team, trying out for the drama club, or being part of a group that parties every weekend may be more important than homework. Many youngsters have not developed good study habits and waste a lot of time because they are so disorganized.

Some adolescents are very self-conscious and, for them, giving oral reports before a large class is an unbearable ordeal. These youngsters can benefit from a group that helps them practice in a more protective setting where they can overcome their fears.

The conflict between athletics and school work can be a bitter one. Boys and girls who are outstanding in sports but mediocre in everything else naturally want to capitalize on their talents. Yet today they must maintain a certain grade level in school in order to be allowed to play. On the other hand, teenagers who work hard but also have athletic aspirations feel that neglecting work to spend all one's time in athletics gives an unfair advantage to those who take this route.

Career Choice

What one will be when one grows up is a central question for teenagers. The implications of any particular career choice, however, are not usually clear to adolescents. They often have limited information on which to base their choice. When youth were asked by employment counselors to describe the life and work involved in various careers with which they were familiar, youth from poor families, particularly, could only describe one or two careers and had little understanding about what life-style they would require. Poor youth, minority groups, and adolescents of all classes who are failing in school are caught in the dilemma of what they may want to do as opposed to what may be possible for them. For example, in a group of girls, aged thirteen to fifteen years old from low-income families, the question was asked, "What do you want to be?" Their answers included: teacher, nurse, social worker, psychologist, and geologist. Later they were discussing going to work and were asked, "What kind of work would you look for?" The general response was, "Cleaning or washing dishes, I suppose, or maybe working at MacDonalds." The lack of expectation that their dreams can be realized is a great stumbling block for many youth and often results in their failing to try. Youth employment programs that were started in the sixties and continue today have tried to bring together opportunities for adolescents to learn skills for living and working, to obtain work experience, and to see visible and accessible channels for advancement, but these only reach a small number of youth.

Parents' aspirations can also be a problem. One group of high school teenagers was struggling with this problem:

"Nothing but an A will satisfy my father."

"I come from a Navy family and my father was disappointed I wasn't a boy, but now I can go to the Naval Academy even though I'm a girl."

"My parents want to see me become a doctor like my Dad and

his father, but I can't see all those years in college. I want maybe to get into boat building or something."

"I have to take on my family business but I couldn't care less. I want to write."

The Transition to College and Work

Frequently high school curricula do not adequately prepare students for the unstructured, more demanding academic reality of college. College freshmen who have had histories of academic achievement suddenly find themselves failing exams. In Counseling Center groups, these youngsters find support as others share their struggles in adapting to the requirements of independent study.[39]

College choice itself can be overwhelming for some youth. If parents are not knowledgeable, teenagers can flounder; even youth with strong parental support find themselves faced with a monumental task. There are so many colleges that it is difficult to know where to start. Students often don't know what they want or how to choose, and they struggle to get organized and send in the appropriate papers before deadlines. Busy counselors don't always have the time to give individualized attention, but a group of adolescents can work together in approaching their problems. Some adolescents just can't face the thought of making a choice, a commitment to a life-long career. They think of going to work every day for the rest of their lives and they shudder. For some of these youngsters, getting experience in different kinds of work before settling down to a particular choice can be a solution. Furthermore, teenagers should know, or be made aware, that in this rapidly changing world they may have to change careers several times before reaching the age of retirement.

Minority groups still face discrimination. A group of black youth who had tried to find permanent jobs through job training programs were discussing the problems they had encountered in coping with prejudice. In training to become cooks, they found repeatedly that whites who had started later were appointed before them to the permanent positions. They became aware that power and influence were vital factors in success. On the other hand, it was also difficult for them to distinguish when it was their own problem that was delaying their advancement.

Many youth who are in trouble despair of being able to develop a satisfying life for themselves in any socially acceptable way. Their problems are reflected in depression; giving up and ceasing to try; retreating into apathy; negativism and drugs; infantilism or illness; hitting back at the adult work in angry defiance or delinquency; becoming pregnant; searching for excitement in dangerous activities, such as drug dealing or gambling, in the hope of instance success; living in a grandiose or fantasy world; or even threatening suicide.

The teenager must somehow be able to hope for a successful life. Teenagers must be helped to know their own capacities and talents, to learn what their interests are. They need help in developing the skills and identifying the channels that will take them where they want to go. In the group, teenagers can see how they frequently precipitate their own difficulties, can test new ways of relating to others such as co-workers and employers, and can plan new approaches to ways of behaving outside the group.

Western culture leaves the adolescent in an ambiguous position. At times these youngsters are expected to shoulder adult responsibilities, while they are also being treated as children. Adolescents are sensitive to this ambiguity and to their own as well as the adults' mixed attitudes. In groups, comments like these give testimony to the adolescent's search for identity:

"Do they call you mister on your job?"

"If they thought you were a child they would call you Clarence."

"I tell you like this, just because you are twenty-one, it really doesn't mean you are a man. You can be twenty-one and act the age of twelve."

"That's right. Then there are some younger people who can act like they are older, like they are grown."

"I think a man is a man if he accepts responsibility and obligation."

"What makes a woman?"

"Same thing, a woman in age, but in mind maybe a different thing."

"You think this group has been passing as adults?"

"No. Average adolescents."

Smoking, Drinking, and Drugging

The so-called gateway drugs—tobacco, alcohol, and marijuana—are adopted by young teenagers for many reasons. They may be in a neighborhood or school where these habits are the norm. They may have grown up in families where one or all these habits were part of the family culture. They may use the substances to feel grown up; to feel part of the group; to allay anxiety, pain, and depression; to gain a high; or to bolster self-esteem. They may agonize over the choice, may be able to take or leave the substances, or may become quickly hooked on one or all. Because it is an issue in American culture today, however, substance abuse will inevitably be discussed at some point in teenage groups, whether they are for socializing or treatment, specifically for substance abuse, or general in nature.

Schools and neighborhoods vary greatly in the extent to which substance abuse is a problem. Within a school there may be sharp divisions. Many hard-working, successful students keep away from all these substances. Those who are keen on athletics may not feel able to succeed unless they take steroids. The students who consider themselves avant garde, those who are failing, and those who have emotional problems are all vulnerable, however. There is relatively little data but it is believed that youth who have dropped out of high school, whether they are working or not, are more likely to be involved in substance abuse.

Schools that have designated the school area as a "drug-free zone" tend to use a variety of groups to prevent drug abuse:[40] groups of student leaders who are trained to set the tone for the rest of the school; classroom groups teaching a range of preventive coping skills, such as assertiveness training and resistance skills; smoking-prevention programs;[41] or rap rooms where students can obtain support and assistance in crises.[42]

Teenagers are sometimes puzzled and resentful about the attitudes of adult society toward different kinds of "bad habits":

"We can be busted for smoking a joint but our parents can get drunk and nobody says a thing."

"My family smokes, why can't I?"

"My mother is always taking tranquilizers when she is anxious, yet she goes through the roof if she finds me with grass."

A college group complains about not being allowed to buy beer:

"Why, a six-pack on a Saturday night is nothing."

"We have to go to my friend's home and get someone over twenty-one to bring us in a keg because we can't go to a bar after the movies. What's the difference between drinking at twenty and twenty-two?"

"My friend drinks too much but he was afraid to go to a counselor because he was doing something illegal, and I didn't know how to get help for him without getting him into trouble."

"Yeah, the trouble with illegal drinking is that if anyone is in trouble it is harder to go for help"

"Well, the law is the law."

"I think the 'designated driver' is a good idea. I'm glad the cops are so tough about drunk driving. It makes everyone more careful."

Stimulants such as crack, cocaine, and "ice" have become obsessions in some circles and groups of teenagers are involved in dealing and using these substances and having sex, with the inherent danger of contracting AIDS. To get drugs some girls have turned to prostitution; then they become pregnant and give birth to drug-damaged or AIDS-infected babies. Increasing numbers of teenagers, however, are aware of the dangers of both "gateway" and hard drugs and are avoiding them. Unfortunately, many adolescents, for one reason or another, are still experimenting and getting hooked. Groups are not only important for the prevention of substance abuse but also for treatment, rehabilitation, and relapse reduction, These latter groups are discussed in more detail in chapter 6.

Teenagers and the Law

Adolescents struggle with the ambiguous status of not being children and not being adults. They are confronted with the reality that if they drop out of school they will be expected to work and pay taxes. At the same time, they may not be allowed to marry, vote, stay out late, or drink alcohol like adults who have reached legal maturity.

For those who do not feel adequate in other ways, defiance of the law may be exhilarating. For example, possessing a gun or stealing cars and driving them too fast may be a way these youth have of confirming their potency. Girls may be expressing their need for love, their daring, or their resentment when they steal from stores.

In a group of girls on probation, they spoke of a few of their reasons for stealing:

"Some people see something they want so bad and maybe they didn't have the money for it and they probably never have the money for it, so it gets on their minds and they just take it."

"Last year, my girlfriend and I, we used to play hooky from school a lot and sometimes we'd go to the grocery store and steal a whole lot of food, you know. We used to steal it and all like that."

"When I steal I don't feel guilty. I just feel nervous and scared after I do it."

The group leader asked what some of the others were feeling, and there were the following comments:

"Sometimes I steal because I am mad, and I don't care if I do get caught."

"I know I couldn't say nothing cause I used to steal, too. Go in the store and see something I want. I would go on and take it. I know what made me stop. I got caught."

"Yes, it's wrong, but I guess they don't think about it anyway as long as it gives them a little bit of enjoyment."

Once teenagers are enmeshed in a delinquent way of life, it is difficult for them to get out of it unless they are helped to change their entire life-style and their circle of friends. They cannot go to work or attend school all day and still stay out with their friends until four in the morning. In some delinquency- prevention and drug-rehabilitation programs, this problem is addressed. A comprehensive program is developed that includes education, work, and opportunities for a different social life. These programs usually include a core group in which a multitude of issues related to self-concept, self-management, and the functioning of society are discussed.

In one human services aide-training program, some of the recreation aides had been at an all-night gambling club that was raided by the police. They were taken to the police station and had barely been able to get to work the next day. The group of aides were discussing the situation:

"Well, I don't see what difference it makes what you do outside of work. Your time is your own."

"On the other hand, you nearly didn't make it to work and the kids would have been disappointed."

"You know, if I were a parent I don't know if I would like my child to be taken care of by someone who spent their nights gambling."

"Isn't it how you are on the job that matters?"

"Maybe it's how you are period that matters."

Eventually the group came round to the idea that perhaps who you are and what you stand for and how you behave when you are off as well as on the job can make a difference, particularly if you work with kids and want them to look up to you and respect you.

Loyalty to the group is strong. The following discussion deals with the retribution meted out to "squealers":

MARK: Like if a boy gets hurt and he tells on that gang, then the gang is going to beat him again, like my brother. See, he was going with this girl, so she started going with this gang, so she told the boy something about my brother, so this whole bunch of boys jumped my brother and he got beaten up. He didn't tell the police what happened, his friend told the police so the boys got put away and when they came back, they were going to beat up the boys who told the police on them.

MR. JONES: What do you other boys say about that, each of you individually?

JIMMY: You mean if we were in his place?

HARRY: I don't know. That would be a hard decision. If you are going to bust down on your friends or not.

HENRY: I ain't going to point the finger at nobody.

In a second discussion, the group struggles with another problem surrounding squealing:

MR. JONES: Do we have a responsibility for something like this? (Silence)

MR. JONES: Is there a right or a wrong thing to do? In this case, is there? I just want your opinion.

JIMMY: It would get out he's a "squealer." If you bust down, they don't want any part of you. They might go out and rob a store or something. How would you feel if you knew these guys had guns and were looking for you?

MR. JONES: Scared and unsafe. But whose responsibility is it? Just the Probation Officer's or everybody's responsibility?

JIMMY: Mr. Jones, I think it's everybody's responsibility.

HARRY: But Joe don't know what to do.

MARK: I don't know. I think I would keep my mouth shut. It's not my duty to turn them in.

HENRY: I would turn them in if they hurt my mother or something like that.

KEN: If Mr. Jones gets into it, they probably will.

JOE: I don't have to tell the police. I just make it clear that I don't want anybody's name mentioned.

Even when the boys would like to get rid of the bullies, fear of retribution is very real and often deters them.

Attitudes toward the law are often pragmatic. For example, the following discussion took place in a group of thirteen-year-old girls:

SALLY: You shouldn't break the law because you will be caught and punished.

CAROL: What is breaking the law?

SALLY: It means that you do something wrong, then you are caught and punished.

CAROL: Are you breaking the law if you cross the street against the red light if nobody is in sight and you are all alone at 3 o'clock in the morning?

SALLY: No, only a fool would stand all alone waiting for a light to change.

CAROL: The lights were put there to stop if there are other people there too."

THE LEADER: So it only matters if you are seen or caught?

SALLY: Well, no, but sometimes the law seems silly.

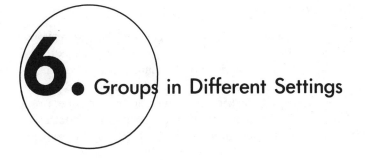

6. Groups in Different Settings

In this chapter we describe groups conducted in different settings—in agencies and institutions and in private practice—and we examine the advantages and constraints inherent in these settings. Groups whose main function is to increase individual capacity for socialization are usually voluntary. Groups that emphasize therapy, rehabilitation, or correction are more often enforced by some authority. Teenagers may join a group because they must, because they want to, or because they gain some satisfaction other than the stated purpose of the group; however, individuals must perceive a need for change and begin to hope for something different for themselves before the group can help them. Any captive group must therefore become voluntary in spirit, a process brought about by a shift from diffuse self-defeating hostility and acting-out to self-motivation for change, before any significant change in behavior can occur.

Institutional Settings

Institutional settings include schools and colleges; recreational and religious programs; work training and employment programs; psychiatric, casework, and community mental health outpatient agencies; substance abuse programs; court and correctional programs; psychiatric day treatment; and in-patient and residential settings. A range of different groups are conducted in these settings. In the first three categories, groups are more likely to be held for education, information, skill development, or crisis management; groups for treatment, rehabilitation, or correction involve increasing amounts of constraint; and more constraint is required as the list continues. Some groups are built into other activities and some are clearly identified as prevention, treatment, or rehabilitation.

Groups in Schools and Colleges

The functions of educational institutions are to prepare young people for social and vocational roles in adult life. The school not only teaches basic educational skills, habits of thought and application, and a wide range of knowledge, but also assists in the transmission of social values and the standards of socially acceptable behavior. Schools provide opportunities for youth to learn how to relate to peers and to authority, to select a career, and to affirm their sexual identity. Training in interpersonal relations should therefore be a significant aspect of a school's responsibilities inside and outside the classroom. Schools are dynamic institutions and administrators and teachers need to understand not only the individual student but also how the management and tone of the institution and the classroom affect the development and behavior of youth. Unfortunately, knowledge of group dynamics in the classroom is often not included in a teacher's general training.

Teachers, through the curriculum, inform students about society. The students learn about physical and psychological development, how different people live, and about their community and different work roles. On trips, they learn of their cultural heritage, get to know their environment, and talk with people in different careers. In the seventies, some school systems encouraged an interactive, humanistic approach in the classroom that included group experiences and exercises to help students understand their feelings.[1] With school desegregation came a concern for intergroup relations in the schools and the tolerance and enjoyment of differences.[2] Berkovitz[3] and Gazda[4] provided excellent summaries of the various groups conducted in secondary schools in the mid-seventies. Berkovitz updated this information in 1989.[5]

In recent years, the federal government has placed more responsibility on schools to teach youth about problems they will encounter concerning the management of their sexual impulses[6] and the need to resist unhealthy habits such as alcohol, drug abuse, and smoking.[7] Social skill training, assertiveness training, the identification of depression, the enhancement of self-esteem have all been targets for the schools.[8] Transitions from elementary school to middle school, to high school and to college have always been problematic for some teenagers who have needed special assistance at these times[9] and peer support groups have been helpful.[10] Guidance and counseling has been an integral part of school systems in educational and vocational planning, and in counseling teenagers who are having difficulty in their peer relations or in dealing with authority.[11] Groups for youth with behavioral and oppositional problems have become popular in some school systems, and therapist/trainers such as Elias,[12] Krieg,[13] and Capuzzi and Gross[14] have developed programs of specific procedures and exercises that are used to train teachers, counselors, and mental health professionals in helping adolescents with these problems.

Conducting groups in school settings has both advantages and constraints. The youth are in the school daily and are more or less a captive group. The school can pressure adolescents to attend and can also lend its authority to the enforcement of certain standards of behavior. The group's reputation in the school is important of course. If it is looked on as highly prestigious, students will join voluntarily. If it is stigmatized as being only for bad, damaged, or stupid youth, students will avoid it. Conducting groups in schools, however, may exclude some of the most troubled youth who may have opted out of the educational system, and for some the school may not be a happy place and not a conducive atmosphere for a group. Furthermore, the school and its staff generally view formal education as their primary task and schedules may conflict. Teachers may prevent students from attending; priority in space and time may be given to other activities; and privacy and confidentiality may not be respected. The youth themselves, in their preformed cliques, may reinforce negative rather than positive values and behaviors.

Personal development and human relations. Both the formal content of the school curriculum and the opportunities for interpersonal relationships within the school as a whole and the classroom in particular should be utilized as counseling material. The homeroom can be a center for discussions on personal development and social adjustment: how boys and girls get along together; how problems are solved; and what is appropriate behavior in dealing with authority. Classroom and school councils are excellent vehicles for enabling youth to take self-responsibility and to put the democratic process into practice. Boy-girl relations stem most appropriately from daily living and from family life education, and the sexual aspects should be dealt with in the context of developing meaningful and tender relationships. Both boys and girls should not only study what goes into marriage and parenthood, but also learn the skills necessary for maintaining a home and rearing a family. Opportunities should be provided for observation and practice in child care, possibly in work-study programs. Literature and movies have been used to supplement formal teaching. Discussions of adult life and marital models can be developed from novels that portray life in various cultures and in different parts of society. Counseling groups, sometimes called personal development groups, can be useful in helping young people learn social skills, work out their identity, and learn how to cope with their feelings.

Sex education has become an important issue in the schools, particularly with the increase in teenage pregnancy and the danger of sexually transmitted diseases such as AIDS. Sometimes these programs are housed in the regular school curriculum. Sometimes they are conducted as part of the counseling department or the school health clinic. Sex is only one part of developing intimate mutually respectful and responsible human relationships and should be dealt with as a normal aspect of such relationships. The problems that are created in the American multicultural scene because of confused and ambiguous attitudes toward sex must be recognized and somehow worked out. Education must be tailored to the level of development and sophistication of the youth. Youth who are already sexually active may not be interested in abstinence but do need to understand and use "safe sex" practices.

Cultural diversity in the schools. The influx of refugees from many countries and cultures who speak many different languages has increased the normal stress of teaching youth from different cultural backgrounds. In one school district in Texas, students reportedly spoke 198 different languages and dialects. Buddy systems, teaching English as a second language, and the establishment of cross-cultural training groups have been some of the solutions. By the end of the century, it is expected that the majority of children in the school systems across the country will be drawn from non-Eurocaucasian minority groups. In the face of this minority competition, the black population has intensified its demands for curriculum relevant to the Afro-American culture and for resources adequate to enhance the performance of black youth.[15]

Drugs in the school. Although marijuana, alcohol, and smoking have been continuous problems over the last twenty years, in the mid- to late eighties two different epidemics have hit some school

177

systems. One has been the use of anabolic steroids by students involved in competitive sports and bodybuilding (with a reported national average use of 7 percent, and an average use as high as 20 percent in some schools).[16] Although the authors know of no formal group approaches used to prevent or treat this problem, coaches and team leaders are obviously critical influences and the athletic meetings can be the arena for discouraging this practice. Education about the dangerous effects of anabolic steroids and human growth hormone, however, should be included in the regular drug education programs mandated by the federal government to be held in schools The other epidemic has been the use of crack and cocaine with its attendant violence and social disruption, which has particularly affected inner-city neighborhoods and schools.[17]

Some schools and neighborhoods have mobilized themselves in an effort to be drug-free. School principals must stand firmly behind the ban on drugs in the school, and a prestigious staff member with peer leader support should be in charge of the initiative. Drug education, training in resistance techniques, and the provision of alternative satisfactions have all seemed necessary tools in the fight against drugs. Training in the identification and referral of youth who have become users is necessary for staff, students, and families. Rap rooms overseen by volunteer teachers or specially trained peer leaders have enabled troubled youth to seek help informally. Some schools also hold Ala-Teen or Narco-Teen meetings in the school for youth from substance-abusing families or youth who are themselves abusing drugs and alcohol.

Groups for learning problems. Basic remedial assistance should be furnished to all youth exhibiting learning difficulties. Although many learning problems can be identified in the first few grades of school, many children do not receive the assistance they need until they have already fallen several grades behind and have become discouraged and bored with school. Some difficulties in learning do not appear until adolescence and may be related either to emotional problems or to difficulties with abstract thinking.[18]

Some problems in reading and counting are the result of defective early psychomotor experiences and can be compensated for in adolescence by age-appropriate exercises. For example, a group of girls in middle school who were unable to read were also unable to identify shapes and the different sides of their body. Dancing the "Alley Cat" helped them recognize their right hands and feet from their left. Games that involved matching shapes and colors helped them identify letters of the alphabet. These interventions with the girls had to be supplemented with teacher training.

Emotional conflicts or early experiences can cause children to give up trying to learn. One boy who was surpassed by his younger brother gave up trying in the second grade. In puberty, he was placed in an activity group, gained confidence there, and was able, with coaching, to catch up with his peers. Some young adolescents are extremely self-conscious and cannot face making presentations in class. As a result, they find themselves extremely handicapped in school. An improvisational drama group, conducted by a knowledgeable and supportive therapist, can be effective in helping these youth overcome this difficulty.

At all ages, boys and girls can learn by counseling others.[19] The status and prestige gained from taking this kind of responsibility reinforces the adolescent's need to master the subject matter. Youth can meet together in a training group to learn how to tutor. Discussions include not only the curriculum content but also the understanding of human behavior and how people learn.

Learning problems can also be related to family conflicts. Youth may be rebellious, reluctant to fulfill their parents ambitions, afraid of surpassing their parents, or have the need to remain the baby in the family. In a family group program worked out by Kimbro and others,[20] and duplicated in the schools by Durell,[21] the therapist encouraged families to describe their difficulties, to explore how the members felt about the problems and how they dealt with one another, and to resolve their conflicts and try out new ways of solving problems.

In-school counseling versus referral. To a great extent discerning teachers, in consultation with a counselor or mental health specialist, should be able to deal with many behavioral and emotional problems. A quiet word in the corner of a playground or classroom may be more useful than many visits to a clinic. Homeroom discussions geared to the difficulties and confusions teenagers experience in growing up may go a long way to settle many difficulties that might otherwise become vast and insoluble problems. Counselors should be available for on-the-spot management of crises, as well as in rap rooms where youth can seek assistance without being conspicuous.

Counseling within the school makes it easier to coordinate the various kinds of help and planning that the teenager may need. If adolescents are already opposed to school and are perhaps refusing to attend, however, they may find it easier to respond positively in a setting divorced from their problem. There is also the important question of stigma. Problems should be dealt with as much as possible through normal channels without labeling the youth. Special classes and special treatments single out individuals as being different and may affect their self-esteem. If the teenagers are not able to keep up with their peers or are disrupting the group, however, it may be necessary to create a special situation in or outside the school.

Vocational counseling. The purposes of vocational counseling are (1) to enable pupils to become knowledgeable about career choices—what they involve, how choices are made, what qualifications are required, and what opportunities are available; and (2) to help students be aware of their own interests and aptitudes, make their own decisions in an informed manner, and develop realistic attitudes toward work.

Vocational counseling should start in elementary school with a steady buildup of knowledge about various careers and how one chooses a career. Career education and counseling then continues with more specificity in secondary school.

The following is a description of how a vocational guidance and counseling program might be organized within a secondary school. Large groups can be organized to familiarize students with different jobs and careers through lectures from individuals working in those fields and through films. Working conditions, career requirements, and potentials for advancement should be described. Factual literature on various careers should be available.

Small groups can be organized in which students themselves explore their attitudes toward work and their particular talents; plan trips to increase their knowledge; hold discussions with community leaders and potential employers; learn to assess the conditions and career potentials of jobs and the conditions of the labor market; learn how to obtain information; practice applying for jobs; and learn how to present themselves for a job interview. Role-playing is a useful tool for this purpose.

Many matters must be considered when planning a career. The teenagers must examine their particular personalities and interests, as well as their capabilities. How ambitious are they? How hard do they want to work? Do they want to work inside or outside, with machines, with paper, or with people? How committed to work are they? How important is a successful career? Do they like responsibility, leadership, or to be creative, or are they more comfortable following others and letting others make the decisions? Do they have some outstanding interest or talent that makes their decision easier, or are they all-round people who might do many things well? Are they willing to travel, or work irregular hours? Do they like taking risks, or do they prefer a regular routine? What kind of pace do they like? Do they respond well under pressure? What are their expectations of themselves, their self-concepts and their values? Do they want their work to have social meaning or prominence, or are they mainly interested in earning money or having security? How do they feel about immediate as opposed to deferred gratification? Are they ready to make decisions that may affect them all their lives? Many youth will change in their orientation as they grow older. Changes in technology may require career changes. Nevertheless, it is valuable for adolescents to begin to think about these different dimensions.

Vocational counseling with the average teenager implies clarification of desires, needs, and feelings, rather than basic changes in attitude. With youngsters who have been unsuccessful, however, who have given up hope for the future, who lack basic tools for adult living, who are delinquent, rebellious, and defiant or passive and depressed, infantile, dependent, or irresponsible, the group itself can become an important reinforcing tool to help these adolescents manage their lives more adequately. The group can help them learn to feel better about themselves, clarify the skills they will need and how to obtain them, and give them support as they begin to catch up with their peers. Remedial and special learning and job opportunities must be available for these youth so they can experience success and see clearly how they can advance.

Apart from including the failing students, vocational counseling groups should initially be unselected. Later, if students become more knowledgeable about what they want, interest groups can be developed. The emphasis of each program should relate to the particular school population and the opportunities offered in the community, as well as nationally. Counseling meetings could run the length of two class periods and be scheduled throughout middle school, enabling students to become knowledgeable about a wide variety of careers and learn whether they are available in their community or whether they would have to leave the area to pursue them.

Work experiences closely linked to education and training can also help students learn more about what particular jobs entail, make more realistic choices, and develop good work habits. Counseling and classroom groups should relate to these work experiences so that principles about working can be identified,

182

problems arising out of the job ironed out, and practice linked to theory, which is taught more formally. In such groups, leaders are both counselors and teachers. They are responsible for maintaining a connection with the work supervisors; bringing up difficulties in their groups; helping members deal with issues; and helping members identify work requirements and learn what is permissible, what will get them into trouble, and why. At the same time leaders set standards and expectations and implicitly transmit a value system to the youth. They act as resources for the group, show them how to obtain background information, and how to discuss the theoretical principles related to their experiences. Some high schools schedule the basic school curriculum and the work experiences on different days so that youth can, in fact, hold part-time jobs. Curriculum and work experiences are often related so that what is learned academically can be seen to have practical relevance. This is particularly true of mathematics, health, the physical, social, and psychological sciences, transcultural learning, economics, and accounting.

If students plan to continue their education, counseling should help them examine and consider different colleges, what these offer and require, and whether financial support is possible. If parents are unsophisticated, students will need help in applying to colleges and in meeting application deadlines.

Whatever the youth wish to do, individual counseling must be offered to help students make specific plans. Counselors should also work with groups of parents so they, too, can be knowledgeable about the vocational choices available to their children. Counselors must also keep in touch with local employers, general employment trends, and higher educational administrators so they can better help the students.

Vocational and employment counseling must extend beyond school into the individual's entry job and continuing employment whether it is the school or an outside agency, such as the United States Employment Services: Youth Division, that becomes the approved organization. Many youth flounder after they leave school because they do not really understand how to manage a job or do not know where to obtain continuing education or advanced work experience when they are ready. Links between education and employment need to be clarified, gaps bridged, and the information about them readily available to youth. Some educators and employers, in fact, encourage individuals to continue their education and training as part of their work week and pay them to do so, so that education, instead of being confined to a few short years, can continue throughout one's life. This is particularly important in the modern world where technological change leads to career obsolescence.

Recreational Settings

Beyond the family and school, recreation is certainly the most important institution in Western society for personality development, socialization, and education of children and youth. Every play activity has potential to improve self-esteem, cultivate sound interpersonal relationships, develop social and activity skills and self-control, and to broaden general knowledge of the world.

The purpose of the recreational program may vary. Primary concern and emphasis may be placed on affecting the climate or values of the target community or group, on helping individuals develop themselves and their relationships, or on carrying out the recreational program itself. A drawback of many sports and recreational programs has been their extreme competitiveness. The enjoyment of the activity is lost in the stress generated by the need to win. A second drawback is the exclusivity of selection, that is, only the best can play. We believe that all youngsters should be able to participate and be encouraged to do the best they can at their own level.

Church and settlement house programs, as opposed to scouting and special interest groups, have often attempted to influence the neighborhood, as well as the individual, by bringing a large proportion of local youth into the program. One church, concerned about the rise in teenage pregnancy in its neighborhood, developed a provocative pregnancy-prevention seminar group, in which all aspects of having a baby were explored. This appeared to be successful as evidenced by a dramatic drop in the incidence of teenage pregnancy in the community, which remained low for a couple of years. It seemed that the peer leaders and group values were affected. When the leaders left the group and were replaced by others who had not been exposed to the program, however, the rate began to rise again.

Programs also vary in the degree to which the group's conduct is structured and activities preplanned, whether members participate in planning as well as carrying out the program, and the amount of conformity to the group's rules and standards that is demanded of members . Many poor youth, as well as many who are delinquent, defiant, addicted, individualistic, or disturbed, have found themselves excluded on this last point. For example, the scouting movement, which is highly structured and emphasizes character development and performance, demands obedience to rules, regular attendance, and has in the past insisted on parental participation. Some settlement houses and social group work programs that have been organized as clubs with formal dues, structured committees, set programs, and rigid behavioral and attendance requirements have foundered on the conflict between the "good guys" and the "bad."

For those who have opted out of the regular institutions, various programs have been developed over the years. In the fifties it was detached workers and roving leaders[22] who moved out to the local gangs to offer them whatever assistance or program they would accept. They attempted to influence the youth directly or to affect the youth by changing the antisocial nature of the group culture.[23] In the seventies drop-in centers and coffee houses became popular, and in recent years there have been Outreach programs to the "shooting galleries" and "crack houses." "The Door" in New York City and "Aunt Martha's Place" in Chicago have been models for a multipurpose service center under one roof.[24] Youth can obtain any service they need. They may just wish to drop in for recreation, or they may want counseling or legal advice, a health examination, or assistance in obtaining employment. Some youth counseling services, in addition to providing information, referral, and crisis management, also run programs on the lines of "Outward Bound"[25] in which the youth go on wilderness trips that challenge their skill and ingenuity and build their self-confidence. They learn to trust one another and to work as a team. Some neighborhood centers form intimate recreation groups, led by paid and trained neighborhood adults or youth leaders under professional supervision. These leaders work with the individual members to provide opportunities for the acquisition of a range of new skills. As the youth change their behavior, they influence others and affect the climate of the neighborhood as a whole. In learning how to plan their social activities, they also learn how to get rid of "gate-crashers," maintain sobriety at parties, and relate to members of the opposite sex.

In these groups, members choose and plan their own activities with stimulation from the leader. They are expected to help one another and to work out difficulties that may arise. Although an active and varied program is desirable in itself, activity also promotes interest in others and a habit of taking care of materials. Active games not only improve muscular coordination and self-discipline but necessitate the ability to cooperate and compete with others, to risk success or failure, to work out conflict within the confines of the game. Sedentary games, such as Monopoly, Trivial Pursuit, or geographic card games, teach a segment of formal education, as well as providing practice in reasoning and interpersonal relations. Today there are also many games related to social skill development, such as the Ungame, and to special problems, such as adjusting to divorce in the family. Computer games, when available, teach youngsters to feel comfortable with machines, which is important in today's world. Trips enlarge youth's view of the world and enable them to see how others live, to practice the skills of travel, and to experience the joys of exploring and discovering the unknown. Many young people, particularly from poor or limited backgrounds, are afraid to move physically or intellectually into unfamiliar territory.

186

Youth should learn to savor adventure, and should be stimulated to enter new surroundings, go camping, or travel so that they utilize their weekends and summers imaginatively. . Campfires are wonderful places around which to review values and life goals. In any such program all members take part, and the more competent are expected to help the rest along. Competence, self-respect, mutual esteem, and individual and group responsibility are stressed, along with having fun, and although competence is anticipated in the long run, problems and errors are expected in the here-and-now. The rule is only that problems must be recognized and tackled. It is even more important that activities are not imposed by adults or by a few selected youth. It is preferable to allow the group to struggle with indecision for a week or two while they learn the art of solving problems and reaching a consensus, rather than imposing a program on the group for which members take no responsibility.

The leader clarifies the outer boundaries of behavior that society or the host institution will tolerate, but leaves members free to confront the realities and penalties of stepping beyond these boundaries. Leaders themselves maintain certain standards and values but do not impose them on members. Their views are open to scrutiny, analysis, and evaluation, however.

When program plans are made, the leader assists members in anticipating situations and practicing how to deal with them. If the group wants to give a party, they are encouraged to think through who should be invited, what should be served, what kind of dancing or games will be arranged, and how to prevent drug and alcohol use and other undesirable behavior. Such an occasion provides opportunities for members to test out relationships with the opposite sex in a protected social setting and stimulates discussion of appropriate heterosexual relationships. Dancing and games are also remedial exercises that enhance members' self-confidence and improve their motor coordination.

A variety of activities should be offered, each for its own special value. The arts, for example, offer the opportunity for emotional expression, the chance to perceive the world more intensely and uniquely. The arts require youth to master a variety of skills and media and to expand their knowledge of world cultures and of the life-styles and interests of different peoples.

When youth are trained as leaders in recreation programs, they not only learn a range of recreational skills but also become aware of human needs and development, individual and group functioning, and their own personal conflicts in self-management. In reviewing the issues that will confront the children or adolescents in their groups, these young leaders must work out their own standards and values. Although a few programs enlist youth as leaders throughout the year, the majority of such programs exist mainly during the summertime in residential or day camps, thus serving a dual purpose of furnishing activities enjoyable both to the youth and the children.

Preemployment and Work-Training Programs

In the sixties, as part of the effort to prevent and control juvenile delinquency and to wage war on poverty, a new kind of comprehensive programming was developed, which included integrated education, remediation, skills training, paid supervised work experience, counseling, help with transportation, health, and child day care, as needed. Recreation and group living were often included in a coordinated effort to prepare high-risk youth to lead a successful and independent adult life. Although these programs were directed toward the poverty-stricken, the delinquent, and the school dropout, their model of integrating employment, education, and job and human relations training, in which all components are included as part of the working day, is still an ideal, particularly for youth with multiple problems. Three programs were of particular significance: the Job Corps,[26] the Neighborhood Youth Corps,[27] and the New Careers Training Programs.[28]

Youth employment training programs have continued up to the present, with modifications. The Job Corps has been maintained. The Neighborhood Youth Corps which has two components, a summer jobs preemployment training program and an on-the-job training program, has experienced a number of changes but both components are still financed under the Job Training Partnership Act (1983), which has been amended several times.[29] Some aspects of the New Careers Training Programs, such as entry-level requirements for jobs for technicians and continuing educational links for career advancement opportunities, have been maintained in the Human Services. The Job Corps was established as a residential work-training program with two components. One is a prevocational program for youth who are functioning at a low level academically and who require intensive remediation. This program is run by the Department of the Interior in relatively small (fifty to two hundred youth) conservation camps in rural areas and concentrates on training youth for craft and trade jobs. Training is closely integrated with Trade Union requirements and the youth are well prepared for existing jobs. The second type of Job Corps Center is contracted out to private industry. Many of the centers are much larger than the camps and provide skills training, remedial education, and group-life counseling. These programs have been particularly useful for youth who had to leave their old environments and their former associates in order to make a new start.

The New Careers Training Programs, initially developed at Howard University, concentrate on creating new technical-level jobs for aides and assistants (paraprofessionals) in Human Services.[30] The programs provide individual and group counseling, remedial education, skill training, and supervised on-the job training and experience. In these programs it was necessary to work with employers to accept the training as a qualification for obtaining the job and to establish new entry criteria, as well as to work with the employment and educational institutions, so as to provide for continuing education and training. By so doing, the youth could advance in their careers and eventually become professionals or administrators. It was also necessary to develop new social and recreational ties for the youth so they did not fall back into their old disfunctional social lives. The Core Group,[31] the central medium for counseling, was designed as a reference group to assist aides in developing a common identity as human service technicians and to work out difficulties they experienced on the job. The group pressed the youth to examine these problems and their own behavior in the group. The group also included a basic curriculum in human relations and community organization essential to their work. The program set standards and expectations and made demands on the youth, while providing opportunities to meet those demands. The youth who had previously experienced only failure began to feel differently about themselves as they became more successful. The group leader, often also a technician, established the ground rules of the program, delimited the areas of decision making that were permitted to the members, and taught them how to take responsibility for themselves and assist one another. The leader also maintained close contact with work supervisors so that any job problems could be fed back into the Core Group before they became catastrophic.

The best of the community training programs have incorporated many of the same principles that were developed in the New Careers Training Program. They work closely with employers so that jobs and careers are available once the program is completed. The trainees are taught and counseled in small groups so that an esprit de corps can develop and the counselor can maintain close relationships with the job supervisors. Some early successful programs were those undertaken in park services where the youth were trained in all aspects of landscaping, gardening, and grounds maintenance. Some of these teams later developed landscaping and gardening companies and became successfully self-employed. Another useful program, conducted by the Smithsonian Institute, trained youth as museum exhibition organizers, of which there was a shortage at the time. Three successful programs were run in federal prisons, which led to well-paying jobs in areas in short supply. These were for deep sea divers, dental prosthesis makers, and optical lense grinders. All these programs embodied the principles of realistic training, an identified need, and opportunities for well-paid employment and career advancement. Many of the programs that resulted from the Job Training Partnership Act have had strong prevocational training that included awareness of the world of work, labor market knowledge, occupational information, career planning and decision making, and job search techniques. Trainees have worked together to role-play their performance in job interviews and have practiced making telephone applications for jobs, which their fellow program members have critiqued. Work maturity skills for holding a job and advancing in the enterprise have included learning positive work habits, attitudes, and behaviors, such as punctuality, regular attendance, neat appearance, good work relationships, a capacity to follow instructions, and an ability to show initiative and reliability. Through this kind of skills training, many youth begin to view themselves differently and to identify with a successful self-image. Many programs have also included remedial education and job-specific skills. Youth support one another in these programs, as well as encourage and critique one another.

Summer youth job programs have always been of variable quality. Some have been useful experiences and have included job counseling, remediation, and a continuous experience from summer to summer so that by the time the youth completed high school, they already had experience and training in a particular field. It was not until 1986, however, that remedial education became a mandatory part of the program. Some summer jobs, however, are still no more than busywork and are boring and poor experiences for the youth.[32]

A final government program that included teenagers was the Work Incentive Program for AFDC mothers.[33] (This program requires mothers to place their children in day care and attend remedial education and training in order to obtain gainful work and get themselves off the welfare roles.) In some locations, these mothers have come together in groups to help one another improve their human relations skills, learn about parenting and health care, and combat discouragement and dropping out. In this program, as in the others, education against drug abuse and resistance training have often been included. The need for education in safe sex practices and AIDS prevention has also become critical, both for high school youth and those who are out of school.

College and Precollege Counseling

The transition from school to college and the stress of the first years of separation from the family often reveal problems in the immature student, both in regard to social adjustment and to studying. Students have difficulty making friends, dating, dealing with their roommates, organizing their time, and finding their way around the campus. They sometimes feel lost and lonely or encounter a conflict in standards and values. Foreign students, particularly those from the Third World, often need group counseling to help them understand the ways of an alien culture. Group counseling has been conducted on college campuses on several different levels: groups oriented to the college program[34]; groups focused on socializing and study problems; groups concerned with identity problems and difficulties in self-management; and groups focused on the issues facing young adults, such as family life education, family planning, and substance abuse resistance, as well as therapy groups for those who seek help with more serious problems.

The discrepancy between the standards of various high schools creates trouble for students entering college from inferior school systems. They have been accustomed to being A students and suddenly find themselves failures, which creates a crisis in their self-esteem. To prevent this problem, precollege remediation and counseling have been provided, as well as programs such as Upward Bound,[35] in which high school students who have ability but have been underachieving can attend comprehensive summer programs held on university campuses. The youth are offered a stimulating educational program, remediation, assistance with study habits, work experience, and the opportunity to get to know college students who act as their counselors.

A positive group climate, one that promotes taking advantage of opportunities and insists on mutual respect and concern for each individual, is crucial for success. Elements of excitement, enjoyment, exploration, and a willingness to engage in intellectual conflict and problem resolution and to risk exposure and temporary setbacks are also important ingredients in the group counseling experience.

Therapy and Rehabilitation

When problems are too severe to be managed within the normal settings, several choices of action are available: providing treatment within the school, work place, or recreational setting in special problem-related or behavioral-related groups; referral to an outside clinic, hospital, or special school or residential program; or bringing in a law enforcement agency. Rehabilitation is concerned with the rebuilding of skills and confidence and the remaking of lives after breakdown or in situations of chronic disability. Psychotherapy is concerned with the achievement of change in psychic structure and functioning so that individuals feel more satisfied with themselves, effect more harmonious relationships with their environments, and mobilize themselves to their best advantage to cope with life's demands. All such change is achieved by individuals gaining a revised perspective on themselves and their world, through increased understanding of the self and the environment, and through new experiences. Therapeutic and rehabilitative interventions, as we have already discussed, are undertaken at different levels. Guidance and problem solving can be seen as primarily intellectual interventions; cognitive restructuring focuses on the ways in which individuals perceive and define their problems and their environment, which in turn affects their emotional state and their capacity to cope with situations; psychoanalytically oriented and dynamic therapies are concerned with exploring the underlying conscious and unconscious personality structure, coping mechanisms, and unconscious motivations that drive the individuals; positive reinforcement approaches, abreactive techniques, and activity group therapy include both emotional and experiential elements. Self Help groups provide social and emotional support. Treatments for serious mental illness and addiction may include pharmacological, psychological, psychosocial, and spiritual elements.

All permanent intrapsychic change is made in and by individuals and cannot be achieved against their will. No change will occur unless the forces within patients and clients are, on balance, in favor of making a change. At some level, youth must want to mobilize themselves in a positive direction. When individuals seek or are referred for psychotherapy or rehabilitation, they must recognize that something is not satisfactory about themselves and their functioning, that they are in some way deviant, and that they are not equipped to make the necessary changes on their own. They must seek help from experts and place themselves in a dependent position. At a minimal level, they must accept the authority of the therapist or the therapeutic agent. They must agree to expose themselves and surrender some control over their own lives.

Because adolescence, as a transitional period, is one of maximum insecurity, this posture can be particularly difficult for teenagers. They are changing physically and emotionally. They are struggling to control new drives within themselves that sometimes threaten to overwhelm them and make them fear for their sanity. They are endeavoring to define their changing position in the world, to review old controls and values, and to obtain status as adults on an equal basis with other adults. The acceptance of one's position as a patient can be viewed as going against the life force of the adolescent and is often strongly resisted. This resistance is a major therapeutic problem in treatment and must be either bypassed or overcome. As we have already discussed, some approaches used in normal settings are designed to bypass the resistance and capitalize on the youth's motivations. In this section, however, we are concerned with approaches that meet the resistance head on and strive to use that resistance as a therapeutic tool. It has become clear that often when individuals are given a particular reputation, stereotyped into certain roles, and thus stigmatized by the community, both the organizational structures in the community and the individuals' feelings about themselves conspire to make them live out the role ascribed to them. For example, when individuals are labeled mentally ill or delinquent, people around them relate differently to them. They expect them to be odd, dangerous, or irresponsible; they set them apart and bar them from many opportunities. Teenagers in such situations may become so angry and despairing that they accept the designated role, cease to struggle against the pressures, and behave defiantly in the ways expected of them.

The reluctance that adolescents experience in facing their difficulties and their need for help has been tackled in a number of ways. Authority has been used to force adolescents to attend a group and expose themselves to treatment. The therapist then has the task to help such group members recognize and accept the need to change and to turn the contact into a voluntary one. MacLennan believes that the first interview is critical in assessing and responding to a teenager's attitudes to treatment and that the group therapist should be the one interviewing because transferring from one person to another only makes the task more difficult. Some workers, such as Westman,[36] have found that this initial opposition to treatment can be used as a cohesive force to draw the youth together in the group, where the antiauthoritarianism can be dealt with directly rather than acted out elsewhere. Many authorities have preferred, even in institutional settings, to allow the youth to decide themselves whether or not they will come and have attempted to develop contracts for at least a few sessions of attendance. Attempts have also been made to reduce the opposition to attendance by providing some pleasurable activities, allowing youth to miss disliked alternative functions in order to come to the group, or rewarding them with points or money. In some institutions, cooperation in the therapy group affects the conditions of daily life. The therapists may have the authority to recommend release from the institution or reduced probation if the members perform well in the group, or they may include the group performance in their evaluation of how successful the youth are at work or in training. Generally, the use of authority as part of therapy has been most helpful with teenagers who use denial and who act out their problems behaviorally.

Mental Health Clinics

Mental health clinics include child guidance and community psychiatric clinics, programs for children and adolescents in community mental health center outpatient clinics, family and youth counseling agencies, hospital outpatient clinics, and rehabilitation centers. Most of the youth come in semivoluntarily. They are brought by their families or referred by recreational or school authorities. A few seek help by themselves, and some are ordered to attend by the court as a condition of their freedom. Many health care workers have found that the normal clinic delays and extensive evaluation of classic psychotherapy are too difficult for adolescents to tolerate. Instead, they make an immediate contact with the adolescent at the time of crisis, when a relationship can be established and some tentative hypotheses about diagnoses and treatment needs set up. These are then tested and refined as treatment proceeds. When the problem is an interactive one within the family, it is useful to see the entire family and to refocus the situation as a family problem rather than one only affecting the adolescent. When the focus of therapy will be on the adolescent, it is useful for the intake-worker to be the group therapist so that a transfer will not be necessary.

These clinics deal with youth in crisis: when expulsion from school is threatened, when a girl is about to have a baby, or when youngsters are so unhappy that they threaten suicide. These clinics also try to help youth cope with chronic behavioral problems, psychoneurotic conflicts and symptoms, and what may be the adolescents' tenuous hold on reality. Many youth today are also involved with alcohol and drugs and require specialized treatment for these abuses; many are living in severely disfunctional families. A significant number have been placed in foster homes. Some hospital outpatient programs focus on helping youth deal with chronic diseases and disabilities, such as diabetes, rheumatic heart disease, epilepsy, or physical rehabilitation after accidents. These groups combine education about the illness with efforts to help the youth accept a life-style that will maintain optimal functioning.

Several prominent professionals who have conducted psychotherapy groups for adolescents and their families for many years all agree that the teenagers referred for outpatient treatment today are angrier and more disturbed than similar patients in the past, and are consequently more difficult to treat.[37] This agrees with the statistical analyses of teenage problems that we have already described.

Treatment groups vary from short-term, problem-related counseling to long-term groups that aim at deep-seated character reconstruction. Most therapists focus on everyday realities and experiences within the group. Others, such as Rachman and his followers emphasize identity development and reconstruction,[38] and others, such as Azima, work within a psychoanalytic framework.[39] Cognitive restructuring and interpersonal psychodynamic therapy groups have both been found useful with depressive patients.[40] Groups for potentially suicidal youth have sometimes been conducted with emergency sessions so members can provide mutual support.[41] Groups for youth suffering from chronic schizophrenia need to focus on the management and understanding of the disease; such treatment groups must be closely integrated with case management and rehabilitation programs.[42] As we have described elsewhere, groups for victims focus on helping them overcome their intense emotional reactions, their feelings of loss and betrayal, their anger, and the degradation of their feelings of self-worth.

A wide range of preventive groups, such as life-style educational groups and groups for crisis management and chronic stress management, may also be conducted in outpatient treatment settings. Staff from these organizations set up educational and crisis management groups in schools and work sites, as previously described, and also consult with and conduct group training of the educational and counseling staff from these settings.

Major organizational issues have already been discussed in chapter 4. It is important to have adequate space in which to run groups, particularly those that include activities for the younger adolescents. Recruitment channels are essential so that a sufficient pool of youth is available to provide for well-balanced groups. Time must be set aside for consultation and training for younger workers. The joint responsibilities of the clinics and the therapists must be clearly understood.

In sum, a wide variety of groups are run in outpatient clinics. These may deal with specific problems, help youth cope with the realities and trials of everyday living, or enable them to function with chronic disabilities and handicaps or to explore and resolve conflicts that lie beneath the surface but that affect their behavior nonetheless. Whenever adolescents have a range of problems in their relationships and in their environment, group therapy or rehabilitation must be closely coordinated with any other services involved. The program must be well organized and the lines of authority clearly established.

Substance Abuse Treatment and Rehabilitation

In earlier sections we have described a variety of programs directed toward substance abuse prevention conducted in schools, neighborhoods, churches, settlement houses, and at the work site. The groups we described included education about drugs; resistance training; improvement in psychosocial coping skills and problem solving; assertiveness training; and the development of alternative life-styles. In this section we describe the use of groups in substance abuse treatment, rehabilitation, and relapse prevention.[43] Substances under discussion include alcohol, tobacco, and licit and illicit drugs used for nonmedical purposes.

198

Groups have always been considered a major therapeutic modality in the treatment of substance abuse and addiction, in part at least because the social group's mores appear to play a considerable role in the use and abuse of alcohol, drugs, and tobacco. Groups are also important because substance abusers are frequently expert manipulators of others and use denial as a major defense. Groups of peers understand these games and members can help one another delve into them to get in touch with their real feelings and problems.

Patterns of drug use vary greatly. Different drugs wax and wane in popularity. Many teenagers try a drug a few times, decide they do not like it, and leave it alone; others use drugs infrequently on social occasions. Some individuals use low doses of drugs or alcohol regularly to relax or become stimulated but never use them to excess. There are others, however, who are susceptible to addiction and find it impossible to control their use unless they totally abstain. Some go on binges; still others use some type of drug, alcohol, or tobacco to control their nervous tension or to overcome their depression, grief, or anxiety. Some individuals, when they stop using alcohol, drugs, or tobacco, become completely normal. Others, however, still have psychological or psychosocial problems that require treatment. Such issues as the legality of smoking or of buying or drinking alcohol and, if it is legal, when and where it can be done, and whether it is a criminal offense to possess or ingest a particular drug, all affect treatment. Youth often come to group treatment under duress and the therapist may often have the authority to affect the members' lives directly. Testing for use may be an integral part of treatment.

Until the eighties most drug treatment was directed toward heroin addiction in males. The two major forms of treatment have been drug-free therapeutic communities or the substitution of methadone for heroin use as a more stable drug on which addicts could still function reasonably well in their lives.[44]

Therapeutic communities were originally developed for long-term, possibly lifelong residency. Currently, treatment lasts for about nine months to two years.[45] The residential community is the vehicle of treatment. Its rules are strict and members are required to confront and support one another. A range of groups are conducted in the residence: therapy groups, community groups, drug education groups, counseling groups, and AA groups. The therapy groups focus on the typical games of denial, blaming others, and claiming unrealistic successes. Role-playing is generally used, and points systems may be incorporated for working in the group and for changed behavior in the residence. All activities are concerned with building self-esteem, which is generally low among abusers. Because women are still in the minority, there are usually specially designed groups for women only. A few communities also allow women to bring their children. These communities are very successful for those who remain in them for the entire treatment. There is usually a large drop-out rate during the first three months, however, and particularly during the early days. Because these are drug-free programs, they accept all addictions and many residents today are polydrug users or cocaine abusers. Brook and Whitehead described a therapeutic community for adolescents in 1973.[46] Aso describes a strict and confrontational program,[47] and Haggerty and others developed Project Adapt, a program designed to help delinquent polydrug abusers return to the community.[48] The program includes skill acquisition, group training, case management, and a peer helper program. High-quality methadone maintenance programs also have counseling groups and AA groups attached to them.[49] These programs are specifically designed for narcotic abusers and, consequently, do not contain many adolescents who more frequently choose other drugs, such as marijuana, crack, speed, PCP, or alcohol.

Teenage drug abusers are frequently treated in outpatient programs.[50] Bratter provides an excellent description of his group methods in the treatment of adolescent drug abusers in outpatient and residential settings.[51]

Alcohol treatment programs were first largely designed for middle-aged men, but today they are usually for both men and women, although men are still in the majority. Treatment may include detoxification in a hospital or in the community, thirty-day residential treatment, or day or weekend treatment that includes educational, recreational, and therapy groups and an introduction to Twelve Step groups. Continuing outpatient treatment and support groups for follow-up care in the community are essential components. These programs also admit and treat cocaine, marijuana, and polydrug abusers. Adolescents with alcohol problems are also found in the juvenile justice system and treated there in groups.[52]

Although some adolescents who drink have already become dependent on alcohol, most of those with problems are still in the early stages and can be treated in outpatient settings. Shields[53] and Morehouse[54] have both treated youth in the schools. Some adolescents who are having problems with alcohol also have alcoholic or drug-abusing parents, and Bogdaniak and Piercy describe the therapeutic issues that arise with these youngsters in group therapy.[55] They have difficulty with trust and communication. Generally they suffer from low self-esteem. Often they blame themselves for their parents' difficulties. They tend to deny their own problems with drinking. The group provides them with support, encourages them to view their problems realistically, and helps them develop skills in coping with their difficulties at home and elsewhere.

Programs designed to help individuals quit smoking have often used group methods, including such techniques as behavior modification through rewards or aversion techniques, cognitive restructuring, and anxiety management through acupuncture, imaging, and relaxation. Most methods have limited success, and individuals may have to try several times before they succeed. Schwartz provides an excellent review of the literature.[56] Although many boys and girls start smoking at thirteen, fourteen, or fifteen years of age, there are not many programs designed to treat them. Flay evaluates the Waterloo School Study,[57] an intervention to help children quit smoking.

Because relapse is so common in addictions, specialized relapse prevention groups have been developed in the last few years, many of them following the theories of Marlatt, who believes there is an alteration in thinking sometime before a relapse takes place.[58] Individuals become overconfident. They believe they can return to the same places and consort with the same people who were associated with their addiction. Alternative lifestyles and satisfactions are important components in overcoming the craving to return to substance abuse. Members of relapse prevention groups help one another spot when changes in thinking and behavior are taking place and remind one another of the dangers of overconfidence.

Specialized programs for teenagers have always been in short supply and many teenagers have had to enter detoxification and treatment programs for adults. The recent association of AIDS with intravenous drug abuse and with the combination of promiscuous unsafe sex and crack or cocaine is an added complication. Some therapeutic communities in metropolitan areas have many residents who are HIV-positive, and some have become terminal treatment programs for abusers who have developed AIDS. In these settings, staff and residents must confront the issues of death, dying, and bereavement. There has also been a great shortage of treatment slots for drug-addicted pregnant girls and women, who need both drug treatment and prenatal and postnatal care for themselves and their children.

Inner-city youth who are substance abusers often need more than drug abuse treatment. They often need remedial education, vocational training, and supervised job placement. Once they have become stable and clean, they need hope for a different life, and programs such as those described above under the youth employment and training programs are essential for them.[59]

Acute Psychiatric In-Patient Programs for Teenagers

In recent years there has been an increase in the number of acute care psychiatric units for teenagers, either in general hospitals or in specialized, free-standing psychiatric hospitals and community mental health centers.[60] Emphasis in most of these programs has been on the development of a therapeutic milieu with large group meetings,[61] as well as with open-ended small therapy groups, art therapy, recreation, and school classes. Because most of these patients only stay a short time, generally from a few days to a few weeks, and the numbers of patients are not very large, the age range in the groups is usually quite wide and the groups are heterosexual. Both in the acute therapy groups and in treatment groups for seriously disturbed, long-term psychiatric adolescent patients, there are likely to be two or more therapists as leaders because of the need to be able to keep the group going even if one or more patients becomes very disturbed. Therapists in hospital groups may be any member of the multidisciplinary team. As in other institutional settings, it is important for therapists to have the support of the administration, the team, and the unit staff.

Focus in the short-term groups is on understanding the nature of the illness, recognizing what precipitated the episode, and considering how to make an adequate adjustment when returning to the community. Several writers are concerned with the functions and dynamics of these short-term groups. McGuire describes the phases in dynamically oriented crisis-oriented groups,[62] Zabusky and Kymissis focus on the group as a transitional object in helping teenagers deal with separation-individuation issues,[63] and Bernfield et al. describe the fluctuations between group and individual resistances and task work in the groups.[64]

Some programs also run multiple family groups to help everyone in the family cope with the illness and to understand how families contribute both to the health and dysfunction of their members.[65]

Long-Term Residential Programs for Adolescents with Chronic Mental Illness

Long-term care programs for adolescents with chronic mental illness include a progressive range of semiprotected settings:

vocational rehabilitation and protected work settings, therapeutic foster and group homes, and therapeutic residences. The range of groups resemble those in substance abuse programs but the tone of these groups and some of the content is different. Groups for seriously mentally ill and psychotic patients are much less confrontational than are those for drug abusers. Bardill, for example, found catharsis more helpful than insight in adolescent residential groups.[66] Schizophrenics use a different set of resistance mechanisms—withdrawal, fantasy, and projection—than those used by drug abusers—typically denial, defiance, and projection. Crabhill found, however, that adolescents tend to act out more than adult patients, possibly because there are more very disturbed teenagers with conduct disorders whose parents have found them to be unmanageable.[67] Outcomes may also be different. If substance abusers can remain off the drugs and are not brain-damaged, they can usually return to normal life, whereas a higher percentage of chronically mentally ill patients have reduced functional capacity and some may have to remain in semi-protected settings and sheltered work programs for life. There has been increased interest in the treatment of patients who have both psychiatric and drug abuse problems.[68] Programs are likely to include cross-training of mental health and substance abuse staff and concurrent drug and psychotherapy treatment. Therapeutic day treatment and special educational programs for teenagers may resemble one another, except that they may be run by mental health or school systems, respectively. It has been difficult to obtain college education and appropriate employment for young, bright, seriously mentally ill patients. One program developed by Boston University has designed a small group program for long-term mentally ill adolescents on their college campus.[69] Students learn how to function again in the real world, provide mutual support for one another, and eventually go on to a regular college program but with continued case management and peer support.

Groups in Shelters

In recent years, emergency shelters and group homes have been established for teenagers and families requiring shelter and protection. These have included homes for runaway boys and girls, shelters for homeless families, and shelters for victims of family violence. The teenagers and families do not usually stay long in these places. While they are there, though, plans need to be made for their future, and they need to be supported in dealing with their current emotional and psychosocial crisis. Some of these individuals and families are quite traumatized and require the type of short-term group treatment described in the sections on child abuse and disaster victims. Helping them deal with their anxiety with relaxation and imaging techniques and teaching them how to manage their anger can be useful to them after they leave the shelter. Runaways may need to resolve their feelings about the conditions from which they fled in order to make effective plans for their future. In some shelters the whole family will be seen together, but in others the mother or parents will work in separate groups from the teenagers. As in other settings where there is a constantly changing population, groups are likely to be open-ended with any one member staying only for a short time. In this type of group, issues may come up over and over again and each session needs to have its own focus. Integration of all the services that these youth and their families need is critical for successful outcomes.

Groups in Court and Correctional Programs

Since Aichorn's classic demonstration reported in *Wayward Youth*,[70] there has been a continuing interest in using groups to work with delinquent adolescents. Raubolt has recently reviewed this literature.[71] In recent years, there has been an increased tendency to work with specific categories of delinquent problems, such as sex offenses, violence, drug abuse, or status offenses such as running away, so that one finds fewer articles addressing "delinquents" per se. In this section we examine groups in the various settings where youth in trouble with the law are found.

Juvenile court and probation. The court is first of all a confrontation. Appearance in court makes it necessary for the youth to recognize that they are in trouble and have been breaking the law. The court must first determine whether the youth have performed the acts of which they are accused and then must study how best to help them keep out of trouble in the future. This is achieved through understanding the nature of the problem and deciding on appropriate disposition and treatment. There are three phases: determination that an offense has been committed, study of the youth and their problems, and action concerned with punishment and rehabilitation. The first of these is a legal question, the others are psychosocial as well as judicial. It has always been an open question whether all three functions should be performed by the court or whether it would be preferable to refer the youth, immediately following arraignment, to agencies that specialize in both voluntary and involuntary treatment, reinforced by the authority of the court. Much delinquency is caused by unfavorable social conditions and cannot be remedied without a comprehensive approach to both social and psychological problems. At each stage, groups can be used during social study for treatment in the community and as part of a residential program.

Judges have a range of alternatives at their disposal. They can dismiss the case, warn the youth, insist they report regularly as a reminder of their precarious status, have the probation staff or an outside agency counsel the youth, require community service and restitution, send them into residential treatment, or even treat them as adult criminals if the crime is very serious.

Groups in the social-study phase can be used to confront the youth with the immediacy of their problems, to explore why they got into difficulty, to recognize the need for change, and to examine the alternatives open to them. The youth help one another face reality.

Counseling groups have also been used to monitor the lives of youth on probation and parole, to help them work out their problems in making a more socially acceptable adjustment, and to help them keep out of trouble with the law. Examination of values, reconsideration of their views of themselves as delinquent and deviant, and thinking through alternate ways of dealing with authority, frustration, deprivation, and temptation are prominent activities in these groups. Nevertheless, even when youth become motivated to change their behavior, if conditions in their world remain the same they are likely to relapse. So frequently they are still faced with the same school failure, their friends still continue to be delinquent, and few supportive programs are available to help them obtain substitute satisfactions and a different self-image. Today a high percentage of delinquent youth, particularly in metropolitan areas, are also substance abusers and this problem must also be treated if any change can occur. As an alternative to sending youth out of the community, some correctional systems manage or contract for open residences that are organized as a therapeutic milieu from which the youth go to school or to work each day. The youth work together as a group to decide on the daily management of their lives and to help one another resolve the problems they experience both in and outside the home. Like the drug abuse programs, most of these groups are quite confrontational and may also use transactional analysis techniques or cognitive restructuring as major therapeutic approaches. The group becomes the central change agent through the pressure that is placed on the members to confront problems and to conform to new standards of behavior. The group leaders do not make all the rules or set all the standards, but they continue to confront the youth with reality and refuse to allow them to slide away from problems. These programs are in contrast to the more traditional training school group that is run by a therapist who has no close connection with the program in the institution.

Short-term detention. Short-term detention is used to hold youth who are perceived as being too dangerous to themselves or to the community to live at home pending a court appearance. Although most detention centers are run along authoritarian lines, there are some exceptions. Some make use of milieu and small-group principles, and in these centers groups can be used to manage the units, to develop programs, and to discuss how and why the youth have got themselves into trouble. Even though youth are only expected to stay a few days, the program can be organized to have considerable impact on them. All youth can learn how to plan together in organizing their units. Older youth may be employed and trained as counselors' aides to assist in the supervision of recreation, tutoring in the classroom, or in orienting newcomers. The residents' council becomes an exercise in democracy. Such a program conducted at the D.C. Detention Center in the sixties greatly improved the counselors' ability to know the youth and to maintain control of their units.[72] The unit group, instead of being a shapeless mob, became differentiated into members taking different roles and positions supportive of or against authority. Admittedly, there are problems in using crisis counseling for youth whose situations are sub judice, particularly if they are denying the offense and specific cases cannot be discussed. There are many problems and issues that the youth have in common, however, and these can be examined without prejudicing the judicial process.

Training schools. Modern residential therapeutic communities, whether they are correctional, psychiatric, or substance abuse institutions, have much in common, just as old-fashioned asylums and traditional training schools resemble each other. The latter emphasize control, security, an authoritarian system, and decision making from the top down, and they maintain a staff and inmates who are both held in dependent positions with little communication between them. These levels of noncommunication foster rebellion and conspiracy, as well as game playing between correctional officers and inmates. Many of these earlier asylums and training schools also sent youth back to the community without any transitional support.

The new residences tend to be small in size and emphasize the interrelatedness of all members of the institution and the importance and significance of each person's contribution to the total climate. In such settings, various kinds of groups are preeminent: work groups, recreational groups, living unit management groups, school classes, therapy groups, and groups that include inmates' families, all woven into a consistent therapeutic pattern. Promoting comprehensive programs and a gradual transition back into the community, building up links, connections, and supports, and holding individuals responsible for their actions are the keynotes of these programs. Haggerty describes a well-designed transitional program.[73] Unfortunately, there are all too few of these in the country today.

Private Practice Groups

Although the treatment of teenagers in counseling and therapy groups has been common practice for the last thirty years, for most of this time there were few reports of groups for adolescents in private practice. Sugar[74] and Richmond[75] discuss the problems in setting up private practice groups for adolescents. Recently, however, there has been a noticeable increase in the number of private practitioners who are announcing groups for this population. Six of the thirteen authors in the American Group Psychotherapy monograph on adolescent group psychotherapy show some private practice among their affiliations.[76] In one metropolitan area, a recent list of private practice groups for adolescents included prevention groups such as those for social skills training and personal growth; support groups for teenagers whose parents are divorcing or are chronically ill; groups for youth with learning disabilities or attention deficits; and psychotherapy groups for teenagers with heterogeneous or specific problems.[77] Eating disorder groups for anorexic or bulimic youth have found their way out of the hospital and are being offered in private practice and in outpatient clinics. Adolescents who are substance abusers, promiscuous, pregnant, or suffering from AIDS are also being treated in private practice groups.

Groups for adolescents in private practice present specific management issues that differ, at least in degree, from groups in other settings. Census issues, that is, the need to obtain and maintain a sufficient number of suitable patients, affect recruitment and grouping and decisions regarding the type of group and its duration. Boundary issues, such as the nature of authority, confidentiality, networking with other therapists, and relationships with referring agencies, all have a somewhat different cast when groups are conducted in private practice.

Recruitment, Selection, and Grouping

Whereas schools and hospitals and other residential settings have a "captive" pool of potential group members, and outpatient clinics may have waiting lists on which to draw, private practitioners, unless they see many teenagers in their practice, generally have to engage in special recruitment efforts in order to start a group. Consequently, they must establish referral arrangements with therapists who treat adolescents but do not conduct group therapy, build contacts with schools, physicians, and agencies serving youth, and possibly select a cotherapist who can also contribute potential members.

Decisions regarding whether the group should be homogeneous or heterogeneous, time-limited or long-term, open or closed may also be affected by the problem of obtaining a sufficient number of patients and maintaining them in the group. The issue of heterogeneous or homogeneous group membership involves considerations of gender, age, diagnosis, and cultural and socioeconomic backgrounds. Ideally, private practitioners will follow the same selection guidelines as do leaders in other settings, that is, unless the group's focus is on a discreet problem that makes gender and age inconsequential, they will be guided by developmental needs. Generally, this means a two- to three-year age span and gender-specific groups in early adolescence, with the likelihood of mixed-gender groups among older adolescents. To start with a sufficient number of group members, however, some therapists may broaden the age range or change their approach and conduct gender-mixed groups in early adolescence.

Criteria regarding the issue of problem-specific or heterogeneous groups have already been discussed in chapter 4. Most therapists in private practice, however, are likely to find it more satisfactory to form mixed groups of teenagers with a variety of problems, strengths, and weaknesses, unless there is a clear demand from the community and a satisfactory source of referral for problem-specific groups. For example, a school system may indicate a need for a group for learning-disabled high school students, a children's diabetic clinic may not have the resources to treat youngsters who have difficulty in maintaining the diabetic life-style, or there may be many substance abusing teenagers in the community whose families can afford private treatment. For these teenagers, the commonality of symptoms will provide a foundation for cohesion and curative exploration of defensive strategies. Even though teenagers may come to the therapist with a specific complaint, pregroup evaluation frequently uncovers a common core question such as "Who am I?" which can provide a central focus for a heterogeneous group.

Group Duration

In private practice, the consideration whether to run open or closed groups for teenagers is a critical issue. Because there is no captive pool of potential members, a substantial amount of time and effort must go into apprising the community, schools, youth clubs, churches, and mental health clinics of the existence of adolescent group treatment and generating sufficient referrals to allow for appropriate selection and a workable group size. For this reason, many private practitioners choose to run open-ended groups. These have no specific ending point and members terminate on completion of their treatment goals. When one member leaves the group, another is screened and added. This format reduces the amount of effort the therapist must expend to recruit and screen members at any particular time, and it prevents the group from becoming reduced in size. As we have discussed, however, adding new members tends to disturb the group process. New members reduce the sense of trust and intimacy already established and reinstate a period of "testing." Short-term groups, on the other hand, require considerable effort on the part of therapists to recruit and select members and to establish a working group. Consequently, they tend to be less cost-effective. Adolescents and their parents, however, often find the commitment to a specified period of time less intimidating. The time frame of September to June, with perhaps a break over the winter vacation, is a common practice among private practitioners who work with adolescents in groups. The groups then re-form at the end of the summer for the next September-to-June period. In such an arrangement, if the membership is relatively stable, no new members are added except at the winter and summer breaks. An adaptation that combines the benefits of both closed and open-ended groups is "sequential time-limited groups." In these groups, adolescents contract for a specified period of time— three, six, or nine months—with the option to "renew" their contracts at the end of each group life-cycle. This approach often makes it easier for adolescents to commit to becoming a group member and, once the attachment is formed, to continue with group therapy as long as necessary without feeling "trapped" in treatment. It also promotes the progressive reformulation of goals for both individuals and the group and the option to add new members at these decision points.

At the time of initial contracting, members will have been apprised of the process of adding new members periodically to keep the group membership at a specific census. This, however, does not substitute for reminding the group that another member will be joining the group as soon as an appropriate referral develops. Sufficient time should be allowed for the present members to process their feelings about the change this constitutes for the group.

Solo or Coleadership

The advantages and disadvantages of solo or coleadership have been discussed earlier. There are considerations, however, that are specific to private practice. On the one hand, it is clearly more expensive to run a group with two leaders. Both must be paid. When recruitment is a problem, however, two therapists in private practice frequently decide to pool their patients and run a group together. Each therapist contributes some patients, and some unaffiliated members may also be recruited. This creates a situation similar to the reconstituted family when divorced parents remarry. Old relationships must be reformulated and new roles and alliances developed. This can be particularly useful for teenagers who are facing a similar situation in their lives. Managing this population, however, requires openness among all parties involved so that members of the group are aware of the relationships between the leaders, the members, and the members' therapists. Coleaders must also take time between sessions to exchange their perceptions of what has occurred and to talk over issues that may have arisen between them.

In any setting, problems always arise when a therapist has to leave town or is sick. This may be particularly disruptive in private practice where there is no institutional back-up. When this occurs, coleadership can provide consistency and continuity. Any such absences carry implications for the members, however, and these also need to be explored and understood. The absence of a leader has the potential to create negative feelings that can interfere with group development unless handled effectively. In the case of coleadership, one leader continues to meet with the group during the other's absence, and members have the opportunity to share their immediate feelings about the absence. Solo or coleaders who are able to give their group members advance notice of impending absences are less likely to face negative repercussions when they return, and are modeling norms for effective communication within the group.

Conjoint Therapy

When adolescents are in a treatment group, additional individual or family therapy may also be needed regarding certain problems or to reinforce what is happening in the group. A decision must be made whether the group leader or another therapist will undertake this task. In institutional settings, it is usually no problem to assign responsibility to another staff member who forms part of the treatment team. In private practice, however, another independent therapist must be found and degrees of communication and cooperation worked out with that therapist, the family, and the teenager.

Problems of Attendance

Most adolescents in private practice groups are not mandated to attend by another authority, such as the court or probation authorities, nor are they a "captive" membership as when groups are conducted in schools or residential settings. Consequently, private practice groups depend on the members or their families to assure that the teenagers attend the sessions regularly. It is therefore necessary for group leaders to conduct a substantial amount of pregroup education with members, parents, and significant others. All group members should be responsible for contacting their therapists whenever they are not able to attend a group session.

Even with careful pregroup education, adolescents may feel apprehensive about beginning treatment. To overcome this anxiety, some therapists use a "practice" session that prospective group members may attend before the official starting date of the group. The guidelines for this rehearsal clearly state that this is a time to see who will be in the group, to ask questions about the process, to see the leaders work together, and simply to experience being in a group setting. There is no expectation that members will disclose more than their names and whatever superficial information they feel comfortable talking about. This approach may have a positive effect in reducing "no shows" and early dropouts.

Transportation can be a major problem, particularly for younger adolescents living in suburban or rural areas because they cannot drive. Teenagers, if self-referred, or their families must make arrangements to ensure that transportation is available. Carpooling is sometimes used but is not desirable because it sets up an exclusive relationship between some of the group members. A parent may take responsibility to drive the adolescent to the group or may hire a cab to do so.

One strategy to increase the likelihood of attendance is to conduct a parallel parents' group. This can increase the parents' investment in getting their youngster to group sessions. It can be particularly useful if the parents' group parallels the topics of the adolescent group and the changes occurring through the process of treatment can be mutually reinforced. Some parents may need a different form of therapy, however, and may be reluctant to invest the additional time. One concern is that if parents want to avoid dealing with issues in their group, they may refuse to bring their teenager to the adolescent group session. If parallel parents' groups are conducted, it is important that the respective group leaders work closely together and that everyone is aware of how and what information will be shared.

The Nature of Authority in Private Practice Groups

In contrast to institutional settings where the organization sets policy and is the final arbiter in any infringements, the private practitioner is the authority responsible for establishing and enforcing the rules for the group. Written contracts, discussed with teenagers and their families in the pregroup interviews, state the therapist's rules for group membership that represent the procedural guidelines. In addition to attendance, ground rules may include: punctuality, nonviolence, no smoking, coming to group sober, and no outside discussion of what goes on in the group. Therapists must decide how they and the group members will deal with infringements.

The treatment of substance abuse may involve regular testing to monitor and control relapse. In clinics, the institution takes responsibility for this function. In private practice, however, the therapist must make the arrangements with the teenagers and their families and establish some mechanism for enforcement.

Policies regarding the payment and nonpayment of fees must also be clearly worked out with the teenager and the family before the first group meeting. This again differs in private practice, in that the therapist is directly affected by nonpayment of fees and makes the final decision regarding how this must be handled.

Confidentiality in Private Practice

In private practice groups, confidentiality can prompt a great many difficulties if it is not dealt with during the pregroup contracting session. First, as with all adolescent groups, private practitioners must convey to the members' parents the limits of sharing with them material from the group therapy sessions. Parents will generally want to have some idea of whether or not their youngster is making progress in treatment, and this will require periodic contact with the leader. This does not, however, suggest that parents can be privy to the content of the group sessions. This boundary is best stated when both parents and adolescents are present, but may also be conveyed to parents through a letter outlining what they can and cannot expect to hear about their youngster's progress. Although the exact content of the therapy will not be shared, they can expect to receive monthly memos telling them how their teenager is doing in the group. It is hoped that strongly reinforcing a guideline of confidentiality will make it easier for the adolescent to share intimate struggles and deal with salient life issues without fear of disclosure and subsequent repercussions. There are exceptions, however, to the bounds of confidentiality, mandated by law or professional ethics, such as when adolescents declare in the group that they are about to engage in behavior that is dangerous to themselves or others. Further, therapists must also determine the limits of confidentiality within which they are comfortable. Once the therapists have determined their parameters of confidentiality, it is easier to present firm guidelines to members and parents.

Therapists treating adolescents in groups in hospitals, residential treatment centers, and clinics must decide, with their institutions, the nature and specificity of information regarding group members that can be shared with other members of the treatment team, such as nurses, physicians, and special educators. Similarly, therapists in private practice must decide what they can share with referring sources or others who have responsibilities in the teenagers' lives. Group leaders must communicate clearly with referral sources the type of feedback that can, legally and therapeutically, be provided regarding the adolescent's progress in treatment. It is recommended that practitioners receiving referrals from multiple sources supply a document stating the parameters of feedback to be expected. For example, if Tony's teacher refers him to the school counselor who, in turn, refers him to a private practice group, the teacher, who must continue to deal with Tony in the classroom, may feel a sense of "entitlement" to contact the therapist and check on Tony's progress. Unless there are specific guidelines, such as an agreement that the therapist may offer suggestions for coping with Tony's misbehavior in the classroom but will not discuss what goes on in treatment, the therapist may be confronted with some irate faculty or administrators. If the therapist is going to speak with teachers or others in the teenager's life, the teenager should be informed and understand the purpose and nature of the contact.

A final caveat about confidentiality in private practice adolescent group therapy is the need to establish firm guidelines regarding outside discussion of what goes on in the group. Although this is important in all groups, it may be particularly significant for private practitioners. Members may live in the

217

same neighborhoods or attend the same schools and both families and teenagers could become uncomfortable and angry if neighbors or fellow students learned about the treatment without their consent. Consequently, both during the pregroup contracting interviews and periodically throughout the life of the group, it is important that therapists remind members of their obligation to "keep the group within the group" and to avoid any reference to group members or group discussions outside the sessions.

7. Group Leaders and Their Training

The first requirements of group leaders who wish to work with adolescents are that they respect them and enjoy working with them. The leaders must be observant and sensitive to the teenagers' moods and the meaning of their behavior and must be willing to be genuine and honest themselves. Because adolescents are often confused, the leaders must be clear about their own standards but also open-minded and willing to consider other views. They should be undefensive, willing to reveal aspects of their personal life when it seems appropriate (adolescents need to be led by real people), able to admit they are wrong, and willing to accept a problem-solving attitude toward life. To lead youth, one must have competence, flair, or be attractive to them. Life must be interesting to the leaders if they are going to interest and hold the youth. Leaders need to have energy and vitality. They must be able to endure rough times. Research also indicates that adolescents place a high value on leaders who have a sense of humor.[1] The leaders' capacity to laugh with the youth and at themselves makes the leaders seem more human.

Working with adolescents is difficult and demanding, because the youth often challenge the leaders and stimulate strong feelings in them. Leaders need to know themselves well and to have worked out their own adolescent conflicts before they can work effectively with this age group. Many therapists agree that adolescent groups are the most difficult to lead and maintain that leaders must first have experience with groups for children or adults before they attempt to work with groups of adolescents.

As we have already discussed, adolescents vary greatly, not only in their personalities and general development but also in their subcultures and cliques. Leaders need to learn about these subcultures they will be dealing with, the adolescents' typical behaviors and habits, their values, their style, and their language. Leaders probably should not adopt the language of any particular group but must be able to understand it and, if appropriate, use certain expressions. Some catchwords or stories can gain special meaning for a group and can thus be useful therapeutically. When one listens carefully to the "idle chatter" that goes on in adolescent groups, such as talk of music, movies, or sports, one can often identify certain themes and issues that the teenagers are most concerned with. For example, a discussion of the Superbowl may lead to the exploration of professional athletes' competitiveness and then to a discussion of how members deal with competition in their own lives outside and within the group.

Beyond these basic personal characteristics and knowledge of the culture, the amount of education and training that group leaders must have will depend on the kind of group to be conducted and the nature of responsibilities the leaders are required to carry in regard to the group and the overall program. In recent years there has been a trend to break down the work of the professional into constellations of tasks varying in difficulty and complexity and to train technicians and aides for specific constellations, thus freeing the professional to concentrate on those tasks and responsibilities requiring a higher level of specialized training, background, knowledge, and capacity to exercise initiative and take responsibility.[2] The essential difference between technicians and professionals is that the former, if they move to a different level of group, will require additional training as there may not be much carryover of experience. The professionals, on the other hand, have a background of knowledge and training that they can build on and adapt to new situations and programs, and this makes it easier for them to initiate and develop new programs. Many professionals today, however, lead specialized groups, such as those for the treatment of victims, substance abusers, or adolescents with eating disorders, where they must learn about these patients and their problems and the special techniques for working with them through continuing education and supervised experience. For technicians, efforts have also been made to link technical experience and training to academic education and continuing education and training so that they can advance in their field and eventually become professionals.[3]

As we have seen, a large variety of groups can be undertaken that require different levels of knowledge and skill. For example, an individual who has been specially trained to work with one type of problem does not need to have years of education to conduct well-defined informational groups. Much of the direct contact with patients in therapeutic communities and the groups that are conducted there will be undertaken by staff who may have no more than a high school diploma; however, their daily responses will be crucial to the effectiveness of the program, and many of the opportunities for informal counseling, individually or in groups, occur between the patients or inmates and these junior staff members. The treatment plan and the general therapeutic direction will have been determined by professionals, however. Group psychotherapy that concentrates on enabling members to identify the ways in which they function dynamically, the planning of therapeutic milieu approaches, group consultation, and the training of therapists all require a high level of education and skill.

Many mutual support groups are being run today with indigenous leaders or on a leaderless group model.[4] These groups function well because the leaders and members have similar problems, experiences, and goals, and the leaders can serve as models with whom the members can identify. They are also knowledgeable about the typical resistances that members experience in their attempts to change and understand the underlying meaning of their language and their games.[5] Quite often, these groups will have a professional associated with them, someone they can consult if problems arise that they cannot handle.

It is extremely important that all group leaders, technicians as well as professionals, have a knowledge of individual personality development and functioning, the range of normal and abnormal adaptations, small group theory, and the structure and functioning of communities and institutions. They must also receive orientation in regard to the population with whom they are working and the goals, policies, and practices of their program.[6] All technicians as well as professionals require training in how to observe individuals and groups and an understanding of their own strengths and weaknesses. Such knowledge and training can, of course, be taught at different levels of complexity. It is still true, unfortunately, that general formal education is given primary importance, with specialized knowledge and training coming second. Experience and personality have been given much less emphasis so that it is still possible for persons to have received masters degrees and even doctorates and to be considered fully trained professionals although they have only a limited and elementary capacity to develop relationships and to work with people.[7] If the practice ever becomes general of linking work experience, formal education, specialized training, and personal development into a long-term employment package with education and training considered part of the job and consequently provided for as such, then professionals could begin to function with much greater competence and their training could be concentrated on advanced work. Today the professional still must be taught, like the technician, the basic concepts and tools required to work with groups. Furthermore, current funding practices induce young professionals to move very early into private practice and sometimes to start groups before they have had adequate supervised experience.

There has been a growth in the development of specialized certification for different types of human service counselors. Most training of technicians is still undertaken on the job, and relatively few Associate of Arts and Bachelors degree programs include counseling with individuals and groups.[8] Professional training in group counseling and group psychotherapy may be included as part of a general professional training, may be obtained at a few specialized centers, or may be provided on the job. The American Group Psychotherapy Association has now developed a model and has decentralized training for professionals in its annual institutes and conferences or conferences held by its affiliate societies.[9] Training in groups for special populations is often provided through continuing education workshops.

Most training for professionals assumes that they have all been educated in human biology, sociology, and psychology, including clinical, dynamic, developmental, social, and abnormal psychology, social anthropology, psychological assessment, and elementary methods of research and evaluation. Specialized training is expected to include knowledge of group theory and management, taught experientially and didactically, group observation, supervised experience with individual and group therapy, and some kind of group experience that focuses on dynamic operations in groups and the individuals own self-knowledge and self-management.[10] Work with younger adolescents and children also requires training in the use of play and craft activities and materials.[11] Group psychotherapists who work with patients suffering from serious mental illnesses possibly requiring medication must either themselves be medically trained or work in conjunction with a medical professional or a clinical pharmacologist. Whenever professionals begin work with a new population, they must become knowledgeable about the specific characteristics of that group, their age differences, their socioeconomic and ethnic backgrounds, and their specific problems.

The personality of the therapist is particularly important in working with adolescent groups.[12] Most therapists agree that adolescents want their leaders to be caring, active, and firm. Leaders also need to have resolved the problems they themselves encountered in adolescence[13] and should be aware of their own attitudes and biases and those of the community toward adolescent populations.[14] They also need to be aware of the relationships between the patients, therapists, the group as a whole, and the setting within which it functions. As we have discussed previously, adolescents who have multiple problems generally require multiple interventions so that all their needs are taken care of. Group leaders who work with such teenagers need to participate in the youth service network and be able to assist in providing whatever other resources the teenagers need.

Group Theory and Management

As textbooks of good quality have become available, more and more teaching is undertaken in small group discussions that frequently include elements of both self-study and group study. The important questions of how to train people to carry over what they have learned, how to make abstract concepts meaningful, how to relate theory and practice, and how to teach people to perceive and understand phenomena and to react appropriately with correct timing have not been definitively answered. The material outlined in this book is taught in group discussions in seminar fashion. The group members use their own group experiences and their own reactions to getting acquainted and to working together as a part of their understanding of how people behave and feel. For example, the first session of the course can include an examination of the mechanism of getting acquainted; how the trainer starts the group; what the members' feelings are about giving their names and backgrounds; what they choose to reveal and not reveal; how they feel about being in a new group with strangers; what their expectations are of the group; and why they want to work with teenagers. In these activities, it is possible to begin to teach group concepts:

1. Members coming to new groups expect the leader to show how the group should operate and to work with the members in defining goals. A group contract will be established. If this is not done, members feel deprived, frustrated, and angry. The less the group is structured, the more anxious members will feel.
2. The more initiative leaders take in setting up the group and defining the limits and the more responsibility they assume for the functioning of the group, the more dependency they foster in the members.
3. If a leader asks members to take turns identifying themselves, one can demonstrate that this makes them anxious and self-conscious. It is possible in this way to initiate a discussion about giving names and what people choose to reveal about themselves.
4. Even though group goals may have been stated explicitly beforehand, most members come into groups with hidden agendas, and the early phases of groups are often taken up with an implicit struggle about what the group will actually adopt as its major concern.
5. In this first meeting, it can also be shown how members handle their anxiety in different ways, just as adolescents do when they are introduced to a group. Some members may take the initiative because they find it difficult to tolerate silence. Others may withdraw into nonparticipation. One can also demonstrate in the group how silent members can sometimes be powerful and affect many members by their silence.
6. The character of participation can be examined. In the beginning of groups, interaction is frequently concentrated between the leader and individual members. In a successful discussion group, after a time, participation increasingly becomes horizontal between different members of the group. Dimensions of participation are degree, spread, and quality. Even in a first meeting, one can notice the general tone of the group and make the concept of group climate real.

As the seminar progresses, many other phenomena can be demonstrated that are similar to those experienced in the treatment groups. Trainees are reluctant to expose their uncertainties, inadequacies, and foolishness. They have trouble accepting and facing differences of opinion. It is difficult for them to trust each other and to develop the intimate, supportive, accepting, and explorative climate so necessary for full and meaningful learning to take place. They, too, exhibit problems of dependency and independence, competition with the leader, and sibling rivalry just as groups of adolescents do. They, too, test the leader at times. They are reluctant to accept concepts, rebel against ideas, feel despairing, are bored, or are discouraged that so little is being achieved. Feelings about issues of particular significance to teenagers—identity, sexuality, family constraints and caring, relationships with authority, substance abuse, and peer relations—need to be explored in the training group to increase the members' self-awareness. Their own adolescent experiences are important.

Members play different roles in the seminar group, just as the adolescents do in the treatment groups. Some trainees work hard and try to learn; others try to take over the role of trainer; others remain silent and nonparticipatory; still others become the clowns in the group. Although it is not always useful or even tolerated by the trainees to go too deeply into their roles and defenses, it is possible to help them begin to be aware of their own propensity to take on certain roles. In the discussion, too, as case material is analyzed, many of the attitudes that trainees profess become apparent to them and to the group. In the seminar the values and standards of the trainees should become clarified, for it is important for group leaders, particularly with adolescents, to understand their own attitudes to the everyday behaviors and crucial issues that adolescents must face.

Such personal interactions in a training program draw the group members together and induce an intimacy that makes it possible to observe more clearly all these group phenomena. Because of this intimacy, by the end of the seminar it becomes possible to observe the members' typical feelings concerning the breakup of groups and separation from each other, that is, the process of termination. It is important to emphasize whether or not one plans to help members of a group become conscious of what is going on dynamically between members. Trainees must understand, too, that dynamic interaction is always present in groups and should be understood by the leader.

Although an understanding of group dynamics is obtained in this kind of seminar, as well as in group supervision and group observation, it is useful for group leaders to take part in short-term sensitization groups that focus on experiencing and understanding the dynamics of group formation and dissolution.

Group Supervision

Just as there has been a move toward treating adolescents in groups rather than individually, there has also been a tendency to group leaders together for supervision. Although both these movements have occurred to some extent because of the need to save time, both have also been found to have definite advantages.

When group leaders are supervised together, they can share vicariously in each other's experiences; their knowledge of different groups can be quickly broadened; and they are exposed to a group experience in the supervisory session.

In the supervisory group itself, many of the same phenomena develop that are observable in adolescent groups. The counselors or therapists in the beginning also have difficulty in revealing themselves when they discuss their groups. They, too, exhibit similar problems of dependency and independence, competition with the leader, and sibling rivalry, just as occurs in adolescent groups. If the group does not go well we may see the same group resistances or even scapegoating of a member. It is therefore necessary to develop an intimate, supportive, accepting, and explorative climate so that full and undefensive discussion can take place. While manifest countertransferences and resistances are discussed in terms of the adolescent and supervisory groups, they are not worked through at any particular leader's familial or genetic level. Where leaders have persistent difficulty with any type of problem or adolescent, they are advised to seek psychotherapeutic help outside the supervisory group situation.

The re-creation of the climate or problem that is being described in relation to a counseling or therapy group can sometimes be noticed in the supervisory group. When this happens, the supervisee unconsciously plays the part of the adolescent in that he or she stimulates in the supervisory group members reactions similar to those experienced as a leader in the counseling group. For example, a therapist was describing how group members seemed to tantalize him and hold him off with isolationist obsessional mechanisms. They would complain and then deny their complaints. As the supervisory group tried to help the leader explore this problem, it became apparent that he was holding them off and refusing to reveal his real feelings in the same way that his adolescent group had dealt with him. The members of the supervisory group found themselves feeling tantalized, helpless, and angry in this shadow boxing. When this interaction had been examined, the therapist was better able to deal with his own feelings and with his adolescents in the therapy group.

In general, such supervisory groups should be kept small. When they are too large it is hard to develop sufficient trust and intimacy and one does not have enough time to examine in detail what goes on in the groups. For groups that are held once a week, a supervisory group of four leaders and a supervisor who meet for two hours each week seems sufficient. Each leader has a group that is reviewed and analyzed twice a month for an hour at a time. So that everyone can keep track of the groups, brief summaries on each adolescent are provided and the leaders write processed accounts of the meetings that they will report on and summaries of the others, all of which are distributed and read before the supervisory session. If audiotapes or videotapes are available, group leaders can select particular sections for review by the group. It is generally too time-consuming to review full sessions.

228

The supervisory groups can be set up in different ways, each having its own special advantages from the point of view of the training experience. They can be composed of

1. leaders who are all learning to work with the same type of group, such as analytically oriented psychotherapy groups with mixed neurotic adolescents or recreational activity groups led by junior counselors;
2. leaders who are working with different kinds of groups that are interconnected, such as parent and child groups;
3. leaders who are using the same methods with different populations;
4. leaders who are working with groups where different methods are being used experimentally with similar populations, such as cognitive restructuring and interpersonal groups with depressed adolescents.

Each of these arrangements has some special advantage from the point of view of the training experience:

In type 1, leaders are able to quickly gain a wide experience with a particular technique, problem, or type of adolescent. For example, four leaders supervised together were all leading groups of teenage mothers living in a shelter prior to giving birth to their babies. In comparing the four groups, the leaders were struck by the similarity of the content and sequence and additionally gained a wide and intensive knowledge of the problems and decisions that the teenagers had to face. Several employment counselors working together soon learned the typical problems and attitudes of their adolescent clients.

When four therapists were working with groups of teenage couples attempting to work out their difficulties in adjusting to married life, they were impressed by the pressure each marital partner placed on the group and on the therapist to get them to be on their side and against their spouse. The leaders were able to share with each other the ways in which they dealt with this problem.

This method makes it easy to see how leaders can react differently to the same problem and is helpful in overcoming resistance to examining one's own difficulties. In one recreational group, the girls expressed their defiance by not coming to the table for refreshments. The leader, understanding their need to express their independence, remained relaxed and unconcerned. Another leader, experiencing a similar problem, was unconsciously reminded of her own suppressed desires to act in this way as a child. She was threatened by the angry feelings that she transferred to the children. They sensed that they had been able to upset her, and continued to defy her. The leader was able, with the assistance of the supervisory group, to recognize her own transferred feelings and to reduce her anxiety. She was no longer upset by the children, and their game of defying her in this way lost its interest.

The second model, interconnected groups, is particularly useful in working with families, where supervisees can gain an excellent picture of the ways the different family members function and can build up a realistic view of how parent-child problems mesh.

The third type, in which leaders examine the use of the same method with different kinds of adolescents or problem, allows leaders to gain an excellent idea of the flexibility and limitations of the method. They can learn what is basic to the method and what can be adapted for different types of youth, as with activity interview group therapy with young teenagers who have varying degrees of impulse control.

Finally, the fourth model, in which group leaders work with similar populations but use different methods, such as guidance and therapeutic groups of parents, enables leaders to understand the range of the different methods. They can compare the leadership activities that teach a group how to function at a particular level, and they can learn how to select more easily for different kinds of group therapy.

When groups are lead by cotherapists, there are often issues that arise between them. It is important that both attend the supervisory session, so that the supervision is owned by both. Several teams of cotherapists in the supervisory group can be very supportive when a team runs into trouble. As we have written elsewhere, it is important that cotherapists work out their roles in relation to each other, remain aware of their reactions, and give themselves time after each group meeting to process what has gone on there.

A final advantage of group supervision is the ease with which the supervisor is enabled to move from specific to theoretical discussion. When a number of groups can be compared, generalizations are more easily made. Not only group but also individual and family dynamics are more easily and potently taught by this method.

Although a certain amount of individual supervision is included in the training of beginning group leaders, it is increasingly becoming our practice to work exclusively in small group sessions.

Group Observation

The demonstration group that is observed by a group of trainees and a supervisor and then discussed with the group leader and supervisor is an invaluable training device. It is possible to identify personal distortions and countertransferences in action, observe individual and group phenomena and leadership techniques, and to discuss alternative courses of action. In such a group, it is also possible to examine and discuss the group dynamics that are operative in this as in other groups.

Audiovisual Aids and Simulations

Taped recordings of sessions have been used frequently both for self-study by the leader and for supervisory purposes, as well as for feedback to the group members. Some films and tapes have been produced for distribution, such as Slavson's Activity Group Therapy,[15] the groups at Highfields,[16] and Scheidlinger's sex education films.[17] There are a number of excellent films on adolescent development that are used both for education and prevention and also to enable leaders to examine their feelings in relation to particular issues, such as bereavement, the effects of various drugs, or sexual behavior. Pritchard's *Power of Choice* is an excellent videotape series to help leaders understand teenager's reaction to today's problems.[18] Simulations by members of the training group can also be revealing. A multiple family group model of short-term therapy can easily be simulated by a group of nine to twelve trainees. Role-playing is useful to help supervisees practice different approaches and to obtain feedback from their peers.

Self-Knowledge and Self-Management

There has been considerable controversy as to whether group counselors and psychotherapists should also have taken part themselves in a counseling or therapy group as members. In our view it is important for group leaders to feel the force of the group, to accept that they too have problems, and to understand their own strengths and weaknesses. It is also important that they are able to be nondefensive in their behavior, to expose themselves when tackling problems that occur in their work, and to have empathy for the difficulties that their clients or patients experience in revealing themselves. We believe, therefore, that group leaders should be required to participate in either self-development or treatment groups for at least a year and that they should, as part of this experience, review their own adolescence and understand why they choose to work with this population.

Specialized Training

Beyond the basic training outlined here, there is also a need for specialized training when group leaders plan to use different methods or work with different populations or problems. Activity and activity/interview group therapy has its own procedures, rules, and potential for modification. Many such groups have failed because leaders have undertaken them without any specialized training or supervision. Groups for substance abusers and other addictive personalities require certain procedures and styles, whether conducted in or out of institutions. There are special issues to be considered, such as drug abuse testing and concerns such as understanding the mental changes that take place prior to relapse. Group therapists may need to have specialized training in treating phobias, eating disorders, or the syndromes related to Posttraumatic Stress Disorder. Specialized workshops should be attended, and consultation or supervision obtained, when a leader begins a group in a new area, no matter how experienced the leader may be in other directions.

Evaluation

Just as no program of intervention should be established without a system of quality control, no training should be developed without evaluation. We must know whether the training is proceeding according to plan, whether the trainees are learning what is offered to them, whether they are able to apply it, and whether the result is effective. This implies that all training programs must be well conceptualized and described, that at least spot-checking of the training operations should be undertaken, and that the trainees should be followed up after they leave the program, as well as tested at its end.

Major problems in evaluating training, as in evaluating programs, have been related to uncertainty about goals. Although trainers have usually been clear about the knowledge they felt group leaders should have, they have been much less certain about what kind of person makes a good leader or an effective therapist. Because of this uncertainty, trainers have been reluctant to exclude potential leaders on the grounds of personality except when there are clear indications of irresponsibility, malperception, poor functioning, or persistent contertransferential involvement.

Summary

Since this book was first written, the number and types of groups being conducted have expanded considerably. There has been much more systematization in general of group psychotherapy training. We still lack widely approved models, however, for the training of adolescent group leaders, counselors, and psychotherapists. This chapter incorporates what is essential for the training of group leaders in general and what is specifically necessary for adolescent group psychotherapists and counselors. The leaders' capacity to understand their own feelings and reactions to adolescence, their knowledge of adolescent development and subcultures, their capacity to deal with their own stress, and their training in group process and group methods in general are all critical elements in the makeup of an effective group leader.

Notes

1. The Group as an Agent of Change

1. Shaw, *Group Dynamics.*
2. H. E. Durkin, "Boundaries and Boundarying"; Minuchin, *Family Therapy;* Bowen, *Clinical Practice.*
3. Cartwright and Zander, *Group Cohesiveness;* Budman et al., "Preliminary Findings," 175–94.
4. Von Bertalanffy, *General Systems Theory.*
5. Sherif and Sherif, *Reference Groups.*
6. Yalom, *Group Psychotherapy.*
7. Lebon, *The Crowd.*
8. Redl, "Group Emotion," 573–96.
9. Bion, *Experience in Groups.*
10. H. E. Durkin, "Boundaries and Boundarying"; J. E. Durkin, *Living Groups.*
11. Von Bertalanffy, *General Systems Theory.*
12. Bales and Cohen, *SYMLOG.*
13. Lacoursiere, *Life Cycle of Groups.*
14. Dies, "Adolescent Groups," 59–70.

15. Draiss, "Building Cohesiveness," 22–28.
16. Corder et al., "Structured Techniques," 413–421.
17. Rogers, "Basic Encounter Group."
18. Erikson, *Identity*.
19. MacLennan and Felsenfeld, *Group Counseling*.
20. Hall, *Silent Language*.
21. Wolff, *Georg Simmel*.
22. Borgatta and Bales, "Reconstituted Groups," 302–20.
23. Slavson, *Group Therapy*.
24. Schachter, "Deviation, Rejection, and Communication."
25. Speer, "Nonverbal Communication," 383–487.
26. Birdwhistell, *Kinesics and Content*.
27. Berne, *Games*.
28. Bass, *Organizational Behavior*.
29. Lieberman, Yalom, and Miles, *Encounter Groups*.
30. Lewin, *Resolving Social Conflicts*.
31. Festinger, "Group Attraction," 152–63.
32. Lewin, *Resolving Social Conflicts*.
33. Stanton and Schwartz, *The Mental Hospital*.
34. Berger, "Communication Process," 29–35.
35. Moreno, *Who Shall Survive?*
36. Scheidlinger, "Peer Group Revisited," 387–97; MacLennan, "Scapegoating," 38–40.
37. Lewin, *Field Theory*.
38. Homans, *The Human Group*.
39. Moreno, *Who Shall Survive?*
40. Bales and Cohen, *SYMLOG*.
41. Hill and Hill, *Interaction Matrix*.
42. Moos, *Evaluating Treatment Environments*.
43. Leary, *Diagnosis of Personality*.
44. Schutz, *FIRO*.
45. Whitaker and Lieberman, *Psychotherapy*.
46. Berne, *Games*.
47. Lippitt and White, "Leadership and Group Life."
48. Azima and Dies, "Clinical Research," 193–223.
49. Dies and Mackenzie, *Integrating Research and Practice*.
50. Azima and Dies, "Clinical Research," 193–223.

2. Adolescents and Their Cultures

1. Gilligan, *In Another Voice.*

2. National Center for Health Statistics, "Advanced Report on Final Mortality Statistics"; Bureau of the Census, "School Enrollment: Social and Economic Characteristics of Students" (October 1986), *Current Population Reports,* series P20, no. 429 (Washington, D.C.: 1988); Flanagan and Jamieson, eds., *Sourcebook on Criminal Justice Statistics, 1987.*

3. Sherif and Sherif, *Reference Groups.*

4. Gilligan, *In Another Voice.*

5. Dryfoos, *Adolescents at Risk.*

6. Hofferth and Hayes, *Risking the Future;* Hodgekinson, *The Same Client; Statistical Abstracts; Vital Statistics.*

7. Hodgekinson, *Demographics.*

8. *National Household Survey—1985,* 38, 49, 81, 92-93.

9. *Data from the Drug Abuse Warning Network.*

10. Hofferth and Hayes, *Risking the Future.*

11. Seibert and Olson, eds., *AIDS.*

12. Kegeles, Adler, and Irwin, "Condoms," 460–61; Melchert and Burnett, "Attitudes," 293–98.

3. General Considerations in Group Counseling and Group Psychotherapy

1. Pritchard, *Power of Choice.*

2. Raubolt, "Group Psychotherapy with Delinquents," 143–62.

3. Berkovitz, "Group Therapy in Secondary Schools," 99–124; Kraft, "Overview of Group Therapy with Adolescents," 461–80.

4. Slavson and MacLennan, "Unmarried Mothers."

5. Bratter, "Alcohol and Drug Addicted Adolescents," 163–92.

6. MacLennan, "Group Psychotherapy with Girls," 25–41.

7. Scheidlinger, "Group Treatment of Adolescents," 102–11.

8. Ibid.

9. Botvin, "Prevention Research."

10. Hamburg, *Life Skills Training;* Goldstein, Reagles, and Amann, *Refusal Skills;* Copeland, "Cognitive-Behavioral Approach," 394–403.

11. Dryfoos, *Adolescents at Risk.*

12. Office of Substance Abuse Prevention, *Prevention.*

13. Wisconsin Clearing House, *Alcohol and Other Drug Problems;* Virginia Council on Coordinating Prevention, *Resource Guide.*

14. Scheidlinger, "Group Treatment of Adolescents," 102–11.

15. Rachman, "Identity Group Psychotherapy," 21–42.

16. Azima, "Confrontation, Empathy, and Interpretation," 3–19.

17. Copeland, "Cognitive-Behavioral Approach," 394–403; Bloom, *Group Therapy with Adolescents*.

18. Krieg, *Behavior Problems;* Elias and Tobias, *Problem Solving/Decision Making*.

19. Brody, *Women's Therapy Groups*.

20. Slavson, *Group Psychotherapy*.

21. Moreno, *Who Shall Survive?*

22. Rogers, Kohut, and Erickson, "Similarities and Differences," 125–40.

23. Truax and Carkuff, *Toward Effective Counseling*.

24. Berg and Landreth, *Group Counseling*.

25. Cassano, ed., *Social Work*.

26. Berne, *Games*.

27. Ibid.

28. Harman, "Gestalt Group Therapy," 473–83.

29. Rachman, "Identity Group Psychotherapy," 21–42.

30. Glasser, *Reality Therapy*.

31. Elson, *Kohutian Seminars*.

32. Gilligan, "Adolescent Development Reconsidered," 63–92; Bull and Neck, "Implications of Developmental Theories," 529–34.

33. Yalom, *Theory and Practice*.

34. Bion, *Experience in Groups*.

35. Skynner, *Group Analysis and Family Therapy*.

36. Schinke and Gilchrist, *Life Skills*.

37. Meichenbaum, *Stress Inoculation Training*.

38. Terr, "Treating Psychic Trauma," 3–20.

39. Pecukonis, "Aggressive Adolescent Females," 59–76.

40. Scheidlinger, "Group Treatment of Adolescents," 102–11; Schaefer, Johnson, and Wherry, *Group Therapies;* Stein and Davis, *Therapies for Adolescents*.

41. Corder et al., "Pretherapy Training for Adolescents," 699–706.

42. McCorkle, Elias, and Bixby, *The Highfields Story*.

43. Hall, *The Silent Language*.

44. The Ungame.

45. Child's Work/Childsplay, The Love Game.

46. The Institute for Mental Health Initiatives, *Learning to Manage Anger*.

47. Linesch, *Adolescent Art Therapy*.

48. Frances and Schiff, "Popular Music as a Catalyst," 393–98.

49. Miller, "Spontaneous Use of Poetry," 223–27.

50. Weber, "Effect of Videotape and Playback," 213–28.

5. Major Themes and Problems in Adolescent Groups

1. Shure and Spivak, *Interpersonal Cognitive Problem Solving*.

2. Botvin, "Life Skills Training Program."

3. Schinke and Gilchrist, *Life Skills Counseling*.

4. Kramer and Frazer, *The Dynamics of Relationships*.

5. Leaman, "Group Counseling," 144–50.

6. MacLennan, "Group Psychotherapy with Girls," 5–41.

7. Rachman, "Identity Group Psychotherapy."

8. Hendren et al., "Eating Disorders," 589–602.

9. Ibid.; Thornton and Deblassie, "Treating Bulimia," 631–38; Lieb and Thompson, "Anorexia Nervosa Inpatients," 639–42.

10. Thornton and Deblassie, "Treating Bulimia," 631–38.

11. Lieb and Thompson, "Anorexia Nervosa In-patients," 639–42.

12. Osterheld, McKenna, and Gould, "Group Psychotherapy of Bulimia," 163–84.

13. *Drug Misuse,* 89–109.

14. Robertson and Mathews, "Preventing Adolescent Suicide," 34–39.

15. Pritchard, *Power of Choice*.

16. "Adolescent Suicide."

17. Botvin, "Life Skills Training Program"; Shaffer, "Prevention of Youth Suicide," 611–13.

18. District of Columbia Board of Education, personal communication.

19. Doyle and Bauer, "Post-Traumatic Stress Disorder," 275–88; Terr, "Psychic Trauma in Children," 3–20; Yule and Williams, "Post-Traumatic Stress Reactions," 279–98.

20. Doyle and Bauer, "Post-Traumatic Stress Disorder," 275–88.

21. *Child Abuse and Neglect*.

22. Kitchur and Bell, "Sexual Abuse Victims," 285–310; Verbur, Hughes, and deRius, "Female Adolescent Incest Victims," 843–59; Knittle and Tuana, "Intrafamilial Sexual Abuse," 236–42.

23. Berliner and MacQuivey, "Adolescent Victims of Sexual Abuse."

24. Carozza and Heirsteiner, "Female Incest Victims," 165–75.

25. Serrano, "Reconstituted Families."

26. Axelrod, Cameron, and Solomon, "Shy Adolescent Girls," 616–27.

27. Botvin, "Life Skills Training Program"; Schinke and Gilchrist, *Life Skills Counseling;* Kramer and Frazer, *Dynamics of Relationships.*

28. Outward Bound Programs.

29. *Experiment with Travel.*

30. *The Door: Program Description.*

31. Mueller and Higgins, *Guide to Prevention Programs.*

32. Dryfoos, *Adolescents at Risk.*

33. Mueller and Higgins, *Guide to Prevention Programs,* ibid.

34. Shure and Spivak, *Interpersonal Cognitive Problem Solving;* Botvin, "Life Skills Training Program"; Schinke and Gilchrist, *Life Skills Counseling.*

35. "A Three-Letter Word for Love"; Scheidlinger and Gordon, *About Sex.*

36. Rosenberg and Rosenberg, "Sex Education for the Family," 235–41.

37. *When Jenny When?*

38. Gardner, "College Students."

39. Ibid.

40. Office of Substance Abuse Prevention, *Prevention.*

41. Ibid.

42. Berkovitz, *When Schools Care.*

6. Groups in Different Settings

1. Hunter, *Encounter in the Classroom;* Jacks and Keller, "A Humanistic Approach," 49, 61–69; Sigal, Braverman, and Pilon, "Effects of Teacher-led Curriculum," 3–9; Garfield and McHugh, "Learning Counseling," 381–92.

2. MacLennan, "Community Mental Health Professionals."

3. Berkovitz, ed., *When Schools Care.*

4. Gazda, ed., *Theories and Methods.*

5. Berkovitz, "Group Therapy in Secondary Schools," 99–123.

6. Gordon, "What Kids Need to Know," 22–26; Nash, "Group Guidance and Counseling Programs," 577–83.

7. Dryfoos, *Adolescents at Risk;* Flay et al., "Social Psychological Smoking Prevention Programs"; Bangert-Downs, "School-Based Substance Abuse Education," 243–64; Tobler, "Meta-analysis," 537–67; Dignan et al., "Risk Reduction Program," 103–96.

8. Botvin, "Life Skills Training Program"; Wodarski, *Preventive Health Services;* Swift and Spivack, *Alternative Teaching Strategies;* Pease, "Social Skills Training Group," 229–39; Hamburg, *Life Skills Training;* Sarason

and Sarason, "Cognitive and Social Skills," 908–18; Morganett, *Skills for Living.*

9. Valene and Amos, "High School Transfer Students," 40–42; Kirshner, "Freshmen Group Counseling Program," 279–80.

10. Gordon, "Youth Helping Youth," 48–53; Tindall and Salmon-White, *Peers Helping Peers;* McKelvie, "Evaluation of a Model," 7–14.

11. Rushton, "Girls Comprehensive School," 267–84; Blum, *Group Counseling;* Durell, "Multiple Family Group Therapy," 44–52.

12. Elias, *Treating Adolescents.*

13. Krieg, *Group Leadership Training.*

14. Capuzzi and Gross, *Youth at Risk.*

15. Gibbs and Huang, eds., *Children of Color.*

16. Windsor and Dimitru, "Anabolic Steroid Use."

17. Dryfoos, *Adolescents at Risk,* 150–74; Office of Substance Abuse Prevention, *Prevention;* Tobler, "Meta-analysis," 537–67.

18. Coche and Fisher, "Learning-Disabled Adolescents," 125–42; Brolin and Gysters, "Career Education," 155–59; Garfield and McHugh, "Learning Counseling," 381–92.

19. Fine, Knight-Webb, and Vernon, "Selected Volunteer Adolescents," 189–97; Allen-Meares and Shapiro, *Adolescent Sexuality;* Lenihan and Kirk, "Treatment of Eating Disorders," 332–35.

20. Kimbro et al., "Multiple Family Group Approach," 18–24.

21. Durell, "Multiple Family Group Therapy," 44–52.

22. *Reaching the Unreached.*

23. Couvillon, *Teenage Pregnancy Prevention.*

24. "The Door Program," 161–63; "Aunt Martha's Place," 161–63.

25. Outward Bound Programs.

26. "Job Corps."

27. Vontress and MacLennan, *Neighborhood Youth Corps.*

28. MacLennan, "New Careers," 135–41.

29. United States General Accounting Office, *Job Training Partnership Act.*

30. Klein and MacLennan, "Groups in Job Training," 424–33.

31. Ibid.

32. United States General Accounting Office, *Summer Youth Jobs Program.*

33. United States Social Security Administration, Work Incentive Programs.

34. Kirshner, "Freshmen Group Counseling Program," 279–80.

35. United States Department of Education, Upward Bound Program.

36. Westman, "Hospitalized Delinquent Adolescents," 275–86.

37. The professionals referred to include Berkovitz, Brandes, Scheidlinger, and Sugar, all of whom expressed their opinions in personal communications in 1991.

38. Rachman, "Identity Group Psychotherapy," 21–41.

39. Azima, "Confrontation, Empathy, Interpretation," 3–19.

40. Copeland, Jr., "A Cognitive-Behavioral Approach," 394–403; Reynolds and Coats, "Treatment of Depression," 657–60.

41. Robertson and Matthews, "Preventing Adolescent Suicide," 34–39.

42. Pepper and Ryglawicz, "Guidelines," 4.

43. Glynn, Leukenfeld, and Ludford, eds., *Preventing Adolescent Drug Abuse*.

44. National Institute on Drug Abuse, *The Therapeutic Community*.

45. Schenkman, *Second Genesis*.

46. Brook and Whitehead, "Adolescent Amphetamine Abusers," 10–19.

47. Aso, *Say It Straight*.

48. Haggerty et al., "Delinquents and Drug Use," 439–56.

49. Shikles, *Methadone Maintenance Programs*.

50. Birmingham, "Adolescent Substance Abusers," 123–33.

51. Bratter, "Alcohol and Drug-Addicted Adolescents," 163–92.

52. O'Gorman and Ross, "Children of Alcoholics," 43–45.

53. Shields, "Busted and Branded," 61–81.

54. Morehouse, "Children of Alcoholic Parents," 4–11.

55. Bogdaniak and Piercy, "Adolescent Children of Alcoholics," 569–88.

56. Schwartz, "Smoking Cessation Methods."

57. Murray D.M. et al., "Prevention of Cigarette Smoking," 274–88.

58. Daley, ed., *Relapse*.

59. Rachin, ed., "Alcohol Problems and Minority Youth."

60. Stein and Kymissis, "Adolescent In-patient Group Psychotherapy," 69–84.

61. Altshuler, "Teen Meeting," 348–52.

62. McGuire, "A Time-limited Dynamic Approach," 373–83.

63. Zabusky and Kymissis, "Identity Group Therapy," 99–109.

64. Bernfeld, Clark, and Parker, "Adolescent Group Psychotherapy," 111–26.

65. McClendon, "Multiple Family Group Therapy," 14–24; Elizura and Davidson, "Treatment of Adolescents and Their Parents," 83–92.

66. Bardill, "A Behavior Contributing Program," 333–42.

67. Crabhill, "Hospitalized Adolescents," 147–58.

68. Pepper, *Dual Diagnosis Program.*
69. Anthony, *Educational Rehabilitation Program.*
70. Aichhorn, *Wayward Youth.*
71. Raubolt, "Group Psychotherapy with Delinquents," 143–62.
72. MacLennan and Belton, *Receiving Home Counselor Training.*
73. Haggerty et al., "Delinquents and Drug Use," 439–56.
74. Sugar, *The Adolescent in Group and Family Therapy.*
75. Richmond, "Observations," 57–62.
76. Azima and Richmond, eds., *Adolescent Group Psychotherapy.*
77. Schutz, *List of Therapists.*

7. Group Leaders and Their Training

1. Tramontana, "Psychotherapy Outcomes," 424–50; Hurst et al., "Determinants of Cohesiveness," 263–77.
2. Grosser, Henry, and Kelly, eds., *Nonprofessionals.*
3. MacLennan, "New Careers," 135–41.
4. Grosser, Henry, and Kelly, eds., *Nonprofessionals.*
5. MacLennan, "Personalities," 177–85.
6. MacLennan, "New Careers," 135–41; MacLennan and Felsenfeld, *Group Counseling; Guidelines.*
7. Grosser, Henry, and Kelly, eds., *Nonprofessionals;* MacLennan, "New Careers," 135–41.
8. True, "Training New Mental Health Personnel," 383–92.
9. *A Personal and Flexible Training Program.*
10. *Guidelines.*
11. *Children's Committee Draft Guidelines;* Slavson and Schiffer, *Group Psychotherapies for Children.*
12. MacLennan, "Personalities," 177–85; Slavson and Schiffer, *Group Psychotherapies for Children.*
13. MacLennan, "Personalities," 177–85.
14. MacLennan, "Influence of the Cultural Environment on Adolescents," 140–49.
15. Slavson et al., *Activity Group Therapy.*
16. McCorkle, Elias, and Bixby, *The Highfields Story.*
17. *Three-Letter Word for Love;* Scheidlinger and Gordon, *About Sex.*
18. Pritchard, *Power of Choice.*

Bibliography

"Adolescent Suicide: Recognition, Treatment, and Prevention." *Research Treatment for Children and Youth,* vol. 7. American Association of Children's Research Centers, 1989.

Aichhorn, A. *Wayward Youth.* New York: Viking Press, 1935.

Allen-Meares, P. and C. H. K. Shapiro. *Adolescent Sexuality.* Binghamton, N.Y.: Haworth, 1989.

Altshuler, A. "Teen Meeting: A way to Help Adolescents Cope with Hospitalization." *American Journal of Maternal and Child Nursing* 2 (1977): 348–52.

Anthony, W. *Educational Rehabilitation Program for Young Schizophrenics.* Boston, Mass.: Boston University, 1985.

Aso, E. G. *Say It Straight.* Norman, Okla.: Golden, 1983.

"Aunt Martha's Place." In J. G. Dryfoos, *Adolescents at Risk: Prevalence and Prevention,* 161–63. New York: Oxford University Press, 1990.

Axelrod, P. L., M. S. Cameron, and J. C. Solomon. "An Experiment in Group Therapy with Shy Adolescent Girls." *American Journal of Orthopsychiatry* 14 (1944): 616–27.

Azima, F. J. C. "Confrontation, Empathy, Interpretation." In F. J. C. Azima and L. H. Richmond, eds., *Adolescent Group Psychotherapy,* 3–19. Madison, Conn.: International Universities Press, 1989.

Azima, F. J. C. and K. R. Dies. "Clinical Research in Adolescent Group Psychotherapy: Status, Guidelines, and Directions." In F. J. C. Azima and L. H. Richmond, eds., *Adolescent Group Psychotherapy,* 193–223. Madison, Conn.: International Universities Press, 1989.

Azima, F. J. C. and L. H. Richmond, eds. *Adolescent Group Psychotherapy.* Madison, Conn.: International Universities Press, 1989.

Bales, R. F. and S. P. Cohen. *SYMLOG: A System for the Multiple-Level Observation of Groups.* New York: The Free Press, 1979.

Bangert-Downs, R. "The Effects of School-based Substance Abuse Education." *Journal of Drug Education* 18 (1988): 243–64.

Bardill, D. R. "A Behavior Contributing Program of Group Treatment for Early Adolescents in a Residential Treatment Setting." *International Journal of Group Psychotherapy* 27 (1977): 333–42.

Barth, R. *Social and Cognitive Treatment of Children and Adolescents.* San Francisco, Calif.: Jossey-Bass, 1986.

Bass, B. M. *Leadership, Psychology, and Organizational Behavior.* New York: Harper, 1960.

Berg, R. and G. Landreth. *Group Counseling: Fundamental Concepts and Procedures,* 2d ed. Muncie, Ind.: Accelerated Development, 1990.

Berger, M. M. "Notes on the Communication Process in Group Psychotherapy." *Journal of Group Psychoanalysis and Process* 11 (January 1969): 29–35.

Berkovitz, I. H. *When Schools Care.* New York: Brunner Mazel, 1975.

Berkovitz, I. H. "Application of Group Therapy in Secondary Schools." In F. J. C. Azima and L. H. Richmond, eds., *Adolescent Group Psychotherapy,* 99–123. Madison, Conn.: International Universities Press, 1989.

Berkovitz, I. H. Personal communication, 1991.

Berliner, L. and K. MacQuivey. "A Therapy Group for Female Adolescent Victims of Sexual Abuse." In M. Rosenbaum, ed., *Handbook of Short-Term Therapy Groups,* 101–118. New York: McGraw-Hill, 1983.

Berne, E. *Games People Play.* Brattleboro, Vt.: The Book Press, 1964.

Bernfeld, G., L. Clark, and G. Parker. "The Process of Adolescent Group Psychotherapy." *International Journal of Group Psychotherapy* 34 (January 1984): 111–26.

Bion, W. R. *Experience in Groups.* New York: Basic Books, 1961.

Birdwhistell, R. L. *Kinesics and Content.* Philadelphia: University of Pennsylvania Press, 1970.

Birmingham, M. S. "An Outpatient Treatment Programme for Adolescent Substance Abusers." *Journal of Adolescence* 9 (1986): 123–33.

Bibliography

Bloom, R. *Group Therapy with Adolescents*. Columbia, Md.: American Health Institute, 1990.

Blum, D. J. *Group Counseling for Secondary Schools*. Springfield, Ill.: Thomas, 1990.

Bogdaniak, R. C. and F. P. Piercy. "Therapeutic Issues of Adolescent Children of Alcoholics (ADCA) Groups." *International Journal of Group Psychotherapy* 37 (April 1987): 569–88.

Borgatta, E. F. and R. F. Bales. "Interaction of Individuals in Reconstituted Groups." *Sociometry* 16 (1953): 302–20.

Botvin, G. J. "The Life Skills Training Program as a Health Promotion Strategy." In J. Zins, ed., *Health Promotion in the Schools*. New York: Haworth, 1985.

Botvin, G. J. "Prevention Research." In *Alcohol and Drug Abuse Research,* Second Triennial Report to the Congress. Rockville, Md.: National Institute on Drug Abuse, 1987.

Bowen, M. *Family Therapy in Clinical Practice*. New York: Jason Aronson, 1978.

Brandes, N. Personal communication, 1991.

Bratter, T. E. "Group Psychotherapy with Alcohol and Drug-Addicted Adolescents: Special Clinical Concerns and Challenges." In F. J. C. Azima and L. H. Richmond, eds., *Adolescent Group Psychotherapy,* 163–92. Madison, Conn.: International Universities Press, 1989.

Brody, C. M. *Women's Therapy Groups: Paradigms of Feminist Treatment*. New York: Springer, 1987.

Brolin, D. E. and N. C. Gysters. "Career Education for Students with Disabilities." *Journal of Counseling and Development* 68 (November/December 1989): 155–59.

Brook, R. C. and P. C. Whitehead. "A Therapeutic Community for the Treatment of Adolescent Amphetamine Abusers." *Correctional and Social Psychology* 19 (1975): 10–19.

Budman, S. H., A. Demby, M. Feldstein, J. Redondo, and Bruno Scherz. "Preliminary Findings on a New Instrument to Measure Cohesion in Group Psychotherapy." *International Journal of Group Psychotherapy* 37 (1987): 175–94.

Bull, J. D. and D. S. Neck. "Implications of Developmental Theories on Counseling Adolescents in Groups." *Adolescence* 14 (1979): 529–34.

Bureau of the Census, *School Enrollment: Social and Economic Characteristics of Students. Current Population Reports,* series P20, no. 429 (October 1986). Washington, D.C.: Government Printing Office, 1988.

Bureau of the Census, *Statistical Abstracts 1987*. Washington D.C.: Government Printing Office, 1988.

Capuzzi, D. and D. R. Gross. *Youth at Risk: A Resource for Counselors, Teachers, and Parents.* Muncie, Ind.: Accelerated Development, 1990.

Carozza, P. M. and C. L. Heirsteiner. "Young Female Incest Victims in Treatment: Stages of Growth Seen in a Group Art Therapy Model." *Clinical Social Work Journal* 10 (1982): 165–75.

Cartwright, D. and A. Zander. *Group Cohesiveness: Introduction to Group Dynamics, Research, and Theory.* Evanston, Ill.: Row, Peterson, 1953.

Cassano, D. R., ed. *Social Work with Multifamily Groups.* New York: Haworth Press, 1989.

Child Abuse and Neglect. Denver, Colo.: American Humane Society, 1979.

Child's Work/Childsplay. The Love Game. Philadelphia, Pa., Center for Applied Psychology, 1991.

Children's Committee Draft Guidelines for Training Mental Health Professionals as Children's and Adolescents' Group Psychotherapists. New York: American Group Psychotherapy Association, January 1982. Revised and accepted 1991.

Coche, J. M. and J. M. Fisher. "Group Psychotherapy with Learning-Disabled Adolescents." In F. J. C. Azima and L. H. Richmond, eds., *Group Psychotherapy with Learning-Disabled Adolescents,* 125–42. Madison, Conn.: International Universities Press, 1989.

Copeland, E. T., Jr. "A Cognitive-Behavioral Approach to the Group Treatment of Adolescents." *Small Group Behavior* 153 (1984): 394–403.

Corder, B. F., T. M. Haizlip, L. Whiteside, and M. Vogel. "Pretherapy Training for Adolescents in Group Psychotherapy Contracts, Guidelines, and Pretherapy Preparation." *Adolescence* 15 (1980): 699–706.

Corder, B. F., R. Whiteside, P. Kochne, and R. Hartman. "Structured Techniques for Handling Loss and Addition of Members in Adolescent Psychotherapy Groups." *Journal of Early Adolescence* 1 (1981): 413–21.

Couvillon, B. "Proposal for Teenage Pregnancy Prevention Program." Washington D.C.: Family Life Association, 1968.

Crabhill, L. "Hospitalized Adolescents Who Act Out: A Treatment Approach." *Psychiatry* 45 (1982): 147–58.

Daley, D. C., ed. *Relapse.* Binghamton, N.Y.: Haworth Press, 1989.

Dies, K. R. "A Developmental Model for Adolescent Groups." *Journal of Child and Adolescent Group Therapy* 1 (1990): 59–70.

Dies, R. R. and K. R. Mackenzie, eds. *Advances in Group Psychotherapy: Integrating Research and Practice.* New York: International Universities Press, 1983.

Dignan, M. B. et al. "Risk-Reduction Program for Smoking and Alcohol." *Journal of School Health* 55 (March 1985): 103–96.

Bibliography

District of Columbia. Board of Education. Conflict mediation. Personal communication, 1989.

The Door: Program Description. New York City, 1970.

"The Door Program, New York City." In J. G. Dryfoos, *Adolescents at Risk: Prevalence and Prevention,* 161–63. New York: Oxford University Press, 1990.

Doyle, J. S. and S. K. Bauer. "Post-Traumatic Stress Disorder in Children: Its Identification and Treatment in a Residential Setting for Emotionally Disturbed Youth." *Journal of Traumatic Stress* 2 (March 1989): 275–88.

Draiss, J. E. "Building Cohesiveness in an Adolescent Therapy Group." *Journal of Child and Adolescent Psychotherapy* 3 (1986): 22–28.

Dryfoos, J. G. *Adolescents at Risk: Prevalence and Prevention.* New York: Oxford University Press, 1990.

Durell, V. G. "Adolescents in Multiple Family Group Therapy in a School Setting." *International Journal of Group Psychotherapy* 19 (January 1969): 44–52.

Durkin, H. E. "Boundaries and Boundarying: A Systems Perspective." In M. Pines and L. Rafaelson, eds., *The Individual and the Group,* 257–68. New York: Brunner Mazel, 1980.

Durkin, J. E. *Living Groups: Group Psychotherapy and General Systems Theory.* New York: Brunner Mazel, 1981.

Elias, M. J. *Treating Adolescents with Oppositional Conduct and Other Behavior Disorders.* Baltimore, Md.: American Healthcare Institute, 1991.

Elias, M. J. and S. Tobias. *Problem Solving/Decision Making for Social and Academic Success: A School-based Approach.* Washington, D.C.: National Education Association, 1990.

Elizura, G. B. and S. Davidson. "The Treatment of Adolescents and Their Parents in Group Settings in a Psychiatric Hospital." *International Journal of Social Psychiatry* 27 (April 1981): 83–92.

Elson, M. *The Kohutian Seminars on Self Psychology and Psychotherapy with Adolescents and Young Adults.* New York: Norton, 1987.

Erikson, E. H. *Identity and the Life-Cycle.* New York: International Universities Press, 1959.

Experiment with Travel. Kayak Shop: Annual Report, F. Y. 1975. Springfield, Mass., 1975.

Festinger, L. "Group Attraction and Membership." *Journal of Social Issues* 7 (1951): 152–63.

Fine, S., G. Knight-Webb, and J. Vernon. "Selected Volunteer Adolescents in Adolescent Group Psychotherapy." *Adolescent Quarterly* 12 (1977): 189–97.

Flanagan, T. and K. Jamieson, eds. *Sourcebook on Criminal Justice Statistics, 1987.* Washington D.C.: Bureau of Justice Statistics, 1988.

Flay, B. R., K. B. Ryan, J. A. Best, K. S. Brown, M. W. Kersell, J. R. d'Avernas, and M. P. Zanna. "Are Social Psychological Smoking Prevention Programs Effective?" The Waterloo Study. *Journal of Behavioral Medicine* 8 (January 1985): 37–59.

Frances, A. and M. Schiff. "Popular Music as a Catalyst in the Induction of Therapy Groups in Teenagers." *International Journal of Group Psychotherapy* 25 (March 1976): 393–98.

Gardner, M. L. "College Students." In N. S. Brandes and M. L. Gardner, eds., *Group Therapy for the Adolescent.* 45–62. New York: Jason Aronson, 1973.

Garfield, L. and E. McHugh. " Learning Counseling: Tutoring and Group Counseling." *Journal of Higher Education* 49 (April 1978): 381–92.

Gazda, G. M., ed. *Theories and Methods of Group Counseling in the Schools.* Springfield, Ill.: Thomas, 1976.

Gibbs, J. T. and L. N. Huang, eds. *Children of Color: Psychological Interventions with Minority Youth.* San Francisco, Calif.: Jossey-Bass, 1989.

Gilligan, C. *In Another Voice.* Cambridge, Mass.: Harvard University Press, 1982.

Gilligan, C. "Adolescent Development Reconsidered." In C. E. Irwin, Jr., ed., *Adolescent Social Behavior and Health: New Direction for Child Development,* 63–92. San Francisco, Calif.: Jossey-Bass, 1987.

Glasser, W. *Reality Therapy.* New York: Harper and Row, 1965.

Glynn, T., C. Leukenfeld, and J. Ludford, eds. *Preventing Adolescent Drug Abuse: Intervention Strategies.* Research Monograph 7. Rockville, Md.: National Institute on Drug Abuse, 1985.

Goldstein, A. K. W., N. Reagles, and L. L. Amann. *Refusal Skills: Preventing Drug Use in Adolescents.* Champaign, Ill.: Research Press, 1991.

Gordon, J. S. "Youth Helping Youth." *Social Policy* 7 (1976): 48–53.

Gordon, J. S. " What Kids Need to Know." *Psychology Today* 20 (1986): 22–26.

Grosser, C., W. Henry, and J. G. Kelly, eds. *Nonprofessionals and the Human Services.* San Francisco, Calif.: Jossey-Bass, 1969.

Guidelines for the Training of Group Psychotherapists. New York: American Group Psychotherapy Association, 1970.

Haggerty, K. P., K. P. Wells, E. A. Jenson, M. Jeffrey, R. F. Catalano, and J. D. Hawkins. "Delinquents and Drug Use: A Model Program for Community Reintegration." *Adolescence* 24 (Summer 1989): 439–56.

Hall, E. T. *The Silent Language.* New York: Doubleday, 1959.

250

Bibliography

Hamburg, B. *Life Skills Training: Preventive Interventions for Young Adolescents.* New York: Carnegie Council on Adolescent Development, 1990.

Harman, R. L. "Recent Development in Gestalt Group Therapy." *International Journal of Group Psychotherapy* 34 (July 1984): 473–83.

Hendren, R. L., D. M. Atkins, C. R. Sumner, and J. K. Barber. "Model for the Group Treatment of Eating Disorders." *International Journal of Group Psychotherapy* 37 (April 1987): 589–602.

Hill, W. and I. Hill. *Hill and Hill Interaction Matrix.* Los Angeles, Calif.: Youth Development Center, University of Southern California, 1965.

Hodgekinson, H. L. *The Same Client: The Demographics of Education and Service Delivery Systems.* Washington, D.C.: Center for Demographic Policy, Institute for Educational Leadership, 1989.

Hofferth, H. and C. D. Hayes. *Risking the Future: Adolescent Sexuality, Pregnancy, and Childbearing,* vol. 2. Washington, D.C.: National Academy Press, 1987.

Homans, G. *The Human Group.* New York: Harcourt, Brace, 1950.

Hunter, E. *Encounter in the Classroom.* New York: Holt, Rinehart and Winston, 1972.

Hurst, A. G., K. B. Stein, S. J. Korchin, and W. F. Soskin. "Leadership Style Determinants of Cohesiveness in Adolescent Groups." *International Journal of Group Psychotherapy* 28 (1978): 263–77.

The Institute for Mental Health Initiatives. *Learning to Manage Anger.* Champaign, Ill.: Research Press, 1991.

Jacks, K. and M. Keller. "A Humanistic Approach to the Adolescent with Learning Disabilities." *Adolescence* 13 (1978): 61–69.

"The Job Corps: A Dialogue." *American Child* 48 (January 1966).

Kegeles, S. M., N. E. Adler, and C. E. Irwin. "Sexually Active Adolescents and Condoms." *American Journal of Public Health* 78 (1988): 460–61.

Kimbro, E. L., H. A. Taschman, H. W. Wylie, and B. W. MacLennan. "A Multiple Family Group Approach to Some Problems of Adolescence." *International Journal of Group Psychotherapy* 17 (1967): 18–24.

Kirshner, L. A. "A Follow-up of a Freshman Group Counseling Program." *American College of Health Association Journal* 22 (1974): 279–80.

Kitchur, M. and R. Bell. "Group Psychotherapy with Preadolescent Sexual Abuse Victims." *International Journal of Group Psychotherapy* 39 (July 1989): 285–310.

Klein, W. L. and B. W. MacLennan. "Utilization of Groups in Job Training for the Socially Deprived." *International Journal of Group Psychotherapy* 15 (April 1965): 424–33.

Knittle, B. J. and S. J. Tuana. "Group Therapy as Preliminary Treatment for Adolescent Victims of Intrafamilial Sexual Abuse." *Clinical Social Work Journal* 8 (April 1980): 236–42.

Kraft, I. A. "An Overview of Group Therapy with Adolescents." *International Journal of Group Psychotherapy* 18 (April 1968): 461–80.

Kramer, P. and L. Frazer. *The Dynamics of Relationships,* vols. 1 and 2. 3d ed. Washington, D.C.: Universal Press, 1988.

Krieg, F. *Group Counseling with Behavior Problems.* Boston, Mass.: American Group Psychotherapy Conference Workshop, 1990.

Krieg, F. *Group Leadership Training and Supervision: A Manual.* 3d ed. Muncie, Ind.: Accelerated Development, 1991.

Lacoursiere, R. *The Life Cycle of Groups: Group Developmental Stage Theory.* New York: Human Services Press, 1980.

Leaman, D. R. "Group Counseling to Improve Communication Skills of Adolescents." *Journal of Specialists in Group Work* 8 (1983): 144–50.

Leary, T. *The Interpersonal Diagnosis of Personality.* New York: Renald, 1957.

Lebon, G. *The Crowd.* London: Fisher, Unwin, 1920.

Lenihan, G. and W. G. Kirk. "Using Student Paraprofessionals in the Treatment of Eating Disorders." *Journal of Counseling and Guidance* 68 (January/February 1990): 332–35.

Lewin, K. *Resolving Social Conflicts.* New York: Harper, 1948.

Lewin, K. *Field Theory in Social Science.* New York: Harper, 1951.

Lieb, R. C. and T. L. Thompson. "Group Psychotherapy of Four Anorexia Nervosa Inpatients." *International Journal of Group Psychotherapy* 34 (April 1984): 639–42.

Lieberman, Morton A., I. D. Yalom, and M. B. Miles. *Encounter Groups: First Facts.* New York: Basic Books, 1972.

Linesch, D. G. *Adolescent Art Therapy.* New York: Brunner Mazel, 1988.

Lippitt, R. and R. K. White. "An Experimental Study of Leadership and Group Life." In T. M. Newcomb, ed., *Readings in Social Psychology.* New York: Holt, 1947.

MacLennan, B. W. "Training for New Careers." *Community Mental Health Journal* 2 (1966): 135–41.

MacLennan, B. W. "Scapegoating." *Today's Education* 58 (June 1969): 38–40.

MacLennan, B. W. "Community Mental Health Professionals Assist in School Desegregation." In W. L. Clairborn and R. Cohen, eds., *School Intervention,* 207–22. New York: Behavioral Publications, 1973.

MacLennan, B. W. "The Personalities of Group Leaders: Implications for

Selection and Training." *International Journal of Group Psychotherapy* 25 (February 1975): 177–85.

MacLennan, B. W. "The Influence of the Cultural Environment on Adolescents and Their Treatment." In L. R. Wolberg, M. R. Aronson, and A. R. Wolberg, eds., *Group Therapy,* 140–49. New York: Stratton Intercontinental Medical Book Corporation, 1978.

MacLennan, B. W. "Group Psychotherapy with Girls in Early Adolescence: Then and Now." *Journal of Child and Adolescent Group Therapy* 1 (1991): 25–41.

MacLennan, B. W. and S. I. Belton. *Receiving Home Counselor Training and Evaluation.* Training Report no. 6. Washington, D.C.: Howard University Center for Youth and Community Studies, April 1965.

MacLennan, B. W. and N. Felsenfeld. *Group Counseling and Psychotherapy with Adolescents.* New York: Columbia University Press, 1970.

McLendon, R. "Multiple Family Group Therapy with Adolescents in a State Hospital." *Clinical Social Work Journal* 4 (1976): 14–24.

McCorkle, L. W., A. Elias, and F. L. Bixby. *The Highfields Story.* New York: Holt, 1958.

McGuire, T. "A Time-limited Dynamic Approach to Adolescent In-Patient Group Psychotherapy: Psychoanalytic and Crisis Theory." *Adolescence* 23 (Summer 1990): 373–83.

McKelvie, W. H. "An Evaluation of a Model to Train High School Students as Leaders of Adlerian Guidance Groups." *Individual Psychology* 11 (1974): 7–14.

Meichenbaum, D. H. *Stress Inoculation Training.* New York: Pergamon, 1985.

Melchert, T. and K. F. Burnett. "Attitudes, Knowledge, and Sexual Behavior of High-Risk Adolescents: Implications for Counseling and Sexuality Education." *Journal of Counseling and Development* 68 (January/February 1990): 293–98.

Miller, A. H. "The Spontaneous Use of Poetry in an Adolescent Girls Group." *International Journal of Group Psychotherapy* 23 (February 1973): 223–27.

Miner, J. L. and J. Boldt. *Outward Bound U.S.A.* New York: Morrow Quill (paperback), 1981.

Minuchin, S. *Families and Family Therapy.* Cambridge, Mass.: Harvard University Press, 1974.

Moos, R. *Evaluating Treatment Environments: A Social Ecological Approach.* New York: Wiley, 1974.

Morehouse, E. "Working in the School with Children of Alcoholic Parents." *Health and Social Work* 4 (1979): 4–11.

Moreno, J. *Who Shall Survive?* Washington, D.C.: Nervous and Mental Disease Publishing Co., 1934.

Morganett, R. S. *Skills for Living: Group Counseling Activities for Young Adolescents.* Champaign, Ill.: Research Press, 1991.

Mueller, D. and P. Higgins. *Funders' Guide Manual: A Guide to Prevention Programs in Human Services.* St. Paul, Minn.: Amherst Wilder Foundation, 1988.

Murray, D. M. et al. "The Prevention of Cigarette Smoking in Children: A Comparison of Four Strategies." *Journal of Applied Social Psychology* 14 (1984): 274–88.

Nash, K. B. "Group Guidance and Counseling Programs: A Vehicle for the Introduction of Sex Education for Adolescents in the Public School." *Journal of School Health* 38 (1968): 577–83.

National Center for Health Statistics. *Advanced Report on Final Mortality Statistics.* Washington, D.C.: Department of Health and Human Services, 1984.

National Institute on Drug Abuse. *The Therapeutic Community: Study of Effectiveness.* Rockville, Md.: Department of Health and Human Services (ADM) 84–1286, 1984.

National Institute on Drug Abuse. *National Household Survey, 1985.* Washington, D.C.: Department of Health and Human Services (ADM) 88–1586, 1988.

National Institute on Drug Abuse. *Data from the Drug Abuse Warning Network (DAWN) Series,* no. 7, Annual Data 1987. Washington, D.C.: Department of Health and Human Services (ADM) 88–1584, 1988.

Office of Substance Abuse Prevention. *Prevention of Mental Disorders, Alcohol, and Other Drug Use in Children and Adolescents.* Monograph 2. Washington, D.C.: Department of Health and Human Services (ADM) 90–1646, 1989.

O'Gorman, P. and R. A. Ross. "Children of Alcoholics in the Juvenile Justice System." *Alcohol Health and Research World* 8 (April 1984): 43–45.

Osterheld, J. R., M. S. McKenna, and N. B. Gould. "Group Psychotherapy of Bulimia: A Critical Review." *International Journal of Group Psychotherapy* 37 (April 1987): 163–84.

Pease, J. J. "Social Skills Training Group for Early Adolescents." *Journal of Adolescence* 2 (1972) 229–39.

Pecukonis, E. V. "A Cognitive/Affective Empathy Training Program as a Function of Ego Development in Aggressive Adolescent Females." *Adolescence* 25 (January 1990): 59–76.

Bibliography

Pepper, B. *Dual Diagnosis Program for Youth.* Pomona, N.Y.: Rockland County Community Mental Health Center, 1984.

Pepper, B. and H. Ryglawicz. "Guidelines for Treating the Young Adult Chronic Patient." *The Lines* 11 (April 1985), 4.

A Personal and Flexible Group Psychotherapy Training Program. New York: American Group Psychotherapy Association, 1987.

Pritchard, M. *The Power of Choice.* San Francisco, Calif.: Live Wire Video Publishers, 1989.

Rachin, R. L., ed. *Special Issue: Alcohol Problems and the Minority Youth. Journal of Drug Issues* 18 (1985).

Rachman, A. W. "Identity Group Psychotherapy with Adolescents: A Reformulation." In F. J. C. Azima and L. H. Richmond, eds. *Adolescent Group Psychotherapy,* 21–41. Madison, Conn.: International Universities Press, 1989.

Raubolt, R. R. "The Clinical Practice of Group Psychotherapy with Delinquents." In F. J. C. Azima and L. H. Richmond, eds. *Adolescent Group Psychotherapy,* 143–62. Madison, Conn.: International Universities Press, 1989.

Reaching the Unreached. New York: New York City Youth Board, 1952.

Redl, F. "Group Emotion and Leadership." *Psychiatry* 5 (1942): 573–96.

Reynolds, W. M. and K. I. Coats. "A Comparison of Cognitive Behavioral Therapy and Relaxation Training for the Treatment of Depression in Adolescents." *Journal of Consulting and Clinical Psychology* 54 (1986): 657–60.

Richmond, L. H. "Observations on Private Practice and Community Clinic Adolescent Psychotherapy Groups." *Group Process* 6 (1974): 57–62.

Robertson, D. and B. Matthews. "Preventing Adolescent Suicide with Group Counseling." *Journal of Specialists in Group Work* 14 (January 1989): 34–39.

Rogers, C. R. "The Process of the Basic Encounter Group." In J. F. Bugental, ed., *Challenges of Humanistic Psychology.* New York: McGraw-Hill, 1967.

Rogers, C. R., H. Kohut, and E. H. Erickson. "A Personal Perspective on Some Similarities and Differences." *Person-centered Review* 1 (1986): 125–40.

Rosenberg, P. and L. Rosenberg. "Group Experience in Sex Education for the Family." *International Journal of Group Psychotherapy* 26 (July 1976): 235–41.

Rushton, A. "Group Work with Adolescents in a Girls Comprehensive School." *Journal of Adolescence* 5 (1982): 267–84.

Sarason, I. G. and B. R. Sarason. "Teaching Cognitive and Social Skills to High School Students." *Journal of Consulting and Clinical Psychology* 49 (1981): 908–18.

Schachter, S. "Deviation, Rejection, and Communication." In D. Cartwright and A. Zander, eds., *Group Dynamics: Research and Theory,* 223–45. Evanston, Ill.: Row, Peterson, 1953.

Schaefer, C. E., L. Johnson, and J. F. Wherry. *Group Therapies for Children and Youth: Principles and Practices of Group Treatment.* San Francisco, Calif.: Jossey-Bass, 1982.

Scheidlinger, S. "The Adolescent and Peer Group Revisited." *Small Group Behavior* 15 (March 1984): 387–97.

Scheidlinger, S. "Group Treatment of Adolescents: An Overview." *American Journal of Orthopsychiatry* 55 (January 1985): 102–11.

Scheidlinger, S. Personal communication, 1991.

Scheidlinger, S. and S. Gordon. *About Sex.* Bronx, N.Y.: Yeshiva University, Albert Einstein College of Medicine, 1972.

Schenkman, S. *Second Genesis Program Description.* Bethesda, Md., 1989.

Schinke, S. and L. Gilchrist. *Life Skills Counseling with Adolescents.* Baltimore, Md.: University Park Press, 1984.

Schutz, C. *List of Therapists Conducting Groups for Children and Adolescents in the Washington Metropolitan Area,* Spring 1990.

Schutz, W. C. *FIRO: A Three-Dimensional Theory of Interpersonal Behavior.* New York: Holt and Rinehart, 1960.

Schwartz, J. L. *Review and Evaluation of Smoking Cessation Methods: The United States and Canada, 1978–1985.* Bethesda, Md.: National Institute of Health Publication No. 87–2940, April 1987.

Seibert, J. M. and R. A. Olson, eds. *Children, Adolescents, and AIDS.* Lincoln: University of Nebraska Press, 1989.

Serrano, A. *Treatment of Reconstituted Families.* Solomon Islands, Md.: Mid-Atlantic Group Psychotherapy Conference, 1988.

Shaffer, D. "Strategies for the Prevention of Youth Suicide." *Public Health Reports* 102 (November/December 1987): 611–13.

Shaw, M. J. *Group Dynamics: The Psychology of Small Group Behavior.* New York: McGraw-Hill, 1981.

Sherif, M. and C. Sherif. *Reference Groups.* New York: Harper and Row, 1964.

Shields, S. "Busted and Branded: Group Work with Substance Abusing Adolescents in Schools." *Social Work with Groups* 8 (1985): 61–81.

Shikles, J. *Preliminary Findings: A Survey of Methadone Maintenance Programs.* Washington, D.C., GAO/T–HRD–89, 1989.

Shure, M. B. and G. Spivak. *Manual for Interpersonal Cognitive Problem*

Bibliography

Solving for Fourth and Fifth Grade Elementary School Students. Philadelphia, Pa.: Hahnemann Hospital, 1983.

Sigal, J., S. Braverman, and R. Pilon. "Effects of Teacher-led Curriculum-integrated Sensitivity Training in a Large High School." *Journal of Education Research* 70 (1943): 3–9.

Skynner, R. *Group Analysis and Family Therapy*. London/New York: Routledge, 1990.

Slavson, S. R. *An Introduction to Group Therapy*. New York: Commonwealth Fund, 1943.

Slavson, S. R. *The Practice of Group Psychotherapy*. New York: International Universities Press, 1947.

Slavson, S. R. et al. *Activity Group Therapy*. New York: Jewish Board of Guardians, 1948.

Slavson, S. R. and B. W. MacLennan. "Group Therapy with Unmarried Mothers." In S. R. Slavson, ed., *Fields of Group Psychotherapy*. New York: International Universities Press, 1953.

Slavson, S. R. and M. Schiffer. *Group Psychotherapies for Children*. New York: International Universities Press, 1975.

Speer, D. C. "Nonverbal Communication." *Comparative Group Studies* 3 (April 1972): 383–487.

Stanton, R. and M. Schwartz. *The Mental Hospital*. New York: Basic Books, 1965.

Stein. M. D. and J. K. Davis. *Therapies for Adolescents: Current Treatments for Problem Behaviors*. San Francisco, Calif.: Jossey-Bass, 1982.

Stein, M. D. and P. Kymissis. "Adolescent In-Patient Group Psychotherapy." In F. J. C. Azima and L. H. Richmond, eds., *Adolescent Group Psychotherapy*, 68–84. Madison, Conn.: International Universities Press, 1989.

Sugar, M. *The Adolescent in Group and Family Therapy*. Chicago, Ill.: University of Chicago Press, 1975.

Sugar, M. Personal communication, 1991.

Swift, M. S. and G. Spivack. *Alternative Teaching Strategies*. Champaign, Ill.: Research Press, 1991.

Terr, L. C. "Treating Psychic Trauma in Children: A Preliminary Discussion." *Journal of Traumatic Stress* 2 (January 1989): 3–20.

Thornton, L. P. and R. R. Deblassie. "Treating Bulimia." *Adolescence* 24 (1989): 631–38.

"A Three-Letter Word for Love." Bronx, N.Y.: Yeshiva University, Albert Einstein College of Medicine, 1969.

Tindall, J. A. and S. Salmon-White. *Peers Helping Peers*. Muncie, Ind.: Accelerated Development, 1990.

Tobler, N. "Meta-Analysis of 143 Adolescent Drug Prevention Programs." *Journal of Drug Issues* 16 (1986): 537–67.

Tramontana, M. G. "Critical Review of Research on Psychotherapy Outcomes with Adolescents: 1967–1977." *Psychological Bulletin* 88 (1980): 424–50.

Truax, C. B. and E. Carkuff. *Toward Effective Counseling and Psychotherapy.* New York: Aldine, 1967.

True, J. E. "Training New Mental Health Personnel in Group Methods." *International Journal of Group Psychotherapy* 24 (October 1974): 383–92.

The Ungame. Baltimore, Md., Life Cycle Resources, 1991.

United States Department of Education. Upward Bound Program.

United States General Accounting Office. *Job Training Partnership Act.* Washington, D.C., GAO/HRD–85–4, 1985.

United States General Accounting Office. *Summer Youth Jobs Program.* Washington, D.C., GAO/HRD–88–118, 1988.

United States General Accounting Office. *Drug Misuse: Anabolic Steroids and Human Growth Hormone.* Washington, D.C., GAO/HRD–89–109, August 1989.

United States Social Security Administration. Work Incentive Programs.

Valene, W. J. and L. C. Amos. "High School Transfer Students." *Personnel and Guidance Journal* 52 (1973): 40–42.

Verbur, D., R. Hughes, and M. deRuis. "Enhancement of Self-Esteem Among Female Adolescent Incest Victims: A Controlled Comparison." *Adolescence* 21 (1986): 843–59.

Virginia Council on Coordinating Prevention. *Resource Guide of Private Sector Prevention Initiatives.* Richmond, Va.: Department of Volunteerism, 1990.

Vital Statistics: Marriage and Divorce, 1986. Washington, D.C.: National Center for Health Statistics, 1988.

Von Bertalanffy, L. *General Systems Theory.* New York: Brazillier, 1968.

Vontress, R. and B. W. MacLennan. *Counseling in the Neighborhood Youth Corps.* Washington, D.C.: Department of Labor, 1967.

Weber, L. A. "The Effect of Videotape and Playback on an In-Patient Adolescent Group." *International Journal of Group Psychotherapy* 30 (February 1980): 213–28.

Westman, J. C. "Group Psychotherapy with Hospitalized Delinquent Adolescents." *International Journal of Group Psychotherapy* 9 (March 1959): 275–86.

When Jenny When? Topeka, Kans.: Department of Health and Environment, Office of Health and Environmental Education, Film Library, 1979.

Whitaker, D. S. and M. A. Lieberman. *Psychotherapy Through the Group Process.* New York: Atherton Press, 1964.

Windsor, R. and D. Dimitru. "Prevalence of Anabolic Steroid Use by Male and Female Adolescents." *Medicine and Science in Sport and Exercise* (October 1989).

Wisconsin Clearing House. *How to Prevent Alcohol and Other Drug Problems and Promote Health.* Madison: University of Wisconsin, 1990.

Wodarski, J. S. *Preventive Health Services for Adolescents.* Springfield, Ill.: Thomas, 1989.

Wolff, K. W. *The Sociology of Georg Simmel.* Glencoe, Ill.: The Free Press, 1950.

Yalom, I. D. *Theory and Practice of Group Psychotherapy,* 3d ed. New York: Basic Books, 1985.

Yule, W. and R. M. Williams. "Post-Traumatic Stress Reactions in Children." *Journal of Traumatic Stress* 3 (February 1990): 279–98.

Zabusky, G. S. and P. Kymissis. "Identity Group Therapy: A Transitional Group for Hospitalized Adolescents." *International Journal of Group Psychotherapy* 33 (January 1983): 99–109.

Index

Index

Counseling Center groups for college freshmen, 164

Counter-transference, 28

Courts, and delinquent adolescents, 206

Crabhill, L., 204

Crack, 178. *See also* Substance abuse

Crafts: in early adolescent groups, 127–28; job training for, 189

Crisis groups, 74–75, 101, 174, 198

Crisis situations, mental health clinics and, 196–97

Crowds, 10

Crushes, 46

Cults, 154

Culture: changes in, 2–3; and communication, 26; diversity, in schools, 177; factors in adolescent development, 49–60; and personal distance, 23

Dancing, 187

Dangerous behavior, confidentiality and, 217

Dangerous habits, avoidance of, 71

Dangers of adolescence, 140, 146

Data sources for group evaluation, 40

Dating patterns, 58

Day treatment, therapeutic, 204

Death: causes of, 140; fear of, 148–50

Deblassie, R. R., 142

Decision making, in groups, 29–31, 87–88

Deep sea divers training program, 190

Defenses: in group development, 13–15; of group members, 117

Defiance: group leadership and, 27; of law, 168

Deindividualization, 10, 16

Delegation of authority by group leaders, 28

Delinquency, culture of, 53

Delinquent adolescents, 21, 47; and confidentiality, 89; groups for, 68, 85, 128, 205–9; polydrug abusers, 200; programs for, 169–71, 188

Demands, unrealistic, 19

Demonstration groups for leader training, 231

Denial of problems, 116, 118, 127; alcohol abuse and, 201; confrontation and, 90; substance abusers and, 199

Department of the Interior, Job Corps, 189

Dependency: bulimia and, 142; composition of group and, 94; group leaders and, 27, 31, 225; older adolescents and, 140; parents and, 151; and termination of group, 136–37; therapy and, 194; in treatment groups, 65–66

Dependency demand, in group development, 13–14

Depression, 48, 94, 143–45; anger and, 145; bulimia and, 142; and friendships, 153; schools and, 175; treatment groups for, 197

Desegregation of schools, 175

Despair, 143, 165; and rebellion, 55

Detached workers, 185

Detention centers for delinquents, 208

Detoxification programs, 202

Developmental groups, 154

Developmental theory, current, 83–84

Development of groups, 8–10

Deviant groups, 85

Diabetics, groups for, 69

Diagnostic groups, 73–74

Dies, K. R., 17, 39, 41

Index

Index

Index

Index

Index

Index

groups and, 185; in younger groups, 129
Runaways, 205

Safe sex, 59, 177; education for, 192
Same-sex relationships, 154; developmental differences and, 153; in late adolescence, 46; young adolescents and, 45, 95, 131, 139
Satisfactions: change and, 18; from group relationships, 62; from work, 133
Scapegoating, 33–34, 95, 125–26
Schachter, S., 24
Scheduling of group meetings, 68
Scheidlinger, S., 70, 158, 231
Schiff, M., 106
Schinke, S., 141
Schizophrenics: groups for, 96, 197; resistance mechanisms, 204
School dropouts, programs for, 82, 188
School programs, 3–4
Schools, 57, 161–62, 174–75; and group programs, 104; groups in, 67, 76, 175–84, 198; sex education, 155, 158; and substance abuse, 166–67; theoretical approaches to counseling, 83
School year, and termination of groups, 135
Schutz, W. C., 38
Schwartz, J. L., 201
Scouting movement, 185
Seating arrangements, 22–23, 105
Secondary schools, vocational counseling, 181
Secret rituals, 154
Security, and conformity, 85
Sedentary games, 186
Selection of members, 92–96, 107; for indirect counseling groups, 81; for life-adjustment groups, 77;
for private practice groups, 210
Self, 17; acceptance of, 63; responsibility for, 63
Self-awareness groups, 76
Self-concept, 32, 169; change of, 7, 18, 70
Self-consciousness: in early adolescence, 44, 126, 127, 129; and learning problems, 179; and school function, 162
Self-control, play activities and, 184
Self-destructive behavior patterns, change of, 69
Self-determination, 115
Self-disclosure, by group leaders, 19
Self-discovery, 83
Self-esteem, 3, 63, 133–34, 141; in early adolescence, 44; eating disorders and, 142; group participation and, 62; indirect counseling for, 81; and indiscriminate sex, 159; learning disabilities and, 57; play activities and, 184; schools and, 175; self-psychology and, 83; sexuality and, 59; substance abuse and, 200, 201
Self-help groups, 70, 194; problem-specific, 74
Self-identification, in groups, 225
Self-image, 32; parents and, 151; prevocational training and, 191; reference groups and, 48
Self-knowledge of group leaders, 232
Self-management, 7, 70, 169–70; of group leaders, 232
Self-mastery, 133
Self-perception, 117; and communication, 25
Self-psychology, 83
Self-reliance, 17, 74
Self-respect, 18

Index

Index